Envelopes of Sound

DATE DUE

Envelopes of Sound
The Art of Oral History

Second Edition, Revised and Enlarged

Ronald J. Grele

With:
Studs Terkel
Jan Vansina
Dennis Tedlock
Saul Benison
Alice Kessler Harris

New York
Westport, Connecticut
London

cation Data

history / Ronald J. Grele
ed., rev. and enl.

ago, Ill. : Precedent Pub.,
1985.
  Developed from a session at the annual meeting of the Organization
of American Historians, Chicago, April, 1973.
  Includes bibliographical references.
  ISBN 0-275-94184-1
  1. Oral history. I. Terkel, Studs, 1912- . II. Title.
[D16.14.G74 1991]
907'.2—dc20   90-15496

British Library Cataloguing in Publication Data is available.

A hardcover edition of *Envelopes of Sound* is available from
Greenwood Publishing Group, Inc. (ISBN 0-313-28099-1)

Library of Congress Catalog Card Number: 90-15496
ISBN: 0-275-94184-1

First published in 1991

Praeger Publishers, One Madison Avenue, New York, NY 10010
An imprint of Greenwood Publishing Group, Inc.

Printed in the United States of America

♾™

The paper used in this book complies with the
Permanent Paper Standard issued by the National
Information Standards Organization (Z39.48-1984).

10 9 8 7 6 5

Parts of chapters 5, 6, and 7 of the present work appeared in a slightly different
form in the following journals:

"A Surmisable Variety: Oral History and Interdisciplinarity," in AMERICAN
QUARTERLY, Volume XXVII, Number 3 (August 1975) pp. 275-295

"Can Anyone Over Thirty Be Trusted? A Friendly Critique of Oral History," in
THE ORAL HISTORY REVIEW (1978) pp. 36-44

"Listen to Their Voices: Two Case Studies in the Interpretation of Oral History
Interviews," in ORAL HISTORY: THE JOURNAL OF THE ORAL HISTORY
SOCIETY (BRITISH) Volume 7, Number 1 (Spring 1975) pp. 33-42

Contents

Preface to the Paperback Edition
Ronald J. Grele

When I first became interested in the theoretical and methodological problems of oral history interviewing, it was as a result of the rather mundane task assigned to me of editing a set of interviews Charles Morrissey and I had conducted for the Ford Foundation Oral History Project. As I sat, day after day, listening to the tape-recorded interviews and correcting the transcripts, I gradually came to understand that buried within those interviews were patterns of language and thought that typified the world of the narrators and revealed their class perceptions of their roles in history. What I also came to realize is that, through our questions, we were helping them to create their historical narratives; giving articulation to those perceptions.

I came to this understanding with two intellectual debts. The first was to Warren I. Susman who taught me, when I was a graduate student at Rutgers University, that the way one views history is a fact worthy of historical investigation. History, the idea of history, was an object of cultural construction, and an understanding of that construction told us about the culture it took place within. It was this belief that led me to search in our interviews for the particular ideas about history that seemed to govern the building of the oral history narratives, and to try to discover how we, as interviewers, were involved in that process. My view of how such attempts at historical construction could be discovered was, again, derived from the work of Susman, especially his concern with the complex interplay between history, myth, and ideology. More than just a recitation of what had happened in the past, the interviews were examples of the way our narrators mobilized myth and history to create ideologies of potent force to explain the meaning of what had happened to them, and served as a filter through which the history of the Ford Foundation was told.

My second debt was to Louis Althusser. Like many of my generation I had been deeply affected by the political movements of the 1960s, especially the early civil rights movement. Again, as many of that generation had, I became attracted to the writings of early Marx as in *The Economic and Philosophic Manuscripts of 1844,* which seemed to merge a concern with the processes of alienation and political action. With the collapse of the dreams of that decade in the debacle of the 1970s many of us turned to the late Marx, as if we could explain our failures, our exhuberances, the lack of mass appeal of the politics of identity, through an examination of a more structured and materialist Marx. At that time, in that context, Althusser seemed to be required reading. Aside from whatever else one found in Althusser, I found a way to read complex documents, a method that he termed "symptomatic": the search for the problematic behind the text, the combination of things said and unsaid, which revealed the place of the text in the history of theory and science. Although one never used the term, looking back upon that experience now, I suppose it was an early lesson in deconstruction.

Could we, I wondered, discover the deeper expressions of ideology underlying our oral history conversations by searching for the idea of the use of history as the key to that problematic? My first experiments were with the interviews we were collecting for the Ford Foundation. Those experiments sought to uncover, through an analysis of what was said about the history of the foundation and the history of philanthropy, the hegemonic ideology of foundation officers and trustees, many of whom, by any standard, would be recognized as members of the American ruling class. The theoretical basis for that experimentation resulted in the essay published here, "Movement Without Aim." The purpose of that essay was to set out before a group of historians the possibility of looking at oral histories and talking about them in a new way. The aim was to move from the idea of oral history as archival practice to discussing the practice as a conscious act of historiography. The key definition was that oral history was a conversational narrative. That definition provided a way to ground the use of the idea of history in the document itself, and gave some sense of the dialectical relationship involved in its creation. It also allowed me to outline the interplay between the various structures of language, performance, and historical vision in the interview, and to speculate upon the relationship of myth, ideology, and history in that vision. Basic to the discussion was the tension between narrative and historical thought (not an original idea given the long debate about the tension between narrative and analysis in historical presentation, and Susman's use of that tension).

Althusser also led me to works in other disciplines, especially linguistics but also anthropology and folklore, fields where structural analysis seemed dominant. I also began to be concerned with problems of ethnomethodology. On a more practical level, these explorations led me to the work of Dennis Tedlock and the eventual development of the panel at the Organization of American Historians annual meeting where he and I first presented the papers in this volume. Those papers, the interview I conducted with Studs Terkel, and the radio session with Terkel were then combined for the initial publication of this volume.

A more interesting possibility to test in practice the ideas toward which I was groping came when Herbert Gutman and Virginia Yans-McLaughlin asked me to serve as a consultant to a project they had organized to record the oral histories of working class and ethnic residents of New York City. This consulting opened up the possibility of expanding the tentative experiments I had undertaken with the Ford Foundation interviews to the arena of working class history. Would it be possible to find in the testimonies of working class New Yorkers the rich ideological expression and narrative ability that I had found among historically conscious foundation officials? "Listen to Their Voices" is the result of that search. Although, as Yans has recently noted,[1] this essay does not reveal the origins or effects of ideological expression, it does show the complicated manner in which ideologies are expressed, and does show, I believe, how we can understand the mechanics of that expression.

In the process of thinking about the special problems of conversational narratives, I tried to acquaint myself with works in linguistics. At the same time I was asked by editors of the

American Quarterly to contribute an interdisciplinary bibliographic essay on oral history; "A Surmisable Variety" is that essay. Although it now seems dated (I think that I was somewhat naive then about the implications of linguistic analysis), it was one of the first attempts among oral historians to try to draw from other fieldwork methodologies some understanding of the generation of conversation and their cultural construction.

"Can Anyone Over Thirty Be Trusted?" is an attempt to present in a comprehensible form what I thought to be the major theoretical and methodological problems of oral history, and to draw out the implications of those problems for actual fieldwork situations. In a way it sums up much of my earlier thinking but relates that thinking to fieldwork practice. The concern, again, despite some references to the ways oral histories are used, was with their creation. The hope was that if we realized the complexity of the creation we would be more careful and creative in the use of oral histories. The essay was also an attempt to raise questions about the growing popularity of oral history and the enthusiasm that seemed to dominate our thinking, and to mediate what was then becoming a more and more obvious tension between those who saw oral history as a movement and those who insisted it was a discipline.

Shortly after the publication of that essay I was fortunate enough to make contact with a group of European historians who had been asking many of the same questions I had been asking about oral testimony, but coming to startlingly different answers. I had also become editor of the *International Journal of Oral History,* which allowed me to bring to the attention of an American audience the work of these scholars, as well as a number of American scholars in different disciplines who were interested in the same questions of narrative modes, conversational analysis, ideology, and subjectivity. Much of this work was directed to understanding the relationship between the interviewer and his or her informant, the relationship between historian and source, and the intersubjectivity of that relationship.

In some sense, it strikes me now as a continuation of that 1960s concern about the ways one related to others as a non-elitist and the ways one framed questions about cultural politics.

The last essay in this volume reflects those new concerns. As critics have noted, it is a move away from the questions raised by Louis Althusser to those raised by Paul Ricoeur and other students of narrative. It is also a shift away from the objectivism inherent in Althusser to more difficult questions of subjectivity. Essentially what was involved was a growing concern with both conversation and narrative, and less of a focus on myth and ideology, although both are inherent in the construction of narratives and the construction of methods of analysis. Conversation and narrative are, however, the mediating stages between ideology and field-work practice. In that sense, it strikes me, the last essay on the art of oral history is an expansion of earlier concerns about fieldwork. As the introduction to the second edition indicates, the roster of those who have most effected this shift for me is rather long.

The opportunity to publish this paperbound edition of *Envelopes of Sound* does not, unfortunately, allow a continuation of the debates over the nature of conversation, narrative, and presentation in oral history. For those interested in pursuing such issues, recent work has been particularly rich. Eva McMahan's *Elite Oral History Discourse* is required reading for any discussion of the nature of historical conversations.[2] Two works in narrative, David Carr's *Time, Narrative and History*, and Kristin Langellier's article on "Personal Narratives," are particularly recommended, as is Jo Blatti's *Journal of American History* article on a theory for oral history and public history.[3] The ways in which the questions raised by Langellier and Blatti are reflected in fieldwork situations are explored in James Clifford and George Marcus, *Writing Culture*, and in Sidney Mintz's recent ruminations on his own fieldwork in Puerto Rico.[4]

Most importantly, Michael Frisch's *A Shared Authority* for the first time begins to outline a set of standards and methods for the uses of oral history in public history presentations.[5] The essays

in that volume are of particular value in both their descriptions of
the use of oral history and their thoughtful strictures about how
historians relate to their various publics. My own hope, which I
trust will not sound too arrogant, is that this volume will, when
read in conjunction with *A Shared Authority*, give the student of
oral history a consistent view of both the creation and use of oral
histories, while raising a similar set of questions about the nature
of historical consciousness and its expression.

Without a doubt, the literature in oral history has become self-
consciously critical and sophisticated in the last twenty years. I
would like to think that *Envelopes of Sound* has played and
continues to play some role in that development. It is in that spirit
that this edition is offered to a wider public.

1 Virginia Yans-McLaughlin, "Metaphors of Self in History:
  Subjectivity, Oral Narrative and Immigration Studies," in
  Immigration Reconsidered: History, Sociology and Politics, ed.
  Virginia Yans-McLaughlin (New York, 1990), p. 262.

2 Eva M. McMahan, *Elite Oral History Discourse: A Study of
  Cooperation and Coherence* (Tuscaloosa, Ala., 1989).

3 David Carr, *Time, Narrative and History* (Bloomington, Ind.,
  1986); Kristin M. Langellier, "Personal Narratives:
  Perspectives on Theory and Research," *Text and Performance
  Quarterly* (October 1989), pp. 243-276; Jo Blatti, "Public
  History and Oral History," *Journal of American History*, 77
  (September 1990), pp. 615-625.

4 James Clifford and George E. Marcus, eds., *Writing Culture:
  The Poetics and Politics of Ethnography* (Berkeley, Calif.,
  1986); Sidney Mintz, "The Sensation of Moving, While
  Standing Still," *American Ethnologist*, 16 (November 1989),
  pp. 786-796.

5 Michael Frisch, *A Shared Authority: Essays on the Craft and Meaning of Oral History and Public History* (Albany, N.Y., 1990).

Preface to the Second Edition
Ronald J. Grele

People have always told their histories in conversation. Throughout the ages, history has been passed on by word of mouth. Fathers to sons, mothers to daughters, grandparents to grandchildren, village elders to younger generations, gossips to eager ears; all in their own way tell of past events, interpret them, give them meaning, keep the collective memory alive. Even in our age of general literacy and pervasive media communication "the real and secret history of humankind" is told in conversation, and most people still form their basic understanding of their own past through conversations with others.

When does this become oral history? What distinguishes the swapping of stories from historical conversations? When does the telling of a tale become more than antiquarianism and begin to affect the consciousness of teller and hearer, and of the community itself?

The answer seems clear. The change occurs when historical imagination and criticism are brought to bear upon the tale; when, as Jeremy Brecher points out, the knowledge of the patterns of the past two hundred years is brought to bear upon the memory of the time under discussion. Conversations become historical in the truest sense when a context is formed for the dialogue. That context is provided by the historian, not as someone who holds a degree and therefore a monopoly over interpretation, but as someone who cares about the pastness of the past, who by an act of imagination tries to form a view of change over time which can explain what is being said. It is this dialectic between the telling of the story and the inquisitive and critical mind, whether of the "professional" historian or of the interested neighbor, which gives oral history its real dimension.

This book is about historical conversations, what we have chosen to call conversational narratives. It is about how they are formed, understood and interpreted. It is about the role historians play in their creation. And it is about their importance, not only for the preservation of a record of what really happened in the past, but for our own understanding of ourselves today.

Oral history holds great promise for the increase of our knowledge of the past and of how that past lives on in the present. Yet, as Michael Frisch has pointed out, very often that promise translates itself into an easy exercise in more history, or no history. In the first instance oral history is seen solely as a way to flesh out the record, to get more history for the historian. In the second it is seen as a way to bypass the historian, to get the real voice of the past unaffected by what the historian says or thinks, to get beyond history. It should be neither. Both views ignore the basic dialectic of the interview; the first by denying any interpretive power on the part of those we interview, the second by ignoring the crucial role of the historian in creating the document. Oral history should be a way to get a better history, a more critical history, a more conscious history which involves members of the public in the creation of their own history.

The major concern of this volume is method, but the aim of the discussion of method is to understand how it is that we can create the critical dialogue about the past that is so necessary to preserve our freedom in the present. Because oral history is a way of involving people heretofore uninvolved in the creation of the documents of their past, it is an opportunity to democratize the nature of history, not simply by interviewing them but by seeing that involvement as a prelude to a method which allows people to formulate their own meanings of their past experiences in a structured manner in response to informed criticism. It is a method of developing historical consciousness.

While we are interested in the canons of historical judgment and the rules for interviewing, as they apply to oral history, we are more concerned with the mind revealed through conversation. We accept all the rules of the profession such as: the complementarity of written and oral sources, the need for

basic research before interviewing, the development of a focused research design, etc. But we accept these canons because
they will allow us to create the kinds of documents which can
give us insight into the nature of the historical process itself
and the way in which people live in and with their history.

In the first edition of this work Alice Kessler-Harris saw the
frontier of the discussion about oral history as "that area where
myth, ideology, language and historical cognition all interact in
a dialectical transformation of the word into historical artifact."
That is still the territory with which we are concerned. Equally
important is our concern that, as Harris also noted, oral history
receive the kind of criticism it deserves.

At the time we published the first edition in 1975 it was
frankly experimental and tentative. There had been little
theoretical or methodological debate over the use of and nature
of oral history. Since that time historians in the United States
and especially in Europe have become increasingly interested
in the problems posed by the use of such documents. The
essays added to the original volume, some published in various
journals, reflect that increasing concern and offer a certain
vision of that work and its meaning. They also reflect the
emergence of a community of interest and a community of
concern among oral historians.

Three events have been of prime importance in moulding
that community of interest. The publication of *The Voice of
the Past* by Paul Thompson has given us a basic text. Whether
one agrees or disagrees with Thompson, his work has put oral
history (an event of the past thirty years) into the context of
the study of history since the time of Herodotus, and he has, in
detail, outlined its methodology. *The Voice of The Past* now
stands as the starting point for any serious discussion of oral
history.

Yet, for all its brilliance, that work is in many ways
informed by a fairly traditional view of the historical enterprise
and does not move to new theoretical ground. It must therefore
be located in conjunction with Thompson's latest publication,

Our Common History: The Transformation of Europe. The essays in that volume, most of which are based upon and use a much more complex and less conventional view of history, were originally delivered as papers at the First European International Oral History Conference at Essex, England in March 1979 (as was the essay titled "Listen to Their Voices" included in this volume). This meeting was the second major event in the development of a network of oral historians.

At that meeting, those of us who had been trying to grapple with the problems of interpreting oral data almost alone in our national communities met, and found, in the words of George Rawick, one of the American participants, that we had "comrades" in our struggle to give meaning to our work. Concern with the qualitative methodology of the social sciences, with consciousness and politics, an attempt to construct a science of the subjective, interest in the life history method and workers memoirs, and a common concern with language, ideology and the new social sciences was what united us. What emerged was a community of workers approaching similar problems in different traditions of discourse with a common drive to move beyond simply documenting the past to an understanding of how oral history can change the manner in which we study the past, and how those we interview relate to history and social change. In two meetings since that time and in the pages of the *International Journal of Oral History* (the publication of which is the third event in this recent history) that community has continued to develop and to elaborate its concerns. By giving a focus to these questions, the *Journal* has continued the dialogue begun in Essex.

The first four chapters of this volume reprint the earlier edition of this work: my interview with Studs Terkel, the radio discussion by six oral historians, Dennis Tedlock's remarkable article on the transcription of oral dialogue, and my initial effort to outline a method for understanding an oral history. "Listen to Their Voices," presented at Essex, was undertaken as an example of the type of analysis urged in the concluding essay in the original edition. "A Surmisable Variety," prepared for the *American Quarterly*, was an attempt to sum up the interdisciplinary literature on interviewing and its applicability. "Can Anyone Over Thirty Be Trusted?" was orginally published in the *Oral History Review* and reflects a concern with some of the newer issues in oral history. The concluding chapter was written for this edition and is an attempt to incorporate, with old concerns and a new international perspective, work being done in conversational analysis.

A book such as this owes an intellectual debt to many people. For the most part they are thanked by my footnotes to their work. E. Culpepper Clark, Eva McMahan, Michael Hyde, and Henry Glassie, the first three of whom I know fairly well, the fourth in passing, deserve special mention. Their efforts to understand the nature of historical communication have continued to stimulate me over the years and I have used their ideas and work heavily. They do not, of course, bear any responsibility for the way I have used it. Indeed, I think they may be rather shocked by how it all comes out.

Politically, personally and professionally I am also deeply grateful to: Luisa Passerini, Paul Thompson, Sally Alexander, Mercedes Vilanova, Alessandro Portelli, Lutz Niethammer, Daniel Bertaux, Anna Davin, Raphael Samuel, and Annamarie Troeger. They have alerted me to more potentialities and possibilities in my own work than I can quite handle at this time. Michael Frisch, one of the finest minds in our profession, deserves special mention. For many years he alone, it seemed, knew what it was I was searching for and what I wanted to say about oral history and consciousness. Although not necessarily agreeing with the way I used his help, he has always been willing to extend it. In addition, Jo Blatti and Howard Green deserve special thanks for their critical but kind comments on the concluding essay.

What oral history gives the historian it gives with abundance. It teaches us anew, every day, how important history is to the common cultural enterprise. It shows us again and again how people live with their past and try to make sense of their present. It allows us to enter people's lives in the most extraordinarily intimate ways. Because the people we talk to give us so much, it is our obligation to think carefully about what they are saying and why, and to evaluate carefully what we are given. These essays are offered in that spirit.

Preface to the First Edition
Ronald J. Grele

This book had its origins in a session on oral history at the Annual Meeting of the Organization of American Historians held in Chicago in April of 1973. The session was held in response to the widely shared concern of field workers with the inadequacy of the interviewing and transcribing procedures used in oral history, anthropology and other disciplines using oral testimony. The papers by Dennis Tedlock and myself, reporduced here, attempted to raise these concerns to a higher theoretical level to stimulate the kind of criticism which we believe is needed in the field.

Alice Kessler Harris organized and chaired this session and Saul Benison and Jan Vansina reviewed and commented on our presentations. The importance of the questions raised and the significance of the comments generated enough debate and requests for reprints to lead us to think in terms of seeking a wider audience.

Prior to the Annual Meeting, on the initiative of Professor Henry Cohen of Loyola University I interviewed Studs Terkel, perhaps the best known practitioner of oral history. He in turn, at the suggestion of Professor Alfred Young of Northern Illinois University, invited our panel to appear on his WFMT radio program. My interview with Terkel which appears here as Chapter I, and the radio transcript which appears as Chapter II, are the products of these meetings. They have been included because we felt they raised most of the major issues of oral testimony in a form far more accessible to the general public than our papers, which were prepared for a more scholarly audience.

This book attempts to introduce the general reader to the methods and problems of oral history, and to raise among students the larger and more theoretical issues of our practice. We do not believe these to be antagonistic aims, and therefore we have structured the essays so as to begin on the level of the specific and practical and move gradually on to more complex questions of method, language and theory. It is our hope that when read in this manner the book will progressively increase the reader's understanding of the nature of oral testimony and its use.

To underscore our concern with language we have tried to transcribe Chapters I and II as originally spoken. Because of the limited ability of our normal orthography to convey the spoken word some of our constructions may seem awkward or ungrammatical. There are sentences which are not sentences, odd syntax and strange punctuation in many places. More radically, Dennis Tedlock's essay, designed with the collaboration of Rick Hibberd, extends this concern to an experiment which attempts to find a new means to convey on the printed page the customary distinctiveness of oral language and testimony. When faced with these constructions we urge our readers to read aloud and catch the flavor of the language and its rhythms and cadences. Although this may seem, at first, a burden on the reader, it was our judgment that too much of the richness of the dialogue would be lost if we altered the spoken word to fit a written form, as arbitrary in its way as any other imposed form. We apologize for this inconvenience but trust that our instincts have been sound.

Finally, this book is also a series of essays on historiography because the issues raised in oral history automatically become issues in the practice and use of history. As Saul Benison notes in Chapter II, "It may be that one of the ultimate values of oral history is that it is a magnificent way of training a young historian to do history." If these chapters do that then perhaps we have accomplished as much as any of us can.

Introduction
Alice Kessler Harris

Historians have long felt that written documents lack human direction and spontaneity. Pre-censored and prepared for special purposes, they reveal only formal relationships, and are innocent of the lives of the vast numbers of poor and working people. Yet a long and respectable tradition beckons the historian to use the oral record. It dates back to the ancient Greeks, who collected participants' accounts of warfare and political practice, it travels through the medieval troubadours, it emerges in the nineteenth century from the pens of journalists and social critics. Represented at its best by Henry Mayhew and Jacob Riis, the oral tradition offers extraordinary insights into the lives and struggles of ordinary people.[1]

Twentieth century technology has given us the tape recorder. Like journalism, other academic disciplines have benefited from its capacity to collect and store oral data. Most historians, despite the tremendous advantages their perspective could bring to oral data, long remained reluctant to use it, seeming to agree with Charles Morrissey that "documents written while events were happening" provide the most reliable evidence. In this spirit Allan Nevins conceived and set up the Oral History Research Office at Columbia University. Saul Benison, one of Nevins' early assistants in the venture, describes Nevins' goal in the following words:

> He looked upon it as an organization that in a systematic way could obtain from the lips of living Americans who had led significant lives a full record of their participation in the political, economic, and cultural affairs of the nation. His purpose was to prepare such material for the use of future historians.[3]

In effect, Nevins saw the project as one which would prepare essentially written documents—which would record for historical personages recollections which they themselves had not written and would not write. Except for a small fragment of the original interview, intended to illustrate the subject's voice and style, tapes of the interviews were erased. The written transcript was considered sufficient information.

In the present age of diminished correspondence and increasing face-to-face and telephone contact, many historians saw in the creation of these documents indispensable tools for future assessment of the present. They were bridging what Benison has called a "technology gap." They were creating knowledge that would otherwise not exist: building a library for the future.

Under these circumstances, the historians' role seemed fairly straightforward. Since their purpose was to gather information from significant people about significant events, to create a complement to written documents, historians carefully selected their questions, led their subjects in directions they believed useful, and structured the interview so that the subject would reveal as much about historically significant events and people as possible. They felt little compunction about editing the tape, reviewing its contents with the subject, and encouraging him or her to alter or strike out words or phrases. The tape was treated as a journal article might be, with the subject-author and the historian-editor united in the desire to set down for others one individual's experience of his life.

However, the interposition of the historian, first as interviewer and transcriber and later as analyst, posed serious theoretical problems. The historian who had intervened to create a document had done more than simply use a remnant of the past to help explain an event or synthesize a larger interpretation. Only recently have historians realized that what happened in the course of the interview would affect the content and therefore the historical value of the tape, as the historian in effect became co-author. Critics soon questioned the intrusion of differences between the interviewer and his subjects, arguing that distinctions in dress, speech, and manners imposed on the subject a set of classbound attitudes that inevitably distorted the information that was offered. Others argued that the subject, anxious to please, would attempt to tell the interrogator what he or she thought the interviewer wanted to hear. Still others raised serious questions about the validity of memory, the selection of events to be discussed, and the subtle but important biases injected into an interview by voice tone, body gesture or ideological suggestion.

These conceptual problems, however, have not deterred historians from seeking oral data. Increasing numbers of students of recent history, with tape recorders in their brief cases and cassettes among their note cards, have liberated themselves from dependence on the written word. The social concerns of the late 1960s provided an important impetus. Those who rejected an "elitist" history of leaders and political events wanted to write about the poor and the underprivileged: about people who did not, perhaps could not record their own stories. Oral histories offered a glimpse into the life styles, belief systems and values of ordinary people. Historians with tape recorders could free themselves from the institutional constraints imposed by collections of written sources and documents. As they turned from formal biographical or autobiographical interviews to oral traditions, to songs, myths, folk tales, and poetry, they unfolded a history of workers for whom labor unions were marginal; of women who never participated in clubs or suffrage parades; of immigrants who were not church members or welfare cases.

The historical profession has not yet come to terms with the implications of this kind of material, despite the fact that it paves the way for a new social history which asks questions not about what happened, but about the historical processes of complex societies. Because at its best it posits answers in terms of a dialectical relationship between changing consciousness and social, political and economic movements, such materials deserve far more analysis and criticism than they have so far received.

These exciting possibilities have narrowed a once-enormous gap between history, and folklore and anthropology, and have led some historians to examine the myths and legends embedded in an oral folk tradition as well as to consider the extent to which myths about the past influence the behavior of individuals in the course of their daily lives. The historian who studies this tradition deals, in Richard Dorson's words, not with "the plain unvarnished facts, but all the notions, biases, and reactions aroused by the supposed fact. . . ."[4] It is this larger context that informs Studs Terkel's *Division Street* and *Hard Times*, a plunging into feelings about facts."This is a memory book," he says in his introduction to *Hard Times*. The interview for him, as he reveals in the interview that is transcribed herein, is a record of what people think and how they feel. "I'm like a prospector," he says, "I'm cutting whatever they cut out. They cut out the dust, or the crap, or the coal, or whatever it was, or the rock. . . . Then you weigh it, and then you find a form."

Terkel reveals the political and personal value of his approach in his interview with Ron Grele. The absence of knowledge about the past perpetuates myths about it, and contributes to maintaining the status quo. Denied a sense of history, people feel individual guilt about problems that may in fact be shared. They rarely, he suggests, stop to say, "wait a minute. Didn't something go wrong with the machinery?" Collecting data from ordinary people contributes to developing a shared sense of what happened. Elsewhere Staughton Lynd goes a step beyond Terkel when he argues that this shared consciousness may have instrumental value for altering society. "Rank and file trade unionists," he argues, "want to know the history of the 1920s so that they can respond to the present upsurge of labor militancy armed with analogies of why the CIO unions so rapidly grew bureaucratic and conservative." [5]

Other historians have seen in non-elite oral history a way of understanding patterns of deference and class that have contributed to maintaining a stable society. Tenaciously held and familiar beliefs that emerge during interviews can help to explain contemporary consciousness. Social mobility in America may be more mythical than real, but the historian who hears, as I have heard, dozens of immigrants describe the hope with which they came to America, begins to understand how the myth functions to maintain stratification. Similarly, Richard Sennett and Jonathan Cobb in *The Hidden Injuries of Class* suggest that the idea of sacrificing for their children encourages blue-collar workers to forget their own physical labor and poverty in the interests of a larger goal.

While much remains in dispute, there are some things about oral history with which few would disagree. Where written sources are available, they should be used as background as well as corroboration. Oral data does not exonerate the historian from searching for and using written documents exhaustively. Critical questions about reliability, validity and the representative nature of the data are as essential for oral sources as they are for written material. A cardinal rule is to come to the interview thoroughly informed and then to let the subject do the talking. Those historians who see the interview as more than an archival or data-gathering process, stress the importance of saving tapes. Ideally video tape would be used to preserve gestures and facial expressions, but verbal intonations, silences, and breathing rates which can be heard on an ordinary cassette are also important clues to the emotional affect of the subject. Unlike their colleagues who use whatever happens to be available, oral historians select documents. They must remain conscious of what their subjects represent. In choosing the people they wish to interview, they necessarily introduce their own judgments about the historical process. Why men rather than women? Strike leaders rather than followers? Strikers rather than strikebreakers?

Unlike diaries, letters and personal papers that were themselves responses to the event or period being studied, interviews are created after the fact and reflect the participants' self-conscious attempts to preserve what they remember for the future. The distortions inherent in materials that have been prepared for the historian, as opposed to those which are artifacts of a period or event, may be impossible to gauge. At a

minimum they involve the subject's view of the historical process
and of his or her place in it. The only way to avoid this problem,
as anthropologist Dennis Tedlock aptly illustrates, is to use oral
data that grows out of the culture itself. Tedlock's reconstructions
of Zuni poetry exemplify the collection of data that are already
there. Unlike the oral historian, he has not intervened in creating
it other than by his presence. He has merely switched on the tape
recorder at an appropriate time. To quote Tedlock, "people do
not reveal their ideas of history only when they are conversing
with an interviewer."

Even this, however, has its dangers. Jan Vansina, whose
Oral Tradition: A Study in Historical Methodology remains the
most useful study of its kind, has argued that Grele's concern
with the confrontation of classes and Tedlock's with the confrontation of cultures may obscure the ordinary but idiosyncratic
expressions of one culture or of one class. "Cultural values," he
has argued,

> colour testimonies in three main ways. Through the medium
> of the first informant, they determine the choice of what
> events to record and the significance attached to them.
> Through the medium of certain cultural concepts, chiefly
> those concerning time and historical development, they
> distort chronology and historical perspective. Lastly, they
> make testimonies conform to cultural ideals, thus turning
> them into examples to be followed. [6]

Unless researchers from one tradition understand the cultural
values of another, they may fail completely to understand the
significance and meaning of the testimony. Turning on a tape
recorder is not enough. Informed listening is an essential adjunct.

All of these and other problems are discussed in the
following chapters. The papers reflect the debates about method
and techniques, and focus on the frontiers of the discussion about
oral history—that area where memory, myth, ideology, language

and historical cognition all interact in a dialectical transformation of the word into an historical artifact. In different
ways each of us is trying to address ourselves to the problem of
what the oral historian is all about. Our answers are buttressed
by the performances themselves, for each chapter of this book is a
performance, each unique and each with its own structure, yet all
united by the common concerns already noted above.

In Chapter I Studs Terkel, author of *Hard Times, Division
Street*, and *Working*, three major works using oral testimony, is
interviewed by a formally trained historian, Ronald Grele. In
this section the questions posed about editing, questioning, bias
and oral testimony are themselves contained and answered
within the interview format. Form and content are thus united
and turned in upon each other.

In the second chapter, the tables are turned and Terkel
demonstrates his technique on his WFMT (Chicago) radio
program, deftly throwing queries at, and catching the responses
of five academics. Here, as one would expect, the temper and
tone of the performance differs strikingly from that in Chapter I.
The language is much more formal and precise and the questions
raised and problems discussed are more theoretical and abstract.

Chapters III and IV are extensions of two of the major
questions raised in the first two chapters. Dennis Tedlock is involved
in the vexing problem of transcribing the spoken language into
written form. His essay in Chapter III is both a rendition of the form
of a Zuni poetic narrative and an example of how to render that
narrative so that the poetry becomes simultaneously artifact and
document. As a performance it most resembles a dramatic reading.

The final chapter is a formal paper, originally presented at a
professional meeting and reflecting all the criteria of language
style and tone expected by such groups. In this essay, Grele
sketches out a theoretical framework that tries to come to terms
with some of these problems. He offers us three ways of con-

fronting an interview: a linguistic analysis of the conversation itself, an attempt to understand the personal interaction between the people involved, and a conception of the cultural milieu or "problematic" that the subject brings to the interview.

Each of these performances was originally spoken. All are here reduced to written form. The audience has in effect been eliminated and therefore the richness of gesture and life are gone. What remains is a document that can only mimic the earlier performances.

The past comes to us encumbered with feelings and perceptions that derive from an individual's cultural experience as well as from his unique engagement. Sometimes consciousness of cultural experience is articulated. More often it lies buried deep within a stream of words and their accompanying gestures. As a result oral history presents some pitfalls and a set of theoretical problems to those who would successfully engage in it. It also offers enormous and exciting possibilities. This book will illustrate the insights and the problems faced by historians who use the spoken word as a source. In the process it will, we hope, de-mystify an ancient and universal technique.

1 See Eileen Yeo and E. P. Thompson, eds., *The Unknown Mayhew* (New York: Pantheon Books, 1971), and Jacob Riis, *How The Other Half Lives* (New York: Scribner's, 1902).

2 Charles Morrissey, "The Case for Oral History," *Vermont History* 31 (July, 1963), 146.

3 Saul Benison, "Reflections on Oral History," *American Archivist* 28 (January, 1965), 71.

4 Richard M. Dorson, "The Oral Historian and the Folklorist," *Selections from the Fifth and Sixth National Colloquia on Oral History* (N.Y.: The Oral History Association, 1972), 48.

5 Staughton Lynd, "Guerrilla History in Gary," *Liberation* 14 (October, 1969), 17.

6 Jan Vansina, *Oral Tradition: A Study in Historical Methodology* (London: Routledge and Kegan Paul, 1965), 108.

Riffs and Improvisations
An Interview with Studs Terkel
April 10, 1973
Chicago, Illinois
Interviewer: Ronald J. Grele
Also present: Henry Cohen
                    Nell Gifford

Grele: My first question is a general question: how and when did you start interviewing people?

Terkel: Well the interviewing itself came accidentally. I don't recall the exact moment of doing it. Originally, I was a disc jockey and played recordings and I liked folk music very much; I interviewed some folk singers; Big Bill Broonzy the blues singer whom I knew; people like Woody Guthrie, Pete Seeger, people I knew. I interviewed Marais and Miranda, the South African couple. They were among the early ones. Accidentally it happened, you know, unplanned, the idea of interviewing, itself. And bit by bit, a writer came through town or it might have been a concert artist, and that's how it began.

I remember someone called up once and said: "Gee, I like your interviewing. . . ." You know, "I'd like you to get more people, to talk to more people."

Grele: You were doing a radio show then?

Terkel: It was a radio program originally on an AM station; part of the ABC network. I was a disc jockey playing folk music and jazz. The first interview I ever did as a matter of fact, for a small station, was with Bud Freeman, a jazz tenor sax man and that was, perhaps, '39, '40, around there. Something like that.

Grele: I listened to your program this morning and it occurred to me that there might be a relationship between the kind of music that you particularly like which is almost a vocal kind of music; folk music, jazz, and I was wondering if there was any relationship between that and conversation, sound and voice?

Terkel: I'd say that's a very good observation. I don't know. I hadn't thought about it. I hadn't thought about it consciously but I think it's been with me for a long, long

time; the idea of jazz, particularly jazz, or folk music.
The approach of jazz is improvisational in nature.
There is a beginning, middle and end of jazz, you
know, a skeletal framework and even when it's
arranged there's still a skeletal aspect to it. And so the
performer, when it comes time for a solo, creates as well
as performs and so there's an improvisational air to it.
And it's not the air of the unexpected so much as the air
of allowance for something to happen that you don't
plan for. And so in an interview, somebody says
something and I don't come prepared.

Let's say an author, let's start with that and then we'll
come to the non-celebrated people. I read his book, let's
take our friend of this afternoon, Billington, and it's a
thick book on Frederick Jackson Turner. I go through it
pretty thoroughly. I mark it. I wish I had a copy of it.
It's rather indecipherable, but I make it out. Now that
I've read it, it's there. And he starts talking. I don't
memorize what I've read but I have an idea generally,
and a phrase or two might come to my mind. He says
something and it reminds me of something I've read. I
call it, "the phrase that explodes," whatever it might
be. I'm interviewing a person, let's say a boner at the
stock yards and he tells me about his work. Something
he says, one thing, might open many avenues. And so in
a way it's jazzy in that sense. There's a beginning, a
middle and an end. You see I've read the book of
Billington's. I know a little about this guy; he's a boner
and he lives in a housing project, and he's eighty years
old. I know that much. And he's on welfare or he's
getting a pension check. But from then on you talk and
you're on your own. You're not wholly unprepared.
Now you're very prepared for the author. Unfortunately, it's a rare case that the guys interviewing
authors read the books. That's one of the sad parts. I

have to. I have to or otherwise I couldn't do it because there are standards I have to maintain.

To come back to the matter of the music we talked about: folk music is sort of mythic in nature, often. You know the Child ballads, and I guess I believe more and more in this as I grow older; not in myths, as such, but in the fact that fact is not always truth, you know. Fact is not always truth. Truth is something else. Remember the bombing of Hiroshima? You know that's a perfect case in point; the navigator of the Enola Gay turns out to be a forger and a liar.

Grele: Right.

Terkel: And he wrote a book with a German guy, called *Burning Conscience*, and so people who were criticizing him were saying: "See that? See that? How can you believe this guy; he's a forger, he's a liar. So what the hell's it about?"

Well, John Wain, that is the British writer, the other John Wain, W-a-i-n, did a BBC program on this guy; Claude Eatherley, and he said, "Maybe he's a liar about forging and all this. Maybe facts are not truth. The truth is he was on a plane called the Enola Gay. The truth is we bombed Hiroshima with an atom bomb. That's the truth. The fact is, this guy was a forger and this guy lied. Now what's more important: the truth or the facts?"

Now we come back to me and my program. As I said in the preface of *Hard Times* that you have there. It's a memory book. Right! Remember this kid from the *Red Buffalo*? He used that. This guy, I said "kid", I don't know. But he made something of it and he's right! See, the fact is it's a memory book. Now is what they're telling true or not? Well, there's that sequence I used from *Grapes of Wrath*, it's their truth. So if it's their truth it's got to be my truth, it's their experience. Somebody lived through that time with a certain something he remembers: that scar left on him; the memory is true. It's there. It's like a doctor saying or someone saying, "The guy's not sick because there are no symptoms. We know it's psychosomatic." But he's still sick. The guy can't find the specific cancer or whatever it might be, but the guy's sick.

Coming back to this matter: How a person, how a human is affected, to me is an important thing. Now if someone says, "The guy's a liar," that really doesn't matter to me. This man experienced something at a certain moment in the Depression, or like the forger Claude Eatherley.

Grele: But it raises a very important question for the historian, the distinction you draw between a memory book and history book, and the question that most of us really haven't quite grappled with in our own interviews; that when we interview we're getting someone's memory of an event, not an exact portrayal of that event. Did you begin with this as a conscious notion? Or is it something that evolved out of your own experiences?

Terkel: I think it evolved. I'm sure it did. Oh, I'm certain it wasn't conscious. No, I think it just occurred to me a little slowly. It just occurred to me as it went along. I don't know when it occurred to me. I didn't think of it. I thought, I'm going to talk to survivors of the great American Depression.

Now, the new work I'm on here, this is more specific; it's about work, how work affects most people's lives. Now they're telling what they do specifically. The spot welder at the Ford assembly plant, he's telling what he does eight hours a day. Now I interviewed another spot welder too; first a white guy, then a black guy, then an old lady, then a guy from the mountain country who is a utility man, which is a step above spot welding. But what they're describing is not only true, it's factual. It's the day. Particularly the mountain guy. You often find that people from the non-city areas, black or white, are much more specific as they talk and as a result much more poetic. We'll come to the matter of poetry in a moment; your friend Tedlock and his theory about oral history must be poetry, it can't be prose. We'll come back because he's talking about Indians, Zuni Indians.

But coming back to the matter of this guy, Franklin Legg. He's fantastic! He describes getting up in the morning in its every detail. He says, "I get up, I open one eye and then open the other eye and then I turn on the radio and then I go to the bathroom and I comb my one hair." He says, "I don't like it." Then he says, "I dread that. And then sometimes I have a cup of coffee, sometimes half a cup of coffee. Depends. Routine you know?" And the word "routine" figures. But as he describes it there's a cadence to it. And often you'll find this. And there's the poetry too, in a way. But the work book will be a little closer, I suppose, to facts. Because they're talking about now rather than then.

Did you see "The Sorrow and the Pity", the film?

Grele: No, I didn't.

Terkel: Ahh. You see, well that's what he was doing, in a way. That's a memory picture. You know, "The Sorrow and the Pity," Marcel Ophuls' movie of the French town of Clermont-Ferrand where a great many were in collaboration with the Nazis. But there, too, it's a film about middle age. That's also a memory. But out of it evolves what, in some way or other, higgledy-piggledy, you might call truth.

Grele: The reaction to that film brings up another question concerning the reaction to your book, *Hard Times*: Both the film and the book were generally misinterpreted. Why do you think historians misinterpreted your book? I think Frisch is right on that point.

Terkel: You mean in the *Red Buffalo*?

Grele: Yes. Yes.

Terkel: He made a good point, didn't he?

Grele: Yes.

Terkel: He was quoting all the favorable reviews and saying how they missed the point. As one, the *Saturday Review*, said, it was an, "anthem in praise of the American spirit."

Grele: Yes.

Terkel: And it's "a song". And only two, Murray Kempton and Nelson Algren. Nelson used the phrase "a failure of nerve" and Kempton saw something else. Well they were right. Because if they weren't right we wouldn't be in the mess we're in right now, quite obviously. That's the whole point. Of course they're right. They're right because it's not an anthem to the American spirit. Oh I suppose it was, in a way. It was both. This is a cliche, of course, "When there's a common disaster," this is Ignazio Silone's phrase, "it's every man's disaster." "A general disaster is every man's disaster." And I think Dorothy Day used that a lot. And she was hoping, Dorothy Day was hoping; she prayed for another depression rather than the Vietnam War. From a humanistic point of view she was saying, "Rather a depression than the prosperity of Vietnam." But she romanticizes too, marvelous, beautiful being that she is, she romanticizes. In fact people did grovel, people were humiliated, people did blame themselves, people never questioned society.

The minority did. The minority called the rebels, subversives, the reds, the minority. Or, for that matter, the ultra-right, too, would damn it in their own way whether it be a Coughlin or a Townsend, you know. Not Gerald Smith because Gerald Smith was owned by Henry Ford; well, not that Coughlin wasn't, but the fact is the "extremes," so-called, were critical. I love that word the "extremes," you know, "watch out for the extremists." Do you know Martin Luther King's crack about that? Remember that one? He was asked, "Why do you associate with extremists?" and "Aren't you an extremist?" when he was in prison and these two white clergymen wrote to him. His reply was, "Our Christ was too, and so were the two thieves beside him. But extreme toward what end?" There's something called creative extremism. Well these guys, I felt, in the thirties who led the hunger marches were creative extremists.

But coming back to the misinterpretation. You often hear someone say, "Oh God, the good old days."

Grele: Yes, they seem to.

Terkel: "The good old days." They were horrible old days. You know. But at the same time and we come now to one of the key things; the differences in people. There were people who were very rich, but they didn't flaunt it. They were quiet, they were scared. As some woman said, "What's more frightened than a million dollars." What's more scared than a million dollars? But you see today with television, with everything, you see the gaps, the tremendous gaps between the haves and the have nots. And in the homes of the have nots who have a television set you see all the stuff that is there to buy, but they've no wherewithal to buy. And you see the absolute insensitivity, not that the rich were any more sensitive then; they weren't. As Sally Rand, my striptease friend/informant, points out; they weren't any less insensitive then than they are now. But we didn't have the means of communication that we have today. That's a factor.

Coming back to the period. Of course there was less fear of ragged strangers then because there were so many of them. As says this one waitress, "I didn't fear that strange man as I fear a strange man today. There were so many." You would have had to fear life itself.

Grele: This is a question of both *Division Street* and *Hard Times* but it involves history. In *Division Street* you say that you find people with no past and no future; that they're very "presentist"; that they have no conception of history. And then in *Hard Times* you draw a distinction between history and memory. And then the historians, of course, come in and pose their own historical frame against something that you have done. Do you really find people lack a sense of history?

Terkel: I hate to say that, but yes. Think of what is happening at this moment, if we may talk about the POW's. We have to think about it. It's on my mind right now. And the media plays its role, quite obviously. You know, through the years the media has always played this role of handmaiden, really it has, to established values. Of course there are individual journalists. There's a Heywood Broun, you know, here and there. There's someone who kicks the establishment, now and then, but generally speaking they haven't. Look at today, right now. Are they forgetting what it is that happened? How were the guys captured? What is it they

did? Now take a case yesterday. I was talking to Carey
McWilliams. I sent a comic thing, a satirical article, to
Carey McWilliams of the *Nation* yesterday. I told him,
"Do you want something? I'll send it." He may or may
not use it. It's about the POW's but it also brings us
back to people and a sense of history. I was watching
"Issues and Answers" yesterday and that became the
basis of this article. And two guys, Herbert Kaplow,
who hardly moves his lips, and he's not even British!
and another guy, whose name I don't remember, are
questioning a guy named General Flynn, a POW. And
General Flynn explains the fortitude of the captives. He
says, "We knew why we were there." And this goes on.
And so I'm waiting for someone to say, "Why *were* you
there?" But no one asked! And so then it goes on. Later
on he says, "Well, as we all know, I'm convinced that
Thieu's South Vietnamese government is more stable
than North Vietnam, and by its democratic spirit we
know it will survive any onslaught of socialism." And
no one asked, "Well, how did you come to *that* conclusion General?" And then there's another question at
the end, "And so we were there, and we were
courageous in pursuing our national objective," And no
one asked, "What *is* our national objective?

It's like Nelson Algren's comic figure, Somefellow
Willie, only they didn't even have the curiosity of
Somefellow Willie. Somefellow Willie, and this is by
way of coming back to your question, Somefellow
Willie feels suspicious because he always looks
suspicious to the cops. So one day they invite him into
their squad car. And he says, "Why am I here?" They
say, "Look in the rear view mirror." He looks and they
say, "Don't you look suspicious?" And he agrees. And
so they take him to the station and they fingerprint him.
He says, "Why did you fingerprint me?" They say,

"Well, you know, you haven't knocked anybody on the head yet, but you might." And he agrees because he looked suspicious and felt suspicious. And he hung around the station for weeks waiting to take the lie detector test in case the cops needed him, because he needed them. And so the media needs Nixon because obsequiousness has come so natural. And I'm saying, why are Nixon and Whitehead so heavy-handed, why can't they be like the heroine of John Cheever's short story, *Torch Song*? The girl is so understanding of her men that they all commit suicide because they feel guilty. And so I'm saying these TV men don't need threats. All you do is pat them on the back, that's how the article for the *Nation* goes.

And so coming back, here we are watching this typical show of the returned POW's. We've forgotten that we've bombed villages, how we got there. We're bolstering up a two-bit little phony as we bolstered the phony before him, and they call it the "free world." And so I'm not blaming the people. And so how can they remember the Depression, the young? They're not told about it by their parents outside of a bawling out. But their parents feel guilty. Guilty because, "I didn't work," the Protestant ethic, "I didn't work. Therefore, something's wrong with me." Now, wait a minute! Didn't something go wrong with the machinery? And so historians haven't done it. Commentators certainly haven't done it in any of the media. This is a round-about way of answering your question, "Do people have a sense of history?" No. It doesn't mean they're stupid, it means they've been denied it. And this is the horror. You know, I hate to use that Santayana phrase again that's so much of a cliche now; if you forget the past, you're doomed to re-live it in the future. Here we go again! And now in just this morning's news, one of the POW's who is now an authority on the subject has told Ramsey Clark that the anti-war protestors prolonged the war. And this is accepted as a matter of fact by the media. And so far there has been no comment to the contrary.

Grele: You know, given the dominant ideology of American life, given the relationship of the media to that ideology, wouldn't it be more surprising if these men did begin to question why they were there?

Terkel: Oh, I'm not talking about the POW's. I'm talking about the media. No. I agree with you. Oh, of course! Who were these men? And if we're going to be this brutally specific, who were these guys? Were they the grunts? The guys Tony Herbert, Colonel Herbert describes as the "grunts". They weren't. They were a distance from the others. They were the officers, the professionals.

Do you know Andre Schiffrin? Andre is the editor of Pantheon Publishing, Andre Schiffrin. He's quite remarkable. He's the one responsible for my doing *Hard Times* and *Division Street*. How they came about is interesting and this is connected with oral history. I was interviewing people on the air, on radio and now and then in a magazine called *Perspectives* that the station has reprinted. And Andre Schiffrin of Pantheon, whose father was Pierre Schiffrin, who founded Pantheon Books in Europe with Kurt and Helen Wolff and escaped Hitler; went to France and from Vichy France came over to America. Andre is his son. And even though Random House owns Pantheon, Andre's quite independent, quite autonomous. He published Jan Myrdal's *Report From a Chinese Village* and then he got the idea, how about a report from an American village, Chicago? And that's how it came about. I speak of that in the Preface to Division Street. And Andre then thought, how about a period forgotten? The Depression. And he talked me into it as he did into the current one, the work book.

Grele: When you started *Division Street*, were you trying to get a sense of Chicago as a unit?

Terkel: I don't think so, I don't think it was something unique about Chicago. I was trying to get something unique about an American industrial city. Yes. I think that was it. Chicago was a good case in point.

I live here and know the city fairly well. And so I suppose that's what Andre had in mind too. He liked my interviews. He thought of that. But also I was in Chicago. Not that Chicago is unique. I don't think it is. I don't believe it for a moment. No, it certainly is not.

Grele: Well, you know, you quote Algren's *City on the Make?*

Terkel: Oh, that's right! Yes. Well.

Grele: You know, what Algren says about Chicago could be said about any city.

Terkel: Of course, but Nelson's a lover. He's a lover. He's a lover of the place where he is. And he's a poet, you know? Chicago is like a woman with a broken nose, you know. She may not be the loveliest of lovelies, but she's the loveliest lovely there is. Something like that. Well, of course. He's ideal for a city like this.

Grele: How do you select your interviewees?

Terkel: Again, you see, say for *Division Street*: Well, who were the people in a large American city? A certain kind of woman, a housewife, lower middle class, maybe a woman of the posh class, some woman who has become a professional; individuals mostly.

Let's take Eva Barnes who runs this tavern, to break a stereotype. Here she is; she's ethnic, in other words, she's worked hard. Her father was a gypsy miner in

Southern Illinois, meaning a guy who travelled around. A Lithuanian, she started work at the age of seven; at twelve she was in packinghouse; at eighteen organizing union. "Union," now I didn't say *the* union because very often in Chicago street talk the article is left out, almost Slavic in nature. Many cities are conditioned. You could be like an amateur Professor Higgins.

Grele: Yes.

Terkel: They're conditioned by the largest ethnic group. New York, Jewish. I've got to tell you this story: I was in New York and a cab driver picks me up and his name was Ryan, and his first name was I-u-s-s-i, Iussi. I said, "What a strange name you've got." So the man named Ryan said, "what can I tell you?" I said, "Iussi Ryan, Iussi Ryan. Is that sort of Scandinavian?" "What can I tell you? I had an aunt named Iussi." I said, "Mr. Ryan, you don't sound Irish." He said, "I live in New York." I said, "Have you ever heard of Jussi Bjoerling?" He said, In a Jewish sing-song, "*You* know Jussi Bjoerling?" "You know?" I said, "Your name is Ryan, you sound Jewish." He said, "I live in New York, what can I tell you?" He lets me off at a Yorkville place where I'm going to talk at the YMHA. He said, "It's a Joiman neighborhood." I said, "Yeah." He said, "You go to a Joiman restaurant?" I said, "Ryan!" as much as to say "What can I tell you?" Well, that's New York. O.K.

So Minnesota has a Scandinavian aspect to it. Chicago defintely has a Slavic aspect to it. So Eva Barnes worked unions, you see. Nelson is very good at this—Algren in many of his short stories, because he's covered Polish communities, Polish-American. What were we talking about?

Grele: How you select the people you're going to interview.

Terkel: Ah so! How do I select? Sometimes an individual—in

Grele: that individual is more than one person, you know.

Grele: Yes.

Terkel: In someone who might be the archetype, is the anti-
          archetype, like Eva. So you think she's going to be anti-
          black, a hawk; she turns out to be the opposite. But in
          her thoughts she understands all the feelings of those
          who are hawks and racists. See? That's the thing. So
          sometimes you have to be in that person. And so the
          person generally is a poet. In everybody there's this—
          this again is romantic-sounding—there's a streak of it
          in everyone. What's a greater line than from a woman I
          call Lucy Jefferson? "There's such a thing as feeling
          tone; either you have it or you don't, you know, it's
          either hostile or it's friendly. If you ain't got it baby,
          you've had it." The indifference. And then I later on
          discover "feeling tone" is a word used by Jung. I didn't
          know that. Jung used the word "feeling tone" con-
          tinuously. Isn't that interesting? Now, how did Lucy
          Jefferson come to that, a black woman and Jung?

          Anyway, so selecting the people, I look for certain kinds.
          Sure I want a guy working steel; steel mills. So I found
          this Mexican-American guy. The word "Chicano"
          wasn't used then. And he was very furious with himself.
          But he was a special kind of person. But in this
          uniqueness is also a generalness too. He's a guy who was
          tremendous. He had certain feelings. He wanted to go
          into art, he had feelings about the world, about the
          Spanish Civil War. He said, "I read *Playboy*. I'm no
          good." He said, "I'm weak. I'm no good. I just wreck
          cars. I drive cars around." But in this guy you find a lot
          of things about a steel man. Instead of choosing just a
          clod. Now a clod's important as a man. It's not his fault.
          But there's "The Man With The Hoe." You know. If
          you use just the man with the hoe, nothing's going to
          come out. There has to be someone who, in his own

way, has an articulateness but at the same time is not so atypical as to be so different.

Grele: What is it that leads you in the search for the general ;— is it your conception of what is the general process or the general trend of an historical event like the Depression?

Terkel: I don't know how to answer that.

Grele: Or is it the real reality?

Terkel: I'm really not aware when I do an interview except toward the end; like now, with the work book. Now, I feel certain trends in certain areas, certain positions in my mind. The book is worked out now, pretty well worked out. I'm almost finished with the first draft, you know, and it's pretty well worked out now. But when I first start? What was the first interview for the work book? I don't recall the first one. It wasn't the bus driver? The first one for the work book, I'm trying to recall. He was one of these assembly line guys. He might have been a Ford worker. But at the time you think, "What is life on the assembly line like?" You know Harvey Swados' book, *On The Line?*   .

Grele: Yes.

Terkel: Swados describes the horror. You know, the myth of the happy worker? He described that myth when he did *On The Line* and very good. But it's even worse than what he described. There's a new book that just came by a kid from the *Detroit Free Press* called *The Company and the Union.* Do you know about that one?

Grele: Yes.

Terkel: About the UAW being sweethearts in a way. Not quite sweethearts but it's an arrangement. It's a hell of a book. William Serrin. It's called *The Company and the Union.* And he's right. He describes their lives. They go to the Green Room. The Green Room is the punishment room, you know. And their lives; sure, they get the minimum wage and all that but the union's hardly anything. The steward has to plead with the foreman or the superintendent, you know, to give them another break. It's humiliation continuously. And so this book *The Company and the Union* is right.

Grele: But you begin each book with a conception?

Terkel: Oh yes.

Grele: Chicago? Depression? The thirties?

Terkel: I put down a whole list of the kind of people; say, oh it's going to be someone doing dirty work, you know. Let's see, the maid, the domestic: certainly the automobile, the auto, and the auto becomes a key in the book. The auto's a big—it's divided into seven books or something. Seven big sequences and one by itself; the "Demon Lover." There's an old Child ballad that deals with this strange mysterious evil knight who woos this girl; he takes her away. And she says, "Where do you think we're going?" He says, "To one of the white hills of heaven, my dear." The white hills of heaven. And she says, "Where are they?" "On the dark hills of Hell!" It was the automobile. You know, the Demon Lover. Part of it is the making; the guys at the plant, also a superintendent, and a foreman; and Garry Bryner of Lordstown, he's in it, the young Lordstown union guy who is so wonderful. Then it goes to the parking; the driving; a bus driver, a young guy and an old guy. I mean, a cab driver, bus drivers, interstate truck drivers and the salesmen. And that's called the Demon Lover. Then it goes into something else; communications. Communications; the girl at the switchboard, receptionists, a middle-aged motel switchboard operator, a young telephone operator. And that goes into "a pecking order," I call it. I'm now working with women, see? And now it goes into the young airline stewardess who wants to be a model; goes into a high-fashion model; a model into an actress, a model-actress; and that goes into an executive secretary who loves her boss, you know, quotes him. And that goes into a call girl, and the call girl says, "All that they've been taught to be is what I am successfully doing." You know? And that goes into something else. So that's what I'm working on. That's the way.

Grele: Would you say that that same kind of thought process is behind *Division Street* and *Hard Times*?

Terkel: I don't know. This is a tougher one. This one is a bigger one, this one, because it's work. And work is everything. You know, love and work or work and love.

Grele: In your own mind there is a process there.

Terkel: In my own mind the idea of talking to people. Yeah, I'd say the process of the doing of it is similar. Yes, because it's finding out what is going on inside. A guy I met named Denis Mitchell who was a British film maker, I think influenced me a lot, a lot more than I realized. And Denis came to Chicago to work on a film on Chicago. I was his guide. Remember that film that was banned in Chicago about ten years ago? There were headlines in the papers: Daley banned it. "Daley Going to Punch Denis Mitchell in the Nose."

Cohen: What are you talking about?

Terkel: I'm talking about "Chicago."

Cohen: I never heard of it.

Terkel: Oh, didn't you? Well it was headlined, but it was never seen. It was banned without being seen because someone told Daley they saw it in England and it was not a good image of Chicago. It was a marvelous film. Hardly any narration; they just speak for themselves. But Denis once said he was looking for the "hurts" in people, the "hurts." And I call it the hidden hurts. You know *The Hidden Injuries of Class* by Cobb and Sennett? You know this book, don't you?

Grele: Yes. It's a terrible book.

Terkel: Didn't you like it? It got clobbered recently. Henry just read it. I didn't think it was too bad. I kind of liked it. You mean it continued the ethnic glorification?

Grele: Oh no, no, no, no. What I didn't like about the book was that rather than trying to grasp what people are all about, he just lapses into a strange psychology and calls them adolescents.

Terkel: Yeah, but the "hidden injuries." I like the phrase, "The Hidden Injuries of Class."

Grele: Yes, the title's beautiful.

Terkel: And the hidden injuries of class is the key. See? What I call hidden hurts. And sometimes it's not even class.

Grele: Right.

Terkel: Oh, but class figures a great deal, you know, especially with the matter of status. You know how blue collar people feel, there's no question about it. There's a guy who opens my book. He's almost a grotesque case in point; he's fantastic. His comments in the book are fantastic. He's the one—did you read the *Dissent* issue on the blue collar worker? That's the guy. Remember that opening one?

Grele: Right.

Terkel: About, who built the pyramids? Well, that's Mike. What I see in him is so much turmoil, so much violence against himself. "Why do guys get in fights in taverns?"

He said, "Instead of punching the foreman, we punch ourselves." If anything, if one word comes into my mind, one theme to the work book, it's violence. Violence. It's called "work." I feel like sub-titling it. "Our Daily Violence."

Grele: Is there a relationship between the work and the violence?

Terkel: Oh, my God yes! Oh Jesus! I don't mean just physical, psychic as well. Psychic violence. I imagine you've experienced it, psychic violence. That's the thing. But I would say the quest is the same. The quest is the same; the hurts. Yeah.

Grele: It sounds like the organization of the book on work will follow the pattern of the interviewing. But that was not the case with either *Division Street* or *Hard Times*. I take this from reading *Division Street* which begins with—I wrote the name down, but I've forgotten it now.

Terkel: Florence Scala.

Grele: Florence Scala. Right. And ends with Jessie Binford.

Terkel: Jessie Binford. yeah.

Grele: Both from Hull House, the most ideological and political of the interviewees in there.

Terkel: That's interesting. Gee. That was not planned. That's my point. That came about. You know, I didn't plan that.

Grele: Was this the way you actually did the interviews, you began with Florence Scala?

Terkel: No. Oh no! No, no. Oh no, you interview, just go ahead. The first interview in that book was—Oh Christ! Who the hell was the first interviewee. God! I know Caesar Chavez was the first interview of *Hard*

Times, but I forget who the first was in that one. Oh no, that comes about when you get the interview and then in your mind—Here's the jazz, here's where jazz figures in. I don't know. I'm not a musician, but I know how a jazz artist thinks, one thought leads to another association, one note leads to another. Suddenly you take off on that and you vary on the themes. Well, I had all these interviews and, "What? How to open this?" And Florence occurred to me. Hull House, Florence, Jane Addams, a community. Suddenly the thought came to me and grew.

Florence's friend in the latter days of this friend's life was an old acquaintance, a friend and colleague of Jane Addams, this marvelous old Quaker woman named Jessie Binford. I think she was a Quaker whose father helped found a town, Marshalltown, Iowa, and she went there to die when she was driven out of Chicago. They became friends. In fact, way back some guys planned a play about them, Nathaniel Benchley, and a musical play by Richard Rogers. It never worked out. My approach was to use them as the two figures wandering through. I never told that before; two figures wandering through. Not an *Inferno* sort of, but the idea of wandering through a city, these two women, you know? But that wasn't planned. I didn't think about it as an ideological—but now that you mention it, yes, I suppose.

Grele: Because you're much more aware.

Terkel: I was unaware of my doing it, but I suppose it is so.

Grele: The opening and close of the book are very interesting in that way.

Terkel: That's true. That's true. This one will open with a guy who is very bitter and violent and it's going to close with a marvelous Huck Finn figure; a New York fireman. His father was a drunk, and that's the whole point of it. So this end will close with Huckleberry Finn. He is at heart the kind of guy who is marvelous and funny and fantastic. He's a New York fireman. At the end we have that. And that wasn't planned. I was horsing around. Horsing around has a lot to do with it.

Grele: But in the process of this horsing around the book then becomes a work of art as well as a work of history.

Terkel: I hope so.

Cohen: Did you ever come home from a session, Ron, and find the whole thing wasn't working?

Grele: Yes, I did that when I interviewed Senator Talmadge.

Terkel: You interviewed Herman Talmadge?

Grele: Yes, I got back to the office and there was nothing on the tape.

Terkel: I did that a couple of times.

Grele: So I had to go back and do the interview again.

Terkel: I lost about three or four. I lost Michael Redgrave. I lost a lot of good tapes. Yes.

Grele: We left off talking about the oral history interview and the compilation of the interviews in a work such as *Division Street* or *Hard Times* as a work of art. This raises all kinds of questions about structure, form, language, editing, etc. and I was wondering if you want to talk about it?

Terkel: Well now you've come, of course to the work. How do I work? How does a guy work?

Grele: Right.

Terkel: Well, I have an analogy. It occurred to me about six months ago, or something like that. The analogy is: a prospector for gold in the days of '49, and what they did. First of all they travelled, they leave for a place unknown, never been there before. This is 1849 I'm talking about, the Forty-Niners, right? I'm a prospector for gold. And reading about: either through folk songs, or history, or Mark Twain; the days of 49, the Forty-Niners, the guys who go. What do you do? You go to an unknown, head out, as Huck Finn; head out for the territory. That's what I do; head out for the territory. The guys head out for a place unknown. Then they use a divining rod or whatever they use. They find something, a piece of land. They stake it out. Then they dig and after they dig they hit something and it's ore. It's ore. And they do what with the ore? They refine it. They sift it through water. Out of it comes the dust; out of the dust eventually the bullion, and it's weighed, and there it is.

O.K. Now what do you do? I head out for the territory. I go to see Eva Barnes in Oak Lawn. What am I going to find? I heard about her through a friend of mine. Or, accidentally, there's this Appalachian couple. I leave at 11:30 at night and they're in a grocery store. There's a cab driver. I heard about them through a friend. And the cab driver says, "You're a writer, are you?" Because he saw the tape recorder. "Are you a journalist?" I said, "Well, I don't—I do some writing." "Did you see 'Lord Jim', the movie?" I say, "No. I know it, but I didn't see it." "Well, it's about courage. It's about me. That's why I joined the John Birch Society." So I said, "Could I see you?" I see him the next day.

So it's heading out for the territory. It's an uncharted area. O.K. So that's it. Now you dig. Here's the prospector digging for gold. You're talking, you're probing; something comes out. And there it is: the ore! And someone, Kathy Zmuda, maybe Nellie Gifford, transcribes it. And I get sixty pages. Now then, I sift. This is the water, this is the dust. Out of the sixty pages—the essence: five-six pages, whatever. You get the truth and cut out the fact. I'm like a prospector, I'm cutting whatever they cut out. They cut out the dust, or the crap, or the coal, whatever it was, or the rock, you know. Then you weigh it and then you find a form. Now the prospectors didn't look for a form. I can look for a form and that's part of it. And after the form you edit it again. And there is the book, you think. But there are still your own thoughts that have got to be put down; that's the Preface, Introduction. And finally it comes out. So I say it's prospecting for gold.

Grele: But the prospector, carrying through the analogy, this is purely an analogy, the prospector prospecting for gold has an objective thing that he's looking for and that's the ore.

Terkel: Right.

Grele: And all along the way he has an objective measure to judge what he's going to throw away and what he's going to keep; what is your measure of what you're going to throw away and what you're going to keep?

Terkel: Well, that's even more difficult yet. To step beyond the prospector, I agree. You don't know. Here again it's more uncharted than the prospector, you see? Because now we're not dealing with a material thing called gold, we're dealing with a human being.

Grele: Your ideas and the kind of relationship that's emerged in the interviews do something to the interview.

Terkel: Right. Now something happens in the interview, of course.

Grele: Right.

Terkel: You see a prospector digs. What he finds is inanimate. It shines, it seems animate, but it's inanimate, you know. I'm talking about the animate. Not just animate but beings with souls and minds, and as a result of which they're crazy, you know, as I am. And so you see this is what it is. You have to have that too. Also very sane, but it's both, you know. But mostly they want to survive with some semblance of that soul still intact. And so that's what we're talking about.

But it's exciting, I won't deny it. If it wasn't exciting, I wouldn't do it. Now I'm practically finished with the book, I think, and yet Andre said, "Have you got somebody doing dirty work?" I said, "I've got the maid, I've got a rendering plant, garbage man, sanitation truck driver, a woman from the luggage factory, assembly line guys." So I said, "Yes, I should have a wash room attendant. I haven't got a washroom attendant, so I'll find one." And then maybe the supermarket checker. So I still have a few. It's practically finished. But I've got to stop now. See, the point is once you start something like work you'll never, never finish. You know the story about William Shirer working on the book on the Third Reich. I'm going to ask him if it's apocryphal or not. I assume it's true. It could be true. It seems he kept going and going, and going and Simon and Schuster, his publisher, said "Finish", and he said, "I can't. I'm so far away from the end I've got piles of material." The guy says, "Quit! Stop now." He said, "No, you don't understand, I've got so much more." He said, "Stop now!" And, of course, the editor was right. I've got to ask Shirer when I see him whether it's true or not. I suspect it's true because he could have gone on forever. You see? You can't. . . . So I've got to stop.

Cohen: Some think he did.

Terkel: Well, yeah. And that's also a big problem I'll face in this book. Where am I going to start cutting? When I cut something out that's a problem and it's going to be a big one.

Grele: Your cutting comes after the transcribing?

Terkel: In my own mind I've been cutting, and in the transcribing I've been cutting. Oh, I cut a fantastic amount. See, I've got a sixty-page transcript, like yesterday fifty-five pages, fifty-seven pages from the insurance man, it's going to be six pages. I've done that already, but even more. I mean, even more. It can be refined, and refined.

Grele: In the process of cutting, do you cut out some of your own questions?

Terkel: Oh yes, very much so. Mostly that. Oh yes. I should have brought you something. There's a book coming out and I guess I'm the last chapter. The book is called *Murders and Others* . . . Some guy named Denis Brian did it and there's a sequence on Hemingway and Hotchner and Hemingway's wife; a sequence on Buckley and Vidal; a sequence on Salisbury and the New York *Times* and Talese, and it ends with me. And so one of the aspects was this thing, the guy was asking, "But where do you cut?"

Grele: Cutting out your questions?

Terkel: Cutting out the questions. He asked me if I was either in or out of it? I said, "Well, mostly out of it but every now and then you have to be in it." He said, "Are you objective? And it's what was said about Stendahl way back, I remember Matthew Josephson's biography of Stendahl. He said the guy was objective and subjective at the same time, inside and outside at the same time. Well that's fantastic. I tried that but you see you have a difficult problem; you become involved with the person. At the same time if you become too much involved you lose your own perspective in doing this. On the other hand, the most horrible thing is being cool and detached. Now, R.D. Laing—know, R.D. Laing? It's why psychiatrists, most of them, hate R.D. Laing. They hate him because R.D. Laing challenges their very being, the guys who put the person on the couch and then detach themselves as if they were Olympian figures. Well they're not Olympian figures, they're persons, so is he. Whereas, if that person on the couch or non-couch should realize the guy asking him questions is human too! that's Laing. And so I become, I suppose, like Laing because I goof up a lot. You know, with the tape recorder I goof up, I botch up, it's wrong, you know. And so they like that. They like it. They say, "This guy is not special. He's like me."

Grele: They respond to you—they respond to the questions you ask and by eliminating your questions, aren't you somehow obscuring the relationship that evolves there?

Terkel: No, because it isn't me. See, two things are involved: How do you get the truth about—again truth or fact—about that person. You've got to get it out. Sometimes my questions might intrude in print. I don't need it. Sometimes it's needed. Like yesterday this insurance man—he's funny. He's a Christian Scientist and he sells insurance, nothing stops him. He says, "I've found the harmonious way. We pray, we study, and we look at people not as people but as God intended them to look and the rewards, the life rewards are infinite." I said, "Does it help you as an insurance salesman?" He said, "Substantially." Well, I've got to keep my question in there because it's a very funny thing. Or like the plant manager at Ford, at the very end of the interview said, "It's a matter of managerial—a managerial society— human engineering." I said, "Does that interfere with your relations with people?" He says, "Oh, of course, but it's engineering, that's the important thing." Well anyway that's the point, the question might be needed. Sometimes it's the comic question. I might cut a cruel question, not a question but a comment, see? A big shot I interviewed, he is very pompous, very funny. And he speaks in the third person all the time. He said he had 29 secretaries and, "I write fifty-seven letters a day," and he dictates. "And it's my people, it's my family and I love them. It's not a question of me being the boss, they're my colleagues." I said, "You're sort of a philosopher-king." He said, "I'd put it that way, yes." He said, "I'd put it that way, yes." So I might cut that because that's kind of cruel.

Gifford: Oh, he wouldn't think so.

Terkel: Well, he might like that. It all depends. But some of the reviewers would think it was cruel. No, they'd laugh, but they'd hit him and it would be unfair of me. I've got to watch that. Sometimes I'm tempted. Here's the big problem about cutting out questions; it's funny, it's great, but then you realize *maybe* it might be a little unfair to the person. It's revealing, but then let it be revealed in other ways, without hurting the person personally. It sounds romantic but it's true. It's only fair.

Grele: In your books it's also obvious that in your transcribing or in your editing, you eliminate a lot of the false starts and fix it up grammatically.

Terkel: Sometimes. No, I leave the language pretty much as it is. I don't fix up—

Gifford Except your questions.

Terkel: The questions—no, as far as the language it's the black person's language or a middle class person with his abstract language or whatever it might be; or say, a hard working person using grammatically wrong phrases. I keep the wrong phrases there. Oh sure. Without hurting the person, you know. That's only right. It should be.

Grele: In my interviews I get sentences that can run on a whole page.

Terkel: Oh, then you've got to do editing for some clarification.

Grele: Yes.

Terkel: No, that's imperative. You've got to cut them. Now you've got a big problem. Now you've come to a very big and important problem: how do you still keep it clear? I know you've got people talking.

Grele: At the same time that you retain the flavor of the way they say it.

Terkel: Well, you have to do it the best you can. You cut it. You've got to cut sentences, you've got to chop a phrase off. It's still the person talking. It's still got to be clear to the reader. I know what you're talking about. A perfect case might be: a woman, Maggie Holmes. She's fantastic, she's a black woman, a domestic, a welfare rights leader. Now Maggie was so furious, so angry that when she talked the words flowed and the sentences never finished. But nobody's going to understand it. I know the way she thinks. Now Kathy Zmuda who did the transcript said, "I can't make this out," so I've got to decipher it. I've got to work. I make it out. I know her. It's O.K. I make it out. It involves cutting out so that it comes out fairly clear when I've finished it. So Andre liked her very much. She's fantastic. He doesn't know what had to go into it.

Grele: How do you keep the anger in there?

Terkel: Oh, that's in. Oh Jesus it's in. Well, for example, she names the worst storm in Chicago's history. "Do you remember that storm? Everybody was stuck. And I'd come to the place and the woman I worked for, she says, "Why were you late?' " Remember that big storm? Were you here?

Cohen: I wasn't here yet.

Terkel: It was five years ago. Maggie Holmes said, "She says, 'Why were you late?' And she calls up the employment agency and complains. I take the phone and I say to her on the phone—I'm looking at this woman, I say, '*What do you want?*' I'm looking at her as I'm saying it." Well, that's pretty angry.

Maggie says, "*What do you want?* Everybody's stuck. I got a black child at home who is my life and she's more important to me than any white woman I ever worked for in my life." That's pretty angry. "*What do you want?*" And the woman was scared and she says to Maggie, "Now I want you to go down on the floor here." "Go down on the floor? For what? Go down on the floor? For what? Do you have rubber pads?" For her knees and the wetness. You get rheumatic, you get arthritis, you know? Well it's all there and it's all quite eloquent too, by the way. But! Maggie Holmes in the original telling of it switches back and forth as I do. You see? I'm sitting in a Cleveland Avenue flat and both of us—I know her because I know her mother. Her mother is in *Hard Times*. Her mother is an old fan of mine who listens to me all the time, Emma Tiller, really a remarkable woman. And so I know her daughter, Maggie, and I'm pretty free with her. So I talk and we're both pretty free. Well when you get that on paper it's pretty indecipherable, you know? You've got to cut it out. And so, since I know her, I know pretty much how she thinks. And so that's a case where I know that particular person better than I might somebody else. This is the refining again. You make mistakes, I'm not denying that. You lose things, too.

Grele: Have you ever gotten any feedback on the books from
            the people you've interviewed?

Terkel: That's an interesting thing. Well, now you've got a big
            problem. The problem is you're dealing with human
            beings, not like Pirandello. Pirandello has six characters
            in search of an author, right? And they haunt him. But
            he created them. But these people were created outside
            of me. Now! So a call comes from my friend Rose, who
            is Lily in *Hard Times*, or from Mike who is in this, too.

Grele: And they know who they are?

Terkel: Oh yeah. No, not a question of complaints. No. They're
            friends of mine. I'm talking about my life now
            becoming intertwined with their lives, that's what I'm
            talking about. Oh no, not the complaints. Very few. On
            the contrary, they're sore because the real name wasn't
            used.

            No, the fact is there was only one, a Chicago society
            woman who never said anything, but was a bit
            disturbed about the first book. I called her Mrs. R.
            Fuqua Davies. And she said to some reporter that she
            didn't realize she had said that. But she did.

Cohen: Well, this happens all the time.

Terkel: Huh?

Cohen: Doesn't this happen all the time?

Terkel: Oh yeah. Now, the thing that's exciting, not just in the
            book, but in interviews on the air is that people
            sometimes say, "I never knew I felt that way," which,
            of course, is pretty exciting when you hear that. You
            draw out something that a person himself/herself didn't
            know. That's exciting. No, I've seen one or two cases
            who felt good, the only indignation was that their real
            name was not being used. I said, "Well, I just wanted to
            save you." I didn't know how it would come out and I

didn't want any embarrassment or anything. The problem is a peripheral problem—not peripheral—a number of them become involved in your personal life and you become involved in their lives, and that's the problem. It is, you know. It is. It's a funny one. That's the thing. And there they are. And you brought them out.

Cohen: Right.

Terkel: Oh Rose! Was she special! She's Lily Lowell, writes poetry. She's in *Division Street*, near the end of it.

Grele: Why did you choose to interview young people, especially in *Hard Times*?

Terkel: Well, specifically to show what they do or don't know about the Depression. You know? That was very deliberate, of course. And many are furious because they were never told about it, know nothing about it. I called them "The Inheritors" in *Division Street*, a separate chapter, but in *Hard Times* I intertwined them. But in *Work* there's rather a funny thing called "The Age of Charlie Blossom." There's a kid I met. I call him—it's not his name—Charlie Blossom—and he's a comic figure. He's comic, he's extreme, but very funny. Charlie Blossom is everything that middle aged, middle America is terrified of, and that's Charlie Blossom—this guy. He's a copy boy at the *Sun Times* and he's so funny. He's so phony, too. He's so fantastic. His fantasies are—He's incredible! You just start with him but then it goes. "Who are the young?" There's a kid who edits *The Capitalist Reporter* in New York, and he tells you "how to make it." Then you've got a kid, your friend, Jim Hogan; then you've got a kid named Ken who wants to make it as the biggest salesman; and then you've got a girl who runs the bakery, the bread shop, who has a new technique; then you've got a kid named

Kenny Brown, a motorcycle tycoon who's making millions to show that, basically that you cannot categorize. I guess all the books, if they have one thing in common, it's the anti-stereotype. One thing in common? I would say it's if I'm anti, it's anti-label, basically.

Grele: Label?

Terkel: Anti-label. Anti-stereotype. That's why the words "liberal" and "conservative" have no meaning to me. I'm a conservative. I want to conserve the Bill of Rights, you know? Words have meanings. I want to conserve the freshness of the air. What does that mean, "liberal"? Is Humphrey a liberal? What does that mean, "liberal"? It has no meaning today as we use it today. It has no meaning. It's what is a person on issues? We have to come to specifics. We're back to art again. Art and literature. I mean, it's always specific. You can't be abstract. I know there's abstract art. I realize that. I'm talking about the more abstract you become the more non-human you become. So I have to use this way back you know, inevitably. If you think about "them" it's abstract. "Them" is Vietnam. "Them." And so it's abstract. So you've got RAND, you've got the Hudson Institute, and you've got these guys working on things; "scenarios" they call them. Even the word "scenario," you know. And it's like some of these intellectuals, who say, they like me or like the station I'm on, listeners to our station; they like Mozart, they play chess, they read books; but when it comes to the work they're doing, some of them are working for RAND and what they're doing is killing people, but that doesn't oocur to them because it's abstract, they're solving a certain task. It's "them." But if it's specific, I mean a specific person, then it becomes different, see?

Grele: But your kind of oral history confuses historians. We've been trained for analysis and analysis means to divide them up.

Terkel: Right.

Grele: Liberals, conservatives; analyzing right down and your kind of oral history makes it much more confusing.

Terkel: I hope so. This always comes back to the question you asked way back about do we have a sense of history? I'd say, "No." And it's not meant as a condemnation of the American people, any people. I merely meant that they were conditioned not to have a sense of history.

Grele: Is it that we don't have a sense of history or that we have a sense of the wrong history?

Terkel: No! We've been conditioned not to have a sense of history. We have a sense of the wrong history, too. That's what Marlon Brando objected to, you know? That's why he was so marvelous during the Academy Awards. Here is a perfect case. Consider that evening, that night; a dull, drab marionette show that suddenly comes alive. Alive by truth. Alive by what? Truth! And then you have this dull, talentless girl, Raquel Welch, saying, "I hope nobody else has a cause." And the fact is, this utterly talentless person, you know. That's another part, you see, the utterly nonartistic package, Raquel Welch, saying this about a guy who is the most imaginative actor in film, Brando. But the fact is he made that night which was dull and drab and packaged and just machines were there—nothing else. It was obscene almost in its dullness. I find unimaginativeness obscene. This to me is the horrible obscenity. Where I find the obscenity is, you know, the blunting of the imagination. And if you blunt imagination you blunt humanity. If you blunt humanity, you blunt a feeling outside yourself. Well, what Brando did was make it come alive. And then we come back to that sense of history. He's talking about that in a way, in his own way about that.

Grele: What you're saying is what you find objectionable is the dullness of imagination. In the popular literature it is the middle class, the articulate who are given imagination and it is the working class, the dull, humdrum-a-day people who are denied imagination. Yet, in your own work these are the people you search out.

Terkel: Well I do. I search the middle class too, you see. But this is an interesting point you're making. This is the very thing we're talking about. We laugh—see, now I'm almost convicting myself talking about the romanticization of the ethnic group. I'm saying it's the appeal to the baseness and not to the possibility. The word to me, the key word is "possibility." The moment of obscenity is the blunting of imagination. Now why was it that Brando made that night, that was unimaginative and death, come alive? Because he brought truth into it. It was fiction until he came along, and the most gifted guy did it. See, the most gifted guy did it and the least gifted condemned him; Raquel Welch, you see. I don't know if she's the least, but one of the least gifted. This is what I'm talking about. The package condemns the person. This is what I'm talking about, see? So we're coming back, coming back to the literature you're talking about in which the central figure who is the middle class package—I'm not going to romanticize the working masses—because he's now become, watching TV, the phrases, the thoughts—you know John Lahr, the young drama critic, Johnny Lahr?

Grele: Bert Lahr's son?

Terkel: Who is marvelous—wrote a beautiful book called *The Autograph Hound*, funny and marvelous. He says he finds the cab driver using phrases that he's heard on TV, "No guts, no glory." So they've been contaminated too. I'm saying once you have a blunting of the imagination where there's one view of history that we are number one. Number one! Number one of where? Texas, Nebraska, Baltimore Orioles, Baltimore Colts.

Grele: New York Mets.

Terkel: Yeah, but Number one! And so the cab drivers say— there's this one guy, I use him. I don't know why because cab drivers—but it's the phony myth built up that they're philosophers. They're not philosophers. They work, and most of them are basically pimps at heart because they—it's not their fault because the person in the back of the cab is ordinarily a businessman who is out for a convention and they hope for a tip. And they assume he thinks a certain way. They assume he hates the kids, he hates anti-war protestors, he hates blacks, so they go along with him. And they're the opposite of the independent people; they're the least independent. All service people are that way; waiters, cab drivers, washroom attendants, all of that type. And this is the horror. No one is immune from this illness, you see. But it would seem that the artist to me, if ever the guy had a mission, his own—I don't mean a message mission—his own mission as a person, you know, a vision—it's not to cater to the public. I'm reading Herbert Blau. Herbert Blau's coming to town. He's the guy who was director of the Actors Workshop.

Grele: Right.

Terkel: Actors Workshop. He wrote a marvelous book of essays called *The Impossible Theater*. And one of his points is, since when must the theater say, "We'll give the public what it wants." Who the hell is the public? What does "public" mean? It's an abstract phrase. They're people. What's happened to the theater? Of course you've got to shock them. Of course you've got to shock the audience, and as Lillian Helman says in *Watch on the Rhine*, "Shake them out of their magnolias." That's the job of an artist or a journalist at all times, shake them out of their magnolias. You've got to do that. And this is what we're talking about. I don't know if I do it, but I just try to. Who is this Moby Dick called "the public?" The big white whale, there's also a black whale too.

Cohen: May I ask a question?

Terkel: You can ask anything. This is open.

Cohen: As a regular listener, I think one of the greatest things about this program is the empathy and sympathy that you have with all the people that you have on. On the other hand, I'm rather curious, have you really gone about trying to interview people for whom you have no such sympathy? Could you for example interview a William Buckley or a Raquel Welch?

Terkel: That's a great, that's a good question. I once interviewed Joan Crawford. And it was a very good interview. In fact it was fantastic! There were two different wavelengths. I told her I'd been to South Africa. "You were in South Africa?" And she says, "You know the costumes we wear, Adrian's, they're South African costumes." That wasn't quite what hit me there. See, I was thinking about Apartheid. And the conversation goes on like this for half an hour and then we switch to other things, and I realize that two different wavelengths were involved. And it's a very funny, and revealing, and cruel interview on my part, I thought, Should I play it and be cruel? So I play it. But what happens? What happens is the audience is divided; some say, "Incredible." Others say, "What a

great woman." Now coming back to interviewing
William Buckley. It could be funny. It'd be kind of
funny, in a way. What does it add up to, you see!

I'll switch from persons to issues. Would I have people
on who are for the Vietnam War; who are for capital
punishment; my answer is "No." My answer is no,
because I've got no time. Time's running out on us. The
Vietnam hawks have a forum, the capital punishment
people have a forum, in fact the majority vote for
capital punishment. What I want to know is: What is
there about a society that makes it so vindictive? What
is there about us that makes us so vindictive that we'd
ritualistically kill a person knowing by now that it does
not deter crime?

That interests me. So Vietnam, for or against Vietnam,
I've no time. What is there about us that makes us feel
righteous in bombing people we don't even know? I
want to know what is it about us. That interests me, a
step beyond it. In other words I'm through with high
school debates. I did it, McKinley High School, 1925-
28. I was on the team and we debated either way pro or
con, for or against capital punishment. Should we or
should we not give independence to the Philippine
Islands? Should we or should we not join the World
Court? And we took both sides. But I went through that
period. It's too late now, for me. I've got no time. So my
answer is: "I've got no time." That's it, and so, no.
There's no point to having Buckley on. He's got his
forum. Why?

Cohen: How about Raquel Welch?

Terkel: Raquel Welch? Again, why? It'd be pathetic. It'd be
sad. Why? Maybe if it were an essay or an article on the
packaging of a product. What Joe McGinnis says about
Nixon, you see?

Grele: Yeah.

Terkel: We could do it with Raquel Welch, but that's a clay
         pigeon, you see? But then, why? There are things out
         there that are interesting, not yet done; why must I go
         through this Buckley routine with his polysyllabic
         phrases, go through a routine? What I would say is he
         and I could make a million dollars together if I could be
         his personal manager. I would take him village to
         village. He would be one of a kind, the Neanderthal
         who speaks in polysyllables. Never been! There's never
         been any such species. He'd be insulted and walk off. I
         can't take him seriously. Like in this book now on
         interviewers and his name came up and I said, "Well,
         he's more Frank Fay than Edmund Burke." Frank Fay
         was a comic years ago. He's more Frank Fay than
         Edmund Burke. He's not Edmund Burke, he's a
         vandevillian, you see?

Grele: Yes.

Terkel: So you see, this is also the horror of our day. What's
         happened to our standards? Buckley is justifying ITT in
         Chile. Well, how could you take him seriously? Even
         Kilpatrick disagrees with him. Well, how can you take
         the guy seriously? But he *is* taken seriously. So, why
         should I lend him a forum? Now if I did it as a comic,
         William Buckley, comic, as if to say "Lord Buckley."
         Same name, see? I'd say, "Lord Buckley, you're a
         marvelous, deadpan comic. You're like Frank Fay."
         Well, of course, he'd walk off. But it's true! He's a very
         funny man. But if he weren't funny he'd be a very dull
         man. So I laugh when I see him. I laugh like I laugh at
         serious commercials, you know. I laugh, you know. Or
         I laugh when I hear a commentator. It's very funny, it's
         kind of amusing you know. It's funny. Buckley to me is
         a very amusing deadpan comic. Think about justifying
         Nixon! Well, how can this be, you see? Therefore, I say

he is better than Bert Lahr. In a different way, he's not like Bert Lahr, he's different, more of a straight man. Frank Fay. By the way, I don't know if you remember Frank Fay? He was a great comic years ago.

Grele: Yes.

Terkel: He had Buckley's style, which is sort of a bland, fall-away style. He'd fade, "Fay fading away." I see Buckley, and I laugh. And he's got the guy from Oxford on with him, but I'm still laughing! The only guy who got Buckley sore was Nelson Algren. Nelson would say—when Buckley once said to Nelson, "Weren't you once a member of the left; the Communist group?" He said, "When you were nine years old, Mr. Buckley, didn't you rob a candy store in Keehaukie, New Jersey? You robbed that candy store." He said, "I beg your pardon, sir?" "Yeah, you did, didn't you? I heard. Somebody told me. Somebody told you that I was 'red, see? Somebody told me that when you were nine years old you went in this candy store in the dead of night and you stole peppermint sticks."Buckley said, "This is nonsense." And as Buckley's going on talking, Nelson started singing, "It's only a paper moon." We're going to have to have Nelson talk about this. So Buckley walked off. It was the Barry Farber Show and Buckley said, "This is obscene." Nelson said, "What's obscene?"

It's Not the Song, It's the Singing
Panel Discussion on Oral History
Recorded at Radio Station WFMT. Chicago, Illinois
April 13, 1973
Participants:
Studs Terkel
Jan Vansina
Alice Kessler Harris
Dennis Tedlock
Saul Benison
Ronald J. Grele

Terkel: I suppose one of the big problems today, perhaps in all societies in the world, certainly in our society in the United States, is this break in continuity. So many of the young feel that they don't know what happened before they were born. It may have something to do with the Bomb. It may have something to do with, maybe, the fact that historians have failed. One of the developments today, in which technology plays its role aside from the bomb, is the tape recorder and the development of oral history. And yet it's so old too. During the week of the convention of the Organization of American Historians in Chicago a number of very distinguished oral historians have gathered, and I am delighted to have colleagues around the table right now. Doctor Jan Vansina is a historian and an anthropologist and I suppose if he has a specialty, he's a generalist, I'm sure, but his specialty is African oral history. Dennis Tedlock is an anthropologist specializing in the oral history of the life of the Zuni Indians. Saul Benison is an historian who has been emphasizing, in his work, professional men in medicine and science, although he has other interests as well. Doctor Alice Kessler Harris is an historian, but her interest has been primarily immigrant women and what has happened to them and what their memories are, I suppose, of mothers and grandmothers, and their own observations. Ron Grele is Assistant Director of the Ford Foundation Oral History Project and is generally interested in oral history.

Now where do we begin? It has to be personal, we all know that; something personal about why each of us has found his or her way into it. Jan Vansina, yourself, how did you become interested in oral history?

Vansina: Well, when I was a child I lived most of my childhood in a village, and oral history came about in three ways.

First my mother was very great for funerals; and funerals are places where people learn about their families five or six generations back. You have to learn about them because you identify others by knowing how they are kin, how your families crossed and all that sort of thing. Secondly, when we came back from school, we would have learned about Belgian history and my mother would say, "My great-grandfather fought against the Netherlands in 1830 and here is his stick," and the whole story would come out about a little skirmish. The third way was remarkable. Old farmers would say, "Well this is the place where this village started." Now if you look at the record and the place names and all that, it comes out that it dates to 400A.D. It was unbelievable. A feud for which nobody remembers the beginning, in that village from archival documents can be dated as having started around 1200. So from childhood on I lived—and I may have been an exceptional case—in an oral history climate at home.

Terkel: Isn't what Jan Vansina is saying, doesn't that strike a chord, Alice Kessler Harris?

Harris: Yes. Although I suppose I got into oral history in a somewhat different way, almost by the back door, as it were. I was trying to reconstruct the lives of immigrants such as perhaps some of the people who'd come from Belgium to America, and discovered that the written records are very sparse indeed, and then decided that perhaps the only way to reconstruct family lives and cultural attributes of groups of people that had come to America was to start talking to them. And so I began interviewing people who are now in their 70s, 80s, and 90s and who had themselves come in 1900 and 1910, and their experiences led me into whole new perceptions of what immigration had been for them and how they felt about disrupting their ties with the old world. But that's very different from your tradition, Jan, which is a kind of old world persistent tradition; mine is the tradition of a break.

Terkel: It's a tradition of break, but isn't there a connection? I'm just wondering. Dennis Tedlock's interest is the "New World", North America, Zuni Indians. Alice Harris speaks of a break, people coming to the New World, you come across—you worked with the Zuni Indians; but how come you did this?

Tedlock: That's a very long story indeed and it probably all started with my liking to hear and tell stories when I was a kid. But I don't think at the time I went into anthropology I knew that was why. I had a Boston Irish grandmother who told fairy tales without reading from a book, and a Swedish grandfather who had endless stories about before he came over, and my father used to actually make up stories that went on for hours at a time. For some reason or other I eventually went into anthropology and found myself in Zuni, partly because I grew up in New Mexico not all that far from the Zuni, and there you can find lots of people with very long stories to tell, all passed down by oral tradition. And in this case they go back to the creation of the world, as far as they are concerned. A lot of them are things that we would call myths. They seem to talk about events which to us would have to be imaginary, but even at that they are full of things that really happened. They even tell about a time when the Zunis had no crops and gathered seeds of wild grasses, which would have to have been about fifteen hundred years ago.

Terkel: It's from the personal to something that's still personal but outside yourself. You now come to the Zuni Indian. Do you see what I'm talking about? Saul Benison, in your own way?

Benison: Well, I got into it just by chance. I was trained by Allan
Nevins at Columbia and for a number of years I acted
as his assistant. That's what you did when you didn't
have a job. We had a very strange little man who
showed up every Friday for a seminar. And this strange
little man was Abraham Flexner, who wrote the Flexner
Report on medicine in 1908 and caused a revolution in
medical education. I remember after one seminar he
berated Nevins, who had begun an oral history project,
by saying, "You're wasting your time, you're interviewing third-rate politicians; you're interviewing
mayors, you're interviewing businessmen, but here is
science and medicine and you're doing nothing there."
And Nevins pleaded that he didn't have any money to
do this. Flexner said. "Well, if I got $25,000 for you,
would you do it?" And Nevins said, "Done." After
Flexner left I said, "Who's going to do it?" He said,
"You're going to do it." I said, "What the hell do I know
about medicine? Nothing!" He said, "Well, you have a
Ph.D. from this institution and there are rights and
privileges that go with the degree, and one of the rights
and privileges is to take any course in the University
providing it does not lead to another degree, and I'll
give you a year and a half, eighteen months, and you go
back to school. Study the things you've never studied
before; physics, chemistry, biology." And so it was.
When I came back I said, "I still don't know anything."
He said, "The people who you interview are going to
become your teachers and you're going to know a hell
of a lot, and it all depends on what questions you
pursue." And that's how I got into it.

Terkel: That's interesting, the people you interview are going to
be your teachers. Ron Grele?

Grele: Well I got into oral history because I was looking for a
job and there happened to be a job open interviewing

for the John F. Kennedy Library in Washington. And I went down knowing nothing about oral history, just happened to tie up with one of the men who was really doing some good work in oral history, Charlie Morrissey, and began to read, and he gave me two or three months just to read in the literature of oral history and the background literature of the Kennedys and it was out of that practice.

Terkel: Each for different reasons, yet there's one common denominator here; the interest in the voice, talk, flesh and blood people.

Grele: Oh, I didn't have that when I began.

Terkel: No, you didn't. No, no.

Grele: When I began, I began as an historian and couldn't have been less concerned with the voice.

Terkel: Yes.

Grele: It's only in the interviewing situation that I came to a realization that something else was happening besides history.

Terkel: You and Saul Benison are similar, that is, in a general way through an academic world, but then it became something else. Whereas in the case of Jan Vansina, it was way in the beginning; in the case of Dennis too. But it's open. What's—

Vansina: You see, in my case actually, when I was at the university I was doing medieval history and I was doing something on oral traditions in the middle ages, by the way. But I remember distinctly going over in the week of my preliminary examinations from medieval history to anthropology because I wanted to work with living people. Now I've changed my mind. I know that documents can be living too. But via anthropology you can get back again to the oral world.

Terkel: Something that Saul said could be a catapult for all of us. He said, "The people you interview become your teachers."

Vansina: True enough. You can't live in Africa for a month, or in another culture for a month, without other people teaching you the rudimentary facts of life according to their point of view——how to be polite!

Harris: I think that's true, but I think often what they teach you is not what you expected to learn to begin with. That is, you begin—and this is a point that Ron made a little earlier in the day—you begin by asking questions, and the responses you get are often not answers to the specific questions you ask, but tell you something entirely different. I, for example, have had some interesting experiences with immigrant women who talk about their families in the old country and the way in which those families, for example, revered the fathers in the families, and how things are really different in America because women and children no longer look up to men as they used to look up to them. And they continue to tell you long stories, and yet when you observe how they act when their husbands come home, for example, you see them responding to their husbands in what seems to be very traditional ways; that is, they take the husband's coat, they bring the husband a cup of tea, they bring him a newspaper, and yet you hear them talking about the fact that in America things are really different. And that makes you wonder about whether the answers they are giving you are really answers which apply to their situations or are in a sense myths about their own past.

Terkel: Aren't you talking through on a different wavelength at the moment from the way Jan Vansina's talking? He's talking about people who live where they have been in a culture of which we know so little, we Europeans and whites; and you're talking about people who have split, who have gone from an old culture to a new one.

Harris: Yes. Yes. I think they're very different traditions: that is, I think that people who have left an old culture develop myths and feelings about that culture which people who live in one don't have.

Vansina: Well I disagree. I think they are more similar than you would think because in my own family checking—since I'm now in the business anyway—I check my family every time I go back. I now have a record sixteen years long. Half of these stories are not true. They are an image setting. They are necessary for the pride of someone.

Harris: Oh absolutely! Absolutely! The stories are not true and I think that's just the point, that one builds up a myth which has nothing to do with the reality.

Terkel: Don't we come to something here Dennis, or Saul, or Ron too: the question of memory. What is true and what is not? And we have to kind of question ourselves too. Sometimes the fact may not be literally so and yet be a truth to that person. Don't we come now to something involving memory? Something not documented? Isn't this more challenging?

Benison: You know the question of truth is not really the issue. It's not something that you can specify like a date. Let me give you an example from my own work. One of the people I interviewed was Tom Rivers, who was the director of the Rockefeller Institute Hospital and a very great virologist, and of course I used him as a link to get into the history of the Rockefeller Institute. One day he began to tell me of an extraordinary debate between Simon Flexner, who was the original director of the

Rockefeller Institute and William H. Park, who was the Director of Laboratories of the New York City Board of Health. He said, "You know, they hated each other." That fact was true. They did hate each other. He said, "Do you know why they hated each other? Flexner, in 1899 had gone to the Philippines and he found a bacillus which later bore his name. Actually however the discovery was made by William H. Park, and for this reason they hated each other." In a sense, Flexner had taken Park's work. The truth of the matter is that Park never went to the Philippines, Park had nothing to do with the discovery of the bacillus. The reason that they hated each other was a conflict over the use of cerebral spinal meningitis anti-serum; Park thought that it was dangerous; Flexner, who was the discoverer of the anti-serum, did not, and there was a fantastic debate. There was a debate, that was true—the myth that Rivers retailed to me told me more about Rivers. It told me what the hell Rivers would get excited about, if someone took his work, and so that myth was revealing of Rivers. As a historian, I just had to put a footnote to say, "This is made out of whole cloth and is revealing of Rivers."

Terkel: It's what is revealed of your teacher in a sense; the person you call your teacher. Ron?

Grele: And in the same sense. What Alice is gathering would indicate that the women she's dealing with find it necessary to invent a distinct family pattern in the old country and a new family pattern in this country, despite the fact that the family patterns are probably quite similar. For some reason they have to invent an historical chain of events that would bring discontinuity into a historical process which is actually one of continuity. And what interests me about this memory is the particular use of a vision of history; that their history must be diachronic, it must progress, it must change; something must change because they came to this country when, indeed, those patterns haven't changed or the change exists some place else.

Terkel: Dennis, I think there's something else here: Alice said something else earlier in passing and it was in reply to something Jan Vansina said about the questions you come asking, not the answers you expect. Don't we come to something else now about asking questions? What do you mean, "What to expect"? I mean don't you have to come almost wholly open as though a child, newborn in a way, although you're not a child and you do know. But at the same time isn't there revelation coming here from the people, say the Zuni Indians? What was your experience there?

Tedlock: Yes, part of the whole art of being a good anthropologist is to know when to sit back and listen to what the man is telling you. And there's where all the big rewards are. If you went into the field to prove something you'd just end up finding out exactly what you wanted to find there. There's nothing to it. Fortunately, that's very unlikely to happen; no matter how hard you might try to shape it, the unexpected is always coming out. I have a comment, too, on this business of truth. What the Zunis demand of someone who is telling them a story is that he make it seem like it really happened, and they're not concerned with the historical fact that might be involved in it. They just want to—well, if he's a good story-teller he makes it fact right in front of you. You can see it right in front of you there.

Terkel: Does this strike a thought with you Jan? What Dennis is talking about?

Vansina: Oh yes. This changes from one society to another. The best comment I had was from an old man who was about ninety and whose career was followable through some documents. He said, "You know, truth with us is what everybody says it is now. What was truth twenty years ago is no longer truth now and what is truth now will no longer be truth in the future." He was paraphrasing, without knowing it, a Greek philosopher, and I think he was right. If you really go to the bottom of all those history books and the things which are never said in them but assumed about truth, you will find that each age has its own truth.

Terkel: Through oral history, through somebody talking, a flesh and blood person, you realize what the challenge always is to someone who is a historian; written, traditional or oral. How many written histories when you think about it, are based on what *was* a truth literally so.

Harris: In that respect though, I think, historians and anthropologists are a little different. That is, I think historians really make some attempt to reconstruct the past, and in some ways like the kinds of things you did, for example, in *Hard Times*, they try to recapture the experiences of people then living. They are not as much interested, I think, in the present inter-relationships among people or in how people presently conceive of their lives as they are in how they then experienced either a depression or a crowded family situation or a job or work experience, for example. I think it is in the attempt to put together the ways in which numbers of people experienced, for example, working in a garment factory on the Lower East Side in 1915, that the historian begins to recapture the way it must have felt to live in that period of time for people who don't write letters and who normally we don't read about in books.

Terkel: But yet that woman whom you saw and talked to and who recalls that time in the garment factory in 1915, her attitude today to a great extent is affected by that which she experienced and told to you.

Harris: Absolutely. And her attitude is also reflected in what else has happened to her since then. That is, the woman who worked in the garment factory in 1915 and continued to work for the next thirty years and then retired on a small pension, feels very differently about her experience than the woman, who in 1915 left the garment factory and got married and had children and returns to those years with a kind of romantic image of how nice it was to work.

Terkel: Aren't we talking now also about—Alice has touched on this. This is the part we're just skirting, we're coming to now, our teachers, the people we meet and talk to, they are the historians. Here is where our time is exciting, the tape recorder, and the bottom up approach. Hitherto we've been told by professionals about kings and queens etc. and now from the bottom up we are getting history. Isn't this the exciting part?

Vansina: Oh sure. I mean this is what my childhood was all about. Whatever was told in school was corrected by the villagers and by the working people in the city saying, "No. This was not true. The First World War wasn't all about these generals. I was sitting in the muck". You know how people can talk about wars. This we can now capture and we do.

Harris: This is particularly relevant for women who are trying to recapture their own history because, since women haven't been the leaders and the soldiers and the statesmen, in large measure, in order to reconstruct their lives one really has to begin to ask about ordinary people.

Vansina: One of the most pathetic stories I ever heard was one of a woman who came from a mining town and she told me how all her children, seven of them, died within two months of the cholera plague in the year 1869. Now in the books, you know, it's just one sentence. That interview really makes you feel what a plague is like.

Harris: It also makes you feel what it's like to be a mother in 1869 as opposed to now.

Vansina: Yes. Sure. Obviously.

Terkel: I'm sure that this point concerns you, Dennis, in your work with the Zuni Indians, this point that Alice and Jan are talking about. You know, there's a Civil War song, a Southern song, *All Quiet Along the Potomac Tonight* and one of the lines is, "Not an officer killed, just one of the men." It's Brechtian in its irony. "Just one of the men," and so the cholera epidemic didn't involve a king or queen's death. How is it with the Zuni as far as status is concerned?

Tedlock: The same thing happens to this extent: the sort of official histories of what happened a long time ago are maintained mainly by the native, pagan priests, so it is only within people's memories or the memories of their grandfathers that you begin to get what it was like to live through something for the individual person. Otherwise the whole story of their history is just a story about what the priests were doing leading the people around in search of the middle of the world. Until you get right up into the nineteenth century you don't get a focus on what it must have been like. Sometimes a good narrator will try to recapture that as he imagines what it must have been. He'll even challenge you the listener and say, "Well, what could that have been like, to be that person, to have been alive then?" He might just throw it back to you. He'll give you an answer too.

Terkel: What could it have been like to have been alive then?
          That's interesting. You were going to say something
          Saul?

Benison: Well, what I was going to say was really something
          harsh about professional historians. You would think
          that with this instrument that all of them would go out
          and immediately try to get the experience of the people
          who don't leave letters, who don't leave diaries, whose
          history is essentially oral that they give to one another
          through a generation and by the third generation it is
          lost. No. They don't do this. As a matter of fact what
          Alice does is very unusual. Most oral history projects
          have a conceit. They go to the "movers" and the
          "shakers" and they believe they are getting at the
          history of their times by a great man. It's like going to,
          let us say, the LaFollette Civil Liberties Committee and
          saying, "I am going to find out all about this committee
          by interviewing LaFollette," who is the last person to be
          interviewed. The staff man who did the work is the
          man to interview. This is why I liked your book. It was
          a joy to see Kid Pharoah talk. Or it was a joy to get the
          farmer in Iowa and listen to him. What is more it was a
          joy to hear a seventeen year old speak about the
          Depression because what he said told me what had
          been transmitted to him about the reality of the
          Depression. It would bring me up with a start, for
          example, while I'm talking to a doctor to hear suddenly
          a memory of Del Bissonette playing first base for the
          Brooklyn Dodgers. Now that tells me something about
          that man's childhood, and the impact of how he spent
          his leisure time. We really don't use our imaginations.
          We're really very, very traditional and I think that's a
          shame.

Terkel: Isn't this one of the—Please. I would rather we keep
          this open to anyone. If something Saul said touches

something off, go ahead.

Tedlock: History is, or has been anyway until now, let's say, written by people who wear neckties. It is hard for us to take our neckties off. We're all wearing them as a matter of fact.

Vansina: It's conventional.

Harris: I'm not. (laughter)

Tedlock: You're not.

Terkel: That reveals something of Dennis Tedlock to you.

Harris: Exactly.

Tedlock: Indeed. It also reveals again, that what I said is correct. History *was* written by people who wore neckties.

Terkel: Yes, of course.

Harris: I think in defense of historians though, it should be said that, particularly younger historians, those now coming out of the graduate schools are beginning to ask questions which are asked without neckties, if you like. That is, they are really beginning to ask questions about workers and their experiences, and family life and those experiences, and we particularly noticed at our session a number of members of minority groups, for example, with tape recorders taping the session and obviously very anxious to know what is going on in oral history, and perhaps anxious to use the tape recorder to interview people who ordinarily, as Saul says, would not leave letters. I think that's changing.

Benison: But you know, if you look at black oral history projects, what are they doing? They're capturing the reminiscenses of people who knew Martin Luther King.

Grele: The movers and shakers.

Harris: I'm not so sure about that. For example, there's a recent book by Gerda Lerner on black women which has, in addition to collecting documents and letters, collected the reminiscences of some very ordinary women who work at very ordinary jobs, who are housemaids for example, or laundresses, whose memories provide a real focus for that book.

Vansina: Let me butt in on that. Some of the black people I work with in America pointed out very forcefully that the first and major aim, as far as they are concerned, is not to provide only how life was like in the beginning of this century, but how it was like in the last century and if possible give an identity which goes back as far as it can go back. It is an identity problem.

Terkel: If we could just take a slight pause. I think that's a perfect spot right there; a cliff hanger, this matter of identity problem, of generations as well as minorities and non-whites.

Terkel: Resuming the conversation, Jan Vansina, you were saying something about the seeking of identity through oral history?

Vansina: I think that Alex Haley, for instance, believes that his forthcoming book, *Roots*—

Terkel: Perhaps you should mention that to the audience, Alex Haley's project.

Vansina: Alex Haley traced his own family back through an incredibly lucky set of circumstances all the way back to 1700, and all the way to a specific spot in Africa and this is what his book, *Roots*, is going to be about. He sees this as a book that will tell black Americans that they do have ancestors and they do have a place to come from. This is most nearly what I was saying before.

Grele: You helped Haley on that, didn't you?

Vansina: Yes I did. It was a very colorful story which Haley tells far better than I do.

Grele: Go ahead anyway.

Terkel: Go ahead.

Vansina: One day I came off a freighter in New York harbor and
           there was Haley standing saying, "Are you Doctor
           Vansina?" I said, "Yes." "I'm Alex Haley. Did you write
           that thing on oral traditions?" I said "Yes." He wanted
           to see me.

           Between the docks and Grand Central Station he began
           talking. He said, "I'll come over to where you are." He
           arrived one day. We spent a whole night talking and he
           had documents and he had tales and he wanted to
           know and he wanted to be certain. He said, "The first
           thing my family remembers is the word 'kinte', 'kinte'
           and our ancestor always pointing towards the sea." This
           was in their tradition. I knew that 'kinte' was a
           Mandingo word and it was from a particular West
           African family which once had been very famous. So I
           said, "Look, if you have the money go to Gambia, that's
           your best bet." He had that one word and one other.
           There were two words. Of course, all of this is wild.
           He went to Gambia and he did find the village. I
           checked up on this independently from him through
           Gambian scholars I knew, and students and people. It
           is true. In fact, if Haley cared to do it—he's not going to
           do it in the book—he can now go back all the way to
           1220 because the African part is very well preserved
           since it was an important family there. But that's not
           what he's interested in. He's interested to show how life
           was in slave days, in the days of emancipation,
           Reconstruction, all the way down to his father in the
           Pullman car. That's how he went to college and so on
           and so forth. It will be a fascinating book.

Terkel: Wow! Alex Haley helped Malcolm X in his
           Autobiography, for the audience's illumination.

This is interesting isn't it, going back. Isn't this almost a metaphorical story in a way? It's a true story of Alex Haley, yet it's almost as though it was an opening, it's almost limitless, isn't it?

Vansina: I think the immigrants have the same problem, especially the second generations.

Harris: Yes. That gets us back, I think, to the point we were making at the beginning. That is, that you need a past of your own: that you really can't live in the future unless you know where you come from, and in that sense it's especially important to reconstruct or create myths about your own past which may or may not be true. But to know where you came from is, I think, one of the reasons why immigrants develop and retain stories of their own past. Among Jewish immigrants, for example, in New York, the women I've been working with, there are lovely stories about the *stetl* culture and the kinds of things they used to do in the *stetl* culture. Well any reconstruction of the *stetl*, which is the small Russian or Polish town out of which most Jewish immigrants to America came in the late 1890s or early 1900s, will tell you that these towns were terribly poor. The immigrants really suffered. They lived four and five families, sometimes, to a room in a basement. They had no clothing. They often had no jobs because jobs were simply unavailable. Yet when women and men talk today about those periods, they reconstruct them in terms of the kind of community that existed. The poverty falls by the wayside, and what they remember is the sense of neighborliness with the people whom they then must surely have quarrelled with if they lived four to a room, but whom they remember with tremendous fondness as a community of people.

Vansina: This is one of the dangers in oral history and I want to point it out to the audience. One of my students, as an exercise, was going to study the history of two Jewish-Russian immigrant families. There were two branches of the same family and what happened was that she found out that way back, just before they went to America, the grandmother of one family had been murdered with the Torah by somebody. One branch knew that. The other branch knew who it was. It was somebody of their branch. This was a young graduate student who didn't think very much. So she laid it out and, of course, what she caused was irreparable harm to the people who are living today. This is, I think, something which all oral historians have to be aware of. There is a special code of ethics in this business because you can create more damage in the name of science than you are really producing for historians.

Terkel: Isn't there something else, Jan and colleagues, Alice and Ron and Dennis and Saul, and that's the point you made earlier about remembering the good things, the self-censorship. Our teachers, the people we talk to, are mostly aware of that too sometimes. It's a question not so much of probing as just sticking with it, the idea of . . . I'm sure it's natural, it's human to eliminate from your memory that which is unpleasant or horrible and so you speak of the Depression as "those good old days." There it is again, the communal spirit, yes, but the horrendousness of the four in a room. That's one of the challenges, isn't it? Do you find that Dennis, among the Zuni? I'm curious to know about the Zuni. Is it different among the American Indians, say Zuni Indians specifically? This particular self-censorship?

Tedlock: I think they, most of the people I know, mostly talk about bad things.

Terkel: Is that so?

Tedlock: Seventy-five percent of them, when they're recalling.
            Maybe that's just the kind of history they have had
            recently. Maybe that's really what there is to talk
            about.

Terkel: Yeah, what else is there to talk about when ever since
            Cortez, that's been it.

Vansina: In Nigeria it's very interesting. They remember the bad
            things about the colonial period and some of the good
            things, but that comes out later when they know you
            very well. Then they will tell you some of the good
            things. But there is not one Nigerian oral story about
            the slave trade. Nothing! That's completely wiped out
            although it continued until almost a century ago. They
            just have wiped it out.

Terkel: I guess the challenges are so many but the awareness of
            this is absolutely essential.

Harris: I think that what both Dennis and Jan have pointed out
            though, are the reasons why one really needs to be an
            historian or an anthropologist or someone with some
            kind of training to do oral history, because often what's
            left out is more significant than what's put in, and it's
            only if you know something about a culture or a period
            from other sources, of all kinds, that you can begin to
            judge how the memories reflect not only what's not
            there but what is there. And the way in which that's
            been distorted then becomes a way of understanding
            the pasts of individuals.
            The best story I can think of, in that regard, is the tale
            that I'm sure almost everybody has heard, of the
            Russian-Jewish immigrant who chops off his big toe to
            avoid going into the army. Well, I have no idea how
            many Russian-Jewish men actually chopped off their

big toes to avoid going into the Army, but one hears
that story from virtually every other person who has a
grandfather or father who did this, and who then
trekked across Siberia or across Poland and somehow
managed to get to America. Now whether or not that
story is true, what's interesting about that story is that
the struggle to be free is what remains in people's
memories. They interpret that as, "Look at what a
marvelous country this is because here we can be free,
and in the old country we had to do such terrible things
in order to avoid being enslaved." And so that feeling
about America as being a place of freedom. . . .

Terkel: Which, of course, is in direct contrast to Dennis' observation. Specifically, the thing that Dennis and Jan
both spoke of was two peoples who were specifically
oppressed and exploited and their past taken away.
Whereas you're speaking of someone who is upwardly
mobile, if I can use that terrible phrase, someone who
was escaping a certain kind of oppression who first
came to a land they felt was much better for them and
so glorify that. Whereas the opposite experience is that
of the Indians and of the blacks in Nigeria.

Vansina: This is so true. I can see this from the Flemish
nationalist movement. The Flemings started out being a
minority group, although they were the majority of the
population, never mind. Anyway, by now they are
about equal and these stories begin to circulate. These
are only thirty years old and easily checkable. It is for
the same reasons you gave. They want to say that the
country now is good but previously, at all times, it was
bad.

Grele: But the constant in all of this is the degree of integration
or segregation from the culture. Those people who are
somewhat assimilated into the dominant culture can see

it as a progressive pattern that is leading to something. There is a future that is going to be better than the past. Those who are isolated from the culture or who were exploited by the culture, whose very culture itself was undermined by the dominant culture, cannot look at the dominant historical pattern in the same way.

Benison: I'm listening to this and the question that enters my mind comes because of a peculiar motto that used to be on the coat-of-arms of Brandeis University. It says, "Truth unto its innermost parts." That sounds really grand, but how far should you pursue the truth? How far should this generation look at itself? In what depth? How far do you go? What do you want to leave for the future? What's your audience? Are you collecting oral histories for people to use five years from now, ten years from now, one hundred years from now? What do you leave them? It is here that you get an extraordinary diversity of opinion.

I had a peculiar question that I faced. One of the doctors I interviewed was a very hard drinker. He made no bones about how hard he drank. As a matter of fact, he told me a hilarious story about his drinking. He had been a young intern at Johns Hopkins Hospital, and he and James Dandy, who was a great neurosurgeon, one day just went out of the hospital, boarded a streetcar and started to drink. They drank copiously and then offered a drink to the conductor. When he refused that drink they put him off the streetcar and they took the car through a wild ride through the city of Baltimore. Women fainted, men cursed. Escaping from the car, pursued by the police, they went into the Hopkins Hospital, put on their surgical masks and uniforms, went into the OR; they were completely unidentifiable. I thought it was a very amusing and very revealing story of intern-resident life circa 1910-1912 in Baltimore. The problem that I faced was the wife. The doctor subsequently approved the telling of this story on himself and he died. His wife who was a seventy-six year old lady objected to the story. Not that the story was untrue, but because she thought (according to her system of values) it would leave a miserable picture of her husband who was, really, a very eminent scientist. He didn't believe it. I didn't believe it. My problem was; should I retell the story when the book was printed. I felt that I didn't want to hurt this seventy-six year old lady. There was enough in the interviews to indicate that he was a hard drinker and I took out the story to save the sensibilities of this lady. Now, how much should history know?

Terkel: This is an interesting point that you raise, an ethical point, Saul. But also something else is here. This is a big problem I have, quite specifically, which I can't recount now, with the work I'm on, involving a father and a son and its very revealing. I'm going to ask their permission. The only persons who will know the true meaning are them. The readers won't know a thing about it. But it's something revealing about the father and the son on their job at a service station. But it's a difficult thing. You're right, it is a question of not hurting people, but your story tells us so much about her and status.

A very quick story. Nothing to do with oral history as it does with our lives. I have a jazz friend, a jazz musician. This was in the Forties. He played at the Sherman House in Chicago when jazz was popular. He'd drink a lot. One Saturday night he goes and gets drunk and they climb over the wall of the Chicago Zoo, Lincoln Park Zoo. This good tenor sax man wants to feed the bear. He got into the bear house. He's got the peanuts and he's going to feed the bear and the bear grabs his hand and he bites it. The guy's hand was in a sling for about a month. He's brooding over it and brooding over it. He's playing again and he gets drunk again and he goes over the zoo wall again. He sees that same bear. He puts his hand out and the bear clutches for his hand. He grabs the bear's paw and bites it. (laughter) He bites the paw!

So I tell this story; the man who bit the bear. His wife was furious. She was furious because, just like the wife of your doctor-informant was; the idea of status. It didn't show him in a good light, she felt. It's a marvelous story but here again it tells us about this matter of our relationships with people, one to another and that's a very delicate situation always, isn't it?

Benison: There's one other element. You know what makes life bearable for everybody? The fact that they can have a secret life that they don't reveal to anyone. That secret life can really inform history. This is what I mean.

You could get data on the rise of income in Great Britain from 1800 to 1830 and you could say in statistical terms, "conditions got better". The one thing that's missing are the hopes and aspirations of these people that make those figures viable. Should you go after the dreams? Should you go after the hopes and aspirations? Should you go after the secret life? I'm not sure.

Terkel: That's a tough one.

Grele: There's a line. There's a line. We know so little about even the public lives of most of the people who lived in the past. We know so little about the basic facts of their lives; how they were born, how they died, who died of what, how they ate, that there is plenty of stuff to collect to begin with. Then there's also a line that one keeps that is a line of propriety. Up to a certain point you can sense it in an interview situation that you're getting to a point at which the respondent wants to stop. You sense it. If you have a feeling for the people you can do it.

Tedlock: There's another problem here too. Of course, it's more of a problem among a group of people who do most of their communication in speaking rather than in writing. That is, if you take the stuff down and publish it you are also freezing it. People change their own history. We do it anyway even in writing. They change their history in ways that are necessary to them to make it meaningful to them now, today. What happens when anthropologists publish huge quantities of myths, legends, stories from oral histories of Indian tribes is that then, when those people have those books and read them, they take that to be absolutely correct. Right there it freezes their oral tradition. They daren't change it because now it's in print. That becomes a sort of an authority and in some ways it's too bad because there are very subtle and good ways in which a culture can change itself and its image of itself, which you have ruined if you put down what was supposedly fact at a certain date back there somewhere, or what was supposedly the correct version of a story.

Harris: There's another interesting aspect to that which is, one experience I've had, for. example. People really tell what they want you to know about themselves. That is, they feel as though they ought to be a certain kind of way or to believe certain kinds of things about themselves, and they are reluctant to reveal themselves as not being that way or not feeling those things. In our society that's particularly true of poor people who feel as though they, for one reason or another, ought not to be poor and who pretend, or feel, or express values which they don't act out in their lives. So that when you

write those things down in history you really have to
wonder whether what you are writing is what they
want you to think about them, or whether what you're
writing is something that they really feel about
themselves.

Vansina: I thought academics were strongest at that. (laughter)

Terkel: You know, it's interesting. Alice's point is so deep, this
aspect of, say, talking to hard working people who have
had little formal education. You are there. Cobb and
Sennett in *The Hidden Injuries of Class* touch on this.

Harris: Yes.

Terkel: You see, you are there. I'll never forget just this one
incident, which reveals a great deal though, if you can
do it gently without hurting. A retired railroad
engineer. He talked about his life and his wife was
trying to keep his self-esteem. He told of the
humiliations. She said, "Oh he's good. Not every man
can be a railroad engineer." He said, "Oh yeah they
can. The diesels can do it, anyone can do it." But then
she only talked of one of her three daughters, the one
who was college educated. The other two hardly existed
in the conversation unless I introduced it. It was sad but
revealing. We come to this challenge. That's something
we all have to be aware of.

Harris: I've had that experience with working women who feel
as though they ought not to be working because in a
middle-class culture women, perhaps, shouldn't work.
Thus, although they have been working, some of them,
for twenty, twenty-five and thirty years, when you ask
them about their work, will say, "Oh that's not important. I want to talk about my family or my
husband's work." Their own work is something which,
since they ought not to be doing, they relegate it to the
background.

Benison: You know, there's a great science fiction writer in England named John Wyndham and he once wrote a short story of historians of the future who can travel back and forth in time. But they only have one interdict. They are not supposed to interfere with history. They are merely to act as observers and learn, because once they interfere they may cause irreparable damage by changing the course of history. It's a very interesting note. I would suggest that historians, or people who are engaged in interviewing, somehow transform the person who is being interviewed.

                Let me give you an example of what I mean. The great figure in television news reporting was, of course, Edward R. Murrow, and Edward R. Murrow would have interviews with all sorts of people and show them for an hour on TV. Many of those interviews were extraordinary and very, very good, but I never forgave Edward R. Murrow for one thing. He made these people entertainers and they were not essentially entertainers. Edward R. Murrow at one time was interested in the life of the scientists at the Institute for Advanced Studies at Princeton. So he went down there and he got absolutely gorgeous material from people like Herman Weyl and other physicists and mathematicians there, but he didn't use it. He didn't use it because he said it was dead. "Who the hell is going to be interested in this?"

Terkel: Saul is hitting something that's a challenge to all of us, this very fact of what happens to our teachers as well as to ourselves. This is the end of the first hour and we'll break here for a few moments. Is there something you want to say Ron?

Grele: Where's the bathroom?

Terkel: Ron says he wants to go to the bathroom. (laughter)

This is the perfect ending. This is oral history at its most profound. We have with us Jan Vansina, Dennis Tedlock, Alice Kessler Harris, Saul Benison and Ron Grele and we'll continue the conversation later. What is oral history, the challenge to all of us who engage in it.

Terkel: This is part two of this conversation, which I find very stimulating for very personal reasons. I'm with Jan Vansina, historian and anthropologist whose specialty is African life but who is also speaking about his own childhood in North Belgium, Dennis Tedlock, anthropologist who has lived and worked among the Zuni Indians, Saul Benison whose interest has been primarily in medicine and science and professional men in contrast to the "less educated people" who are the teachers of most of us. Ron Grele of the Ford Foundation Oral History Project and Alice Kessler Harris, historian who has worked among immigrant people from Eastern Europe, primarily. We're talking about effects upon people and effects on us, all of us who are involved in this work. The effect of it on us. Jan you were going to say something on that?

Vansina: I was going to say two things. First, I started, you know, when I was twenty-one and in a foreign culture which created a greater shock. I feel that every time I have conducted an interview that something has changed. My views on lots of things have changed throughout my life because of my work in oral history. The other thing is that when I hear my voice now, and when I was twenty-two, on the tape. This is the first generation, I suppose, which hears its voice aging. It may be poetical but it's terribly sad to hear your voice aging.

Terkel: Need it be sad? Isn't there something else there too, Jan?

Vansina: Sure, not necessarily sad in the sense of the philosophers.

Terkel: But that change. You're thinking now of the physical sound of the voice. But what about the effect on you, Alice? When you talk to the immigrant women who are your teachers. In what way does it alter your view of life or of yourself?

Harris: I think that relates very closely to my own background. That is, I have a feeling that all historians become historians in a search for their own pasts. And that's certainly true of me. I was born in England of a refugee family when the War broke out, and we remained immigrants in England until shortly after the War and then came to America. My own immigrant experience has led me, I think, to search for the experiences of other immigrants. When I listen to them talk, I must admit, I find it very difficult to remain dispassionate. I get very involved with the stories and the tales that they tell.

Terkel: We were just about to come to that theme in a minute. You've introduced a new theme. Sorry, go ahead.

Harris: But it always sort of strikes me as a kind of search for a lost past. I, for example, learned how to read and speak Yiddish when I started doing this, out of the feeling that I was really going to have to speak Yiddish to people whose memories were in Yiddish, and listening to them speak in their own language is a very different thing from listening to them speak in English. My experiences with Italian women, for example, speaking in English and my experiences with Jewish women speaking in Yiddish have been almost totally diametrical. I've come to the conclusion that I can't interview Italian immigrant women, older women, in English any more because the language that they use is not one which represents their tradition.

Terkel: That's interesting. Now the opposite, it seems to me, is someone whose experiences are diametrical to yours, is Dennis Tedlock. You deal with people of your culture and your parent's culture in a general way, whereas Dennis' work is totally alien—Swedish-Irish to Zuni Indians.

Tedlock: Right. But here I am, or there I was, growing up in New Mexico with that sense of ultimate homelessness that any American must feel at some time or another, who is not an American Indian, impressed upon me, too, by the fact that none of my family had been here more than a couple of generations, some for only one. So, there in an environment in which almost everybody around me was of a radically different background, and lots of them were Indians, I guess what I was doing was trying to find out where I was, what is this country, what was it to the people who were here, what does it mean to spring from this earth? It's really quite something to talk to somebody who will, in fact, say just that, "We sprang from this earth." This is something that the rest of us can't say. Archeologists say that the Indians came over the Bering Straits forty thousand years ago. I think one reason that they are so fascinated with that fact is that they want to look aside from this essentially indigenous character of the Indian and see them as one more band of immigrants, never mind that it was ten, twenty, forty thousand years ago and they have been living here ever since.

Terkel: In your case Jan, I suppose when you are in Africa, your experiences would be more closely related to Dennis' than to Alice's.

Vansina: Oh yes. I was with the Kuba for three years and I was due to take a plane, to leave. I had gone through boy's initiation with the other boys; they had lumped me with the seven year old boys and after three years they had said, now you are a grown-up and we can put you in the secret cult tomorrow, the last day I was there. On that side, of course, I've had those experiences.

One I've had here is, of course, the one of migrating myself to the United States and living ten years or twelve years here. This, I suppose would give me a different reading of the same interviews you are collecting now because I would be thinking of other types of questions or feelings than you have.

Benison: I've been changed by working in oral history. When I was younger, I would say, theories of history, large scale movements of men and events just poured from my lips. I was sure I knew what the tendency of history was and I made generalizations about the lives of tens of thousands of people. I did it and I was sure I was right. Now here, I started interviewing individuals; there they stand and they're there and that's what history is all about. It's about individual people and we've never captured their voices before. You know, you get a row of statistics and the statistics say that workers in mines die of black lung at age thirty-five. What does that mean in an individual life? This is where the process of history is. It makes history far more difficult. It was an easy business with grand theory that was telling me what the tendency of history was. Now it is a far more difficult thing and a far more gorgeous thing. Do you know the Blythe volume, *Akenfield*?

Terkel: Oh gosh, yes. That's a great book.

Benison: It's very interesting. Blythe is not a historian, he's a poet. And there is a question he puts to an old farm worker. He says, "What songs did ye sing Davy?" and

Davy looks at him and says "It's not the songs, it was the singing." Here is an extraordinary wisdom which is revealed, and you're never going to get at that wisdom unless you come to the individual person. It makes me revere people far more.

Terkel: Ronald Blythe's story is perhaps worth telling; it's quite remarkable. Ronald Blythe came from a rather aristocratic family, the river Blythe runs through the village that is called Akenfield, some fifty miles or so out of London. He's lived there generations and generations—his family. He didn't know these people. So he took the tape recorder and his shyness and his diffidence was his asset. The fact that he was gentle and they were gentle and he was seemingly inarticulate rather than say, like Mike Wallace, was what helped. It was a different approach and so, as a result, he discovered himself, Blythe did, as he puts it. Blythe wrote about Ronald Firbank. He knew Sylvia Ashton Warner which was in his favor. He was in another world entirely and then he discovered himself. This is the other tremendous aspect which leads, of course, to the big question that Alice touched on. He became emotionally involved. So we come to the question of detachment and involvement, don't we. Where do we go from here?

Grele: Maybe I can begin. The interviewing experience that I've had has been all with elite interviews. It would have to be called that; members of the John F. Kennedy Administration, senators, congressmen, judges, The Board of Trustees, directors, officers of the Ford Foundation, people like that. But there is still—you do become involved with the person whom you are interviewing. There is some kind of dialectical process that occurs in which you are working jointly on something and you come to share the creation itself. In my own mind there's always the problem of detachment because, as a historian, I have to stand back. Although the creation is partly mine it should really be mostly his. On the other hand, I'm concerned about that creation. Yet it has got to be a historical document as well. It's a very peculiar kind of relationship that evolves.

Harris: I'm not so sure that that's not an asset, in some sense. I think that to become emotionally involved, while it's true that it violates the first canon of the historian, which is objectivity, nevertheless, puts you intimately into a situation and thus enables you to understand it in a way, I think, you can't understand it if you remain outside the situation. That is, I think there are advantages as well as disadvantages to being inside.

Grele: One of the advantages, this is interesting. I was talking to a quantitative historian last night and he drew a distinction between his research and his actions as an historian; which was a very interesting kind of distinction. In oral history you can't do that because your research is your practice of history and the two are synthesized somehow so that this dichotomy does not exist in oral history as in quantitative history.

Vansina: I disagree. Perhaps this is the anthropological experience but, you know, you acquire a sort of split personality. In fact, I think the effect of being emotionally involved is also to suspect your own emotions and your own beliefs. It makes you, it's not psychoanalysis but it makes you realize how dangerous it would be if you knew yourself, really, as other people would know you if they knew all about you.

Terkel: On this matter of the split personality, the question is, is there ever such a thing as objectivity? We know now in the world of journalism there's a big dispute going on, which should have gone on long ago, the advocate journalists against the "objective" journalists, whatever that may be. There is no such thing.

At the same time Jan raises the point, how can one be both? This is the challenge. How can one be both? Take yourself, Dennis, you said you were with Zuni Indians; wholly different, you felt alien, it was a strange land to you. Your people had only been there a few generations so you had to be emotionally touched even though you were totally alien to them.

Tedlock: Right. Well, I guess it comes back to that business of trying to deal with that challenge that the man threw out, what could that have been like?

Terkel: What was it like to be there?

Tedlock: What was it like to be those people? What Jan says about split personality is absolutely right. Being somebody working across that large a bridge, I think, you get about as many butterflies in your stomach sometimes as a person can stand. Until, of course, you begin to know the people and be more relaxed with them, it's really very trying at first.

Vansina: You know, there are things like: you're in a village and measles come along. It's nothing. Yet out of the sixty children, ten die because measles are serious and you're the only guy around who can give advice and do things. But the people won't accept it because it's not their way. That's when you really feel the split personality. You ask, should an anthropologist get involved, or should a historian be involved in practical advice when he knows the solution, or should he not? I think anthropologists are divided on the question and I think oral historians, when they face it, are also divided. Should we give this advice or should we not?

Harris: In terms of the interview itself, though, the kinds of
          questions you ask and the way in which you ask them,
          and your voice inflections reveal your own biases and
          put you into the interview, in, as Ron says, a kind of
          dialectical process. So to argue that you can ever be
          objective in an interview itself, I think, is to distort your
          own role in the inverview. That is, you have to become
          a participant and not simply an observer.

Grele: But you become a participant within limited realms.
          When I worked on the Kennedy Project, when I would
          go to interview someone after I had interviewed a
          number of other people, very often I knew more about
          a particular topic than the man I was interviewing.
          There could have come, at a number of times, points at
          which I could have revealed to him something that I
          knew that would govern his actions in the future. Say,
          for example, I was interviewing a senator after I had
          interviewed ten or twelve people in a regulatory agency,
          and the senator was deeply involved in a particular
          policy at that agency. If I had revealed what my sources
          in the agency had told me, to the senator, he would
          have changed his actions and affected their careers. So
          that there's always that, you know. On that particular
          project and on the project I work on now we are in-
          formally sworn to a certain kind of secrecy. We do not
          reveal information. So that while we are participants in
          the interview we are not participants in the on-going
          process of the historical chain of events.

Terkel: But you, Ron, your project is a little different, con-
          siderably. You are dealing with "public", "important",
          in an ironic sense "important", people in contrast to the
          people whom everyone here works with.

Grele: But the people that others interview also have an in-
          tegrity that should be respected. It doesn't differ
          because someone sits on a board of trustees or someone

hangs around in a local bar. Each one is an individual personality and should be respected.

Terkel: Oh yes. This comes back to the earlier question on the first program raised by Saul, on the matter of ethics, about hurting someone privately. It might not be a public hurt, but a private hurt which is a particular problem I have in one case in this project I'm on right now.

Grele: And that's a deeper hurt.

Terkel: What?

Grele: That's a deeper hurt.

Terkel: Well, of course.

Benison: You know, raising questions of objectivity, I think, is playing a ball game off to the side. It does a lot for our feeling of virtue. It does a lot for our feeling of morality, but it ain't the ball game. I think, here, we talk about objectivity as if we were going to emulate scientists and also believing that scientists are completely objective in their work. No. The minute you ask a question you have a bias. You are trying to generalize. Why ask questions of, "Where did you come from?", "Where did you live?" Your bias says, "Gee that's important, it's important to know his genetic make-up, his biological makeup, the place where he was born." It is a bias of the effect of environment on him. There is no such thing as writing "objective" history. It's like reading the telephone book, if you were going to write objective history. It would be a series of names. It would be meaningless.

Terkel: Not only that, even then you might be skipping polysyllabic names, or foreign names too.

Benison: Yes. I mean, my god; if you look at life and the hurts of life. You know, there's a story of Lord Plunkett who was a great milk co-operative organizer. He was speaking up and down Ireland during the time of the troubles in 1916, about milk co-operatives. And he found himself in Northern Ireland. He said, "Ladies and gentlemen, I know that there are differences between Catholic and Protestant. I know there are differences between North and South Ireland. But I'm not here to talk about that problem today. I'm here to talk about milk co-operatives." And for the next two hours he spoke about milk co-operatives. Afterwards, when it was all over, an old Presbyterian farmer came to him and said, "Lord Plunkett, ye spake the trruth tonight, man. Them Papishers will burn!" (laughter)

He heard what he wanted to hear. But, my God! How do you get rid of the passions of life in history? If you do then you're distorting it.

Terkel: Isn't Saul hitting what, I suppose, attracts us all to what we're doing; precisely that, that it is highly personal. We try to be detached and as "objective", whatever that may be, as possible but, we deal with passion, I guess, primarily, rather than with statistics. Isn't that what it really amounts to?

Vansina: I see one big problem which occurs when you are working in the oral history of your own society. In anthropology your major problem is to translate another culture, another way of thinking into the way of thinking of the audience you are writing for. Now the more oral history we do, in this case, the more we realize that there are subdivisions and sub-divisions within sub-divisions, but in what common language are you now trying to translate this? Is this for fellow academics? Is this for middle class subjects? I can see real problems. I can see minorities saying, "I don't care if you write for middle class suburban people, I want you to write for my people and in a different way." We haven't touched upon this problem. I wonder if it has been raised by oral historians.

Benison: It's an important question.

Harris: Historians, I think, have traditionally written for other historians, and with very few exceptions, of whom Allan Nevins is one, people who have been trained as historians see their work as a way of extending scholarly knowledge. I myself think that that might be a mistake and that that needs re-evaluating and we; really, ought to begin writing for, and interpreting our experiences for anybody who wants to read them. But that means asking different kinds of questions sometimes and certainly, learning how to write in different kinds of ways.

Grele: I think that oral history is a tool to democratize the study of history. History is one of the few professions which is really democratic, in the sense that it does not have a special language. Someone does not have to learn a special rhetoric to do history. It's open to the public, to anyone who wants to do it. All they need is a special kind of sense of the past or a desire to know the past. I think that by using oral hstory and by training, or helping people to use the tape recorder and to look at the past in a particular kind of way, we can then turn them loose to do their own history so that they speak, then, to their own people, their own audience, rather than just the narrow audience of historians.

Terkel: Now we're coming to the Grail, now we're coming to what Parsifal has been looking for. This has been raised by Jan and touched upon by Alice and Ron right now. What we're doing is really the beginning of something. Often, I'm sure, you've come across, perhaps, the daughter of an immigrant woman you've met or possibly, quite probably, Jan, in Africa, some young guy who may do what you're doing, and Dennis, maybe among the Zuni Indians. I find it very often the case. Someone's going to do it. "I'm going to do it among my own family," said this girl, and she got a tape recorder. Or said someone younger, because of the nature of energy and vitality. And then, there's a tremendous sense of release, energy has been released now. Whom is it for? Suddenly, they will be writing for themselves and all we do is to open, very slightly, a sluice gate. But there it is.

Grele: But they can do it in bad ways too. Because for the past two hundred years history has, more or less, grown into the domain of a narrow group of priests, in many ways, now when you democratize it, the people themselves may accept all of the erroneous caveats that they have been taught about history, and go out and do their own history in all the wrong ways. So that, they need help and they need help from people who are particularly sensitive to certain kinds of problems in the study of the past. And, I would say to you, Studs, if you turn people on to history like that, you're going to have to make them as aware of the distinction between history and memory that you draw in *Hard Times*. You're going to have to transmit the certain kinds of sensitivity that you have towards the past experiences of the people you interview to them, to that they will do it in that kind of tradition.

Terkel: It need not be, precisely, just the way I did it.

Grele: No, but that same sensitivity.

Terkel: Well, it's there in this sense, if, say, my grandmother has a tape recorder—you could probably talk about this Alice—or Jan—my grandmother, I'll ask her what it was like and suddenly the grandmother, who has been silent, and mute, and sat in the corner, begins to talk. What we're talking about is self-esteem and a sense of personal worth coming into play.

Think of another aspect, the tape recorder. We've touched on this. Oral history is old, older than the printed word. We're talking now about something new but the fact is that it is a sort of resurgence because of technology, something that has been knocked out to a great extent by Gutenberg, in a way. Isn't that so?

Tedlock: Ultimately not only can we replace ourselves as oral historians and anthropologists by turning them on to it, but also, in the process, no reason why, ultimately, books shouldn't be replaced by cassettes if anybody has a tape recorder.

Harris: Oh no! This discussion is really beginning to bother me because you're using the word history in a way in which historians have never intended that it be used. That is, what you are talking about is the collection of data, asking people how they feel about their own experiences and so forth, or putting memories on cassettes. This is simply to record data in a different way. It's not numbers and it's not letters, but it's the equivalent of numbers and letters, interpreted in new ways. What the historian does is say, "what does all this mean?" That is, if you add up the experiences of fifty individuals who record their own childhoods in X way, or who, for example, recall the Depression in a certain kind of way, the historian then comes along and says, "What does this tell us about why people voted for Franklin D. Roosevelt, for example, or about the kinds of political movements that existed in the 1930s." I would deny that a historian can ever be replaced by a cassette.

Grele: I'm in between on this.

Tedlock: If we give the people the same means that you're talking about. The one advantage that we have, as social scientists, is that we have not one or two cassettes, but fifty or a hundred, and that is our one advantage. We can listen to them all and try to make a synthesis.

Harris: But history is not the sum total of discrete experiences, its parts.

Terkel: I think there's a misinterpretation, maybe there's a disagreement between Dennis and Alice, but I don't feel that a book could, ever, be replaced by a cassette. Both are essential today. This doesn't mean that there shouldn't be any knowledge from above, either. This comes back to student participation in universities, it's both, bottom up and top down, not a question of data. I was merely thinking about self-esteem. That's all, do you see? It has nothing to do with data, but something to do with how people live. When old grandma tells a story, I'm talking about her own personal view in relation to her granddaughter, something good happens. This has nothing to do with history. I was simply saying that this opens up so many possibilities, as yet untouched.

Harris: O.K. I'd agree with you there, but, what I would have to say is that, once you find out how people feel about themselves and their own experiences, that question of self-esteem, you still have to go a step further and say, "what does this mean". It can't stop right there. That's why I, for example, would argue with most historians that your book is not history. It is data and I use it as data. I give it to my students and I say, "Here is now a lot of people felt about the Depression, now, how do you interpret it? What sense can you make of this? Those are the questions that historians ask.

Terkel: Let's take a slight pause. I'm sorry, what did you want to say?

Tedlock: Again, if you place the same means in the hands of the people you interview, they can draw their own conclusions, if somebody is interested in some event that happened during World War II and you place in their hands a reasonable amount of tape and film and so forth. Let every man be an historian, and a comparative historian too.

Vansina: This is my line, you know. I've trained African historians and now they have taken over and rightly so, and they are historians. But they are also the people who did not have a voice before. Now some of the books or some of the interpretations are wild, but this is the first generation of African historians. They will integrate, and some of them superbly integrate today, the rigor of the historical method, which is somthing that can be measured, into their data. The important fact to them is, obviously, that it is they who are saying it.

Harris: I think that's important and I would agree with you wholly, there. But I think the distinction between what you're saying and what Dennis has just said is that Dennis would give tape recorders to anybody and say, "Go out and tape and what you come up with will be history". I would respond by saying that a historian trained as Dennis was, would have to train people with tape recorders to see what people say in the context of the myths of a society, of the ideas with which they've been trained, of the particular economic and social characteristics in which they've been brought up and trained, of the political situation of the period in which they're interviewing; all those things are the things that a historian conceives of in broad scope and into which he then fits the interview. The interview doesn't exist by itself.

Tedlock: The only thing that permits him to do that, in the end, is that he has access to more information than anybody else.

Harris: Exactly.

Tedlock: Well?

Harris: And he also has access to historical methodology. He has been trained to ask broad questions about the past.

Terkel: Let's continue. I don't want to end this, but just a slight pause. We'll pick it right up. We'll resume this particular battle.

Back to that whole subject of history and data and people with cassettes and tape recorders recounting their lives and Alice's point that this is not history but data. You were saying in reply to that, Dennis?

Tedlock: I think that the historical view itself, ultimately, is the result, simply, of the access to that much more information. To hear someone telling about their direct experience, their private history, and to know because you've read books, or listened to other tapes of other interviews and so on, that there are other views, it is precisely that kind of comparativeness that makes a historical method and abstract historical ideas possible. If you place, again, the same—if you let people listen to one hundred opinions about a certain event, I think they can spontaneously reconstruct at least a part of what a historian would do anyway.

Grele: Oh, I don't think anybody does anything spontaneously.

I'm kind of torn in this argument because on the one hand, I do feel a very deep obligation to the canons of historical practice, and I think they are very, very important because they do help us learn something from the past. On the other hand, I'm also convinced that these canons, these practices are easy enough for everyone to learn. I do feel that every man can become his own historian, but that being a historian means being a certain kind of person, looking at the world in a particular kind of way. One of the examples I always use, in terms of asking a question; it comes up very often in an interview that people will tell you, "Oh we can't do that that way anymore", or "We don't do that that way anymore". The logical question that most citizens would ask is, "Why can't you do it that way any more?" Then you get a description of the institutional arrangements within which people are acting now. The historical question, however, is to ask, "Why could you do it that way at another time ? or at that time you're talking about." Then you get a description of the past. To ask questions that way, to think of questions that way demands a certain kind of historical thought, a certain way of viewing history, a certain commitment to the pastness of the past. It's very easy to learn. I think everyone can learn it, but it must be learned. It is a special way of looking at the world.

Benison: I'd like to add one thing. I really don't disagree very much with what was said, either by Dennis or Alice. It may be that one of the ultimate values of oral history is that you have a magnificent way of training a young historian to do history, of being aware of the tenuousness of memory, of being aware of the individual in history and his whole experience, of being aware of putting documents and photographs, etc. in juxtaposition to get, in a sense, a picture of the past. The one danger of handing people cassettes is that what you may get is not an inquiry, but a celebration and that is a very grave difference indeed.

Terkel: Not disagreeing with Alice at all, on the contrary of course, you have to have some sort of vision at the end, some sort of vision has to be there as a result of all of this. But, what's wrong with celebration? This is the point. If we accept it as celebration. I don't think Dennis meant for that to be the end-all. When Jan was talking about the young people in Central Africa, one of the key challenges in the moment we live in right now is this gap, probably in every society with a bureaucracy, the gap between the experts, so called, and the many. I'm not thinking about history as such, but about overcoming this tremendous gap that may kill us all, and that involves self-worth, personal worth and self-esteem. And I see this as a tremendously revolutionary instrument.

Grele: It depends on what you're celebrating and how. I really do believe that a view of the past helps one live in the present, that it somehow governs your actions, that it somehow informs your actions, that there's a relationship. A view of the past as celebration has consequences for the way you act in the present and I think that one of the real social dangers of the time we live in is the view of the past as celebration because it makes us incapable of solving certain kinds of very real problems that have absolutely nothing to do with the celebration of the American past.

Vansina: Well, we could escalate a little to point out, for everyone, that history is a very dangerous weapon. It is the weapon we use to indoctrinate our children. It is the way we build ideologies and we all know that wars then come from certain ideologies. Right now, across the world, I would say, the biggest danger is, if the past is used for national celebration, that's all right, but if that leads to a national ideology in a world where nationalism is becoming more and more dangerous, then no! This is what I try to teach my African students. Be proud of your home country, be proud of your past, record it, but, for God's sake don't say that you are good and the others are all worth nothing because if you begin on that line, that is the end.

Grele: And I would argue that it's safer to have history in the hands of the people than it is to have history in the hands of the state and the state historians who would more likely use it for nationalistic purposes than would people who are much more concerned with just how they eat and live and breathe.

Terkel: That is precisely what I think this discussion is about. This is the very point. If people—I don't mean "the people" etc.—if people can have a means of expressing themselves and their sense of being, when so long they've been anonymous as statistics in practically all societies, a great many, that's terribly important. Not that it is the answer. No. Not that he's the historian but that this is a tremendous moment we live in. This is a tremendous instrument and by all means let's use it.

Harris: But you know, Studs, that's in a sense, an illusory kind of self-esteem you're giving people. That is, talking into a tape recorder doesn't make you any better than, or any more valuable than . . .

Terkel: No, I'm talking about, say, some older person, as a case in point, talking about her life to her granddaughter. It's a terribly important thing. She's recognized that person as someone who has brought her something. Both are enriched. She feels good. There's nothing wrong with that. I don't mean that talking into a tape recorder makes you a different person. It's merely one more instrument. It's not everything. By all means Jan is right. But, from the fact that he celebrates his life, if he could see the fact that somebody else's life is not that far removed from his, the dangers of nationalism would be less. There again, nationalism, we have to come to another subject entirely. Don't we? When colonial people suddenly find their identity, they'll find their own tyrants too. That's another subject, isn't it?

Benison: Let me skew this a little. As historians . . .

Terkel: Excuse me. I just want to bid farewell, and I hope we meet again, to Alice Kessler Harris who is, obviously, doing some quite remarkable work among immigrant women in America. Is there a work of yours that we can look forward to seeing soon?

Harris: There are a number of articles which are in process, but they will be published in scholarly journals.

Terkel: There again, we come to that question, don't we?

Harris: Right. The scholarly versus a more popular audience.

Grele: Plug the book.

Harris: Plug the book, *Past Imperfect?*

Terkel: What's the title?

Harris: *Past Imperfect.* It's a collection of essays which I've just edited.

Terkel: Published by?

Harris: Knopf was the publisher. It deals, unfortunately, not with oral history but with traditional history.

Terkel: And Dennis Tedlock?

Tedlock: Yeah. I have to go also, to run out and catch a plane.

Terkel: What of yours, for the people who are listening, is it possible for them to read?

Tedlock: Just last December, the Dial Press in New York released my first book which is called, *Finding The Center: Narrative Poetry of the Zuni Indians.* In that I set forth a lot of oral traditions of the Zunis in a translated form, which if you read it aloud, it's like a script, you will make it sound the way it originally sounded. That's what you're supposed to try to do. It's a story book in a sense, to be read out loud.

Terkel: I know, before you leave, that you have theories about prose and poetry in oral history, too. I know that.

Tedlock: It's simply that, people talk poetry, they don't talk prose.

Terkel: As Dennis leaves, that could be one of the subjects that we could talk about. Thank you very much Dennis Tedlock.

So Jan, and Ron, and Saul, we're talking about the point Alice and Dennis raised, this matter of, I suppose, poetry. "I've been talking prose all my life", said that guy. He said, "I didn't know I was talking prose all my life." That comes into it doesn't it, the talk of people you meet, the poetic nature of it?

Vansina: Right: My belief on the whole question, is, if you do give tape recorders out and people tape things, the experience you have is that they are not so much interested in taping history. They are interested in taping songs and taping what's happening and doing and thus they are, of course, providing documents for other people. If you are a linguist and you listen to these tapes and get the language and you may say, it is poetry. It isn't like written prose; but if you're a linguist then you know that the way we write is always stilted. Isn't it? I mean, it's rare to find a man who speaks and you can just type it and it comes out a book.

Terkel: Isn't this the excitement of oral history?

Benison: The language is, really, one of the exciting things and it's one of the things that historians, as a group, have paid very little attention to. They've not analyzed language. And this is the most social aspect of our heritage. We carry our history in our language. You know, silence is damned important. Inflection; by inflection you can change meaning. Now, the question is, which voices are you going to collect to preserve for the future? Are you going to only collect the reminiscences of seventy year old men? Are you going to collect middle aged men? Are you going to collect kids? There's an English folklorist named Opie who collects the lore and language of children, and reading the Opie volume you get a tremendous insight into how quickly information among communities of children is transmitted from one to another. You talk about Telstar, my God! this is equally fast. You know the poem by Andrew Marvell?

> Had we but world enough and time,
> This coyness, lady, would be no crime.

This is a young guy speaking. He's trying to make someone for an evening. Now, should you collect the young voice? Should you collect the old voice?

I work with scientists and I believe that it would be more profitable for me to collect the biographical data of a relatively young scientist; say forty-five years of age. Why? Because I can come back to him. I can come back to him at age fifty-five, I can come back to him at age sixty-five, if he lives that long. And then, I could do something that no other historian has done; I could actually begin to see his changing ideas, how he has been re-writing his history. So oral history, in a sense, gives you all sorts of options to do things that you have never done before in history, in terms of analysis.

Grele: And if the socio-linguists are correct, you would also find by comparing his voice at age forty, age fifty, and age sixty-five, patterns of social integration there, patterns of social mobility, patterns of social interaction with various kinds of groups, you would find a professionalization of his language that would tell you an incredible amount of information about that man himself.

Vansina: Yes.

Benison: You know, there's one other thing, since I'm wound up, let me say this, and I made this point this morning. We live in an envelope of sound; all sorts of sounds. We blithely speak of the environment and this is one element of the environment that is so evanescent and changing. Here we have an instrument to collect sound; what is it like in the supermarket in 1973? What is it like on the subway train? What is it like in a steel factory, or an automobile factory? We could preserve a part of our environment that historians a hundred and fifty years from now would bless us for. Do we do it? Absolutely not! Because we're still skewed to collecting the movers and the shakers.

Terkel: The makers and the shakers.

Grele: But also, we live in an age in which people have forgotten, really, how to see and how to listen. The most elementary facts of existence have been forgotten. In a sense, oral history, I think, opens up questions about seeing, reading and listening that are very important questions for the culture.

I don't know if you want to get on to this?

Terkel: Go ahead.

Grele: The other day, Studs and I were talking about his interest in jazz and its relationship to conversation and he raised kinds of very sensitive relationships between the two. Do you want to talk about that some, now?

Terkel: What was it? I forgot what I said.

Grele: I asked you, if your interest in jazz and folk music as particular forms of music had any influence on your interest in oral history interviewing.

Terkel: Oh yes. Obviously it did. Sure.

Grele: And you agreed that it did and began to talk about the improvisation in jazz, and its similarity to a conversational narrative.

Terkel: This is what we haven't talked about so far, in the two hours. We've talked about the questions and answers. But we didn't talk about listening and how suddenly, as we listen, something that that person said, suddenly brings something new into the arena. Jazz, as you know, has a beginning a middle and an end. We know that my conversation with my old friend, this old woman of the housing project, the old Appalachian miner who got black lung, begins. I know it's going to end too. That much I know. I also know something about him, generally. But aside from that, there's a flexibility. I'm sure Jan has found this, amazingly, in central Africa.

            Therefore, what he says suddenly alters things for me, and it is like jazz. A jazz soloist gets up. There's an arrangement, a beginning a middle and an end, it's skeletal. But say a Count Basie trumpeter gets up, Joe Newman, say, and he starts playing; well, he's not only interpreting, he's creating as well, because of the flexibility allowed.

Vansina: In Africa, we have run studies to see if the improvisations follow the language we know. To understand that, you have to know that African languages have tones, pitch. So a normal word goes and exaggerates a normal sentence; ìbà bààt ìbà bàát bàát báànyì bààn.* This is a set of tones. When you sing, do you destroy it or not, when you improvize? We find

            *   ⁄ high pitch, ⟍ low pitch (Bushong: there were people, there were women, women had children.)

out that in certain patterns it does, and in others it doesn't. It's a distinction between improvisation where it is not erased and real "music", as they call it, where it is erased. But obviously what you're talking about is dialogue.

Terkel: Dialogue. Now we come, not to the question and answer, but dialogue. So both of us are affected. Ron, you want to say something, Ron?

Grele: There's another dimension to that because it then becomes an art form as well, and the set of structures that you are then dealing with are different, and they raise other kinds of questions; questions of performance, questions of artistic values, worth, etc., and how do you divorce them from the cultural context to look at them objectively. In a sense, your interviews become works of art, as poetry.

Benison: This leads us to the question; who is the audience? Who is the ultimate audience and how does the audience transform the story being told? My God! Do you remember the Mercury Theater?

Terkel: Oh sure, the Orson Welles theater.

Benison: Orson Welles. I remember once, when I was a kid, going to see *Julius Caesar* and they were not old Romans present at all. These were gangsters.

Terkel: It was done, you recall, during the time of Hitler's rise and was like Brecht's *Arturo Ui*, in a way. It was a police state, a totalitarian state.

Benison: The performers were playing to the audience, the audience was affecting the performance. Now, if you're preparing something for a historian a hundred years from now, he is not someone who was there. Is the stuff skewed for him or do we really only present our oral histories to the immediate audience of the present. And this is the problem; the historian has the illusion that he is preparing stuff for the future and that really isn't so.

Grele: I'm preparing stuff for the future, and to do it well, in this sense, I think we should leave performance notes, just as you have performance notes to a drama.

Vansina: The one point, in all of this, which I'm always gotten by, and I was this morning, is that I'm used to African audiences and I'm used to the audience reacting and at historical conventions it is not polite to react. You never get off the ground.

Terkel: Jan is hitting something. Do you know John Neville, the British actor, a marvelous man? He brought Shakespeare to Nigeria. And he said it was so exciting. The audience was reacting to *Macbeth* and *Hamlet* as though they were a sporting event. He said, "fantastic". That's what Jan is talking about, of course. You were disturbed by the silence?

Vansina: My classes, for instance, I've re-arranged my classes in such a way that they do have to react. It comes hard.

            Now that, to transcribe that, and leave it for the future record is very difficult. I think it can be done with film. I've seen experiments where film, sound and notes were all used at the same time, but it's a challenging opportunity.

Terkel: I'm thinking this is about the end of two hours of conversation with five of my colleagues, all oral historians and each in our own way, with Alice Harris and Dennis Tedlock here too, before. We should have, perhaps, one last go-around, each of you. I realize that we're not going to solve everything tonight, obviously all of this is a beginning, everything we've touched on. So, Ron Grele of the Ford Foundation Oral History Project, your thoughts briefly as we go around here, on I don't know what, anything.

Grele: The last thing I want to say would be that, I think that oral history raises the kinds of methodological questions that historians are very uncomfortable with, and that's one of the reasons why they don't like to talk about oral history or oral testimony. They don't want to explore other fields like anthropology, sociology, psychology that deal with oral testimony or other forms of materials. They're very uncomfortable with these questions.

Terkel: Saul? Saul Benison?

Benison: I don't know what to say, except that for me it has opened up a whole new world. It has not only humanized history for me, I think it has made me more of a human being. It is as if you say, really, I'm starting to work with a scientist but it is not only the scientist I'm concerned with. Nothing human is really alien to me now and that's the joy of it. That means you don't look at the watch when you're working. That's what it means.

Terkel: Is there a work of yours Saul, that the audience can look into?

Benison: Several years ago I published an oral history memoir I had done with Doctor Rivers of the Rockefeller Institute and I've just begun one with Albert Sabin, which I have great hopes for.

Terkel: So we'll look forward to that.

Benison: But what I really have to get on top of is two hundred and forty linear feet of records.

Terkel: So the task is ahead. Jan Vansina?

Vansina: Oral history is obviously a powerful tool and it's a very exciting one. I think the dangers fifty years from now will be that we will neglect pictures, pencils, notes and other things which go into history. Perhaps I'm way

ahead of everybody but I see that that's what is happening in Africa right now. We must get into some sort
of balance. But, surely the oral record has brought into
history the lives of ordinary persons and therefore made
it meaningful for ordinary persons again.

Terkel: Is there, Jan Vansina, a work of yours that . . .

Grele: There are hundreds of them. (laughter)

Benison: Boy have you opened something. The bibliography is
           . . .

Terkel: I know he's done a lot. I mean, one that, perhaps,
           might not be too esoteric.

Vansina: Well, most of my work has been written for the local
           audience and therefore hard to read and they're usually
           not in English. There is one on a kingdom just on the
           eve of the arrival of the Europeans, called, *The Tio
           Kingdom.*

Terkel: *The Tio Kingdom.*

Vansina: T-i-o Tio. 1880--1892, which describes how the living
           society was, in a way, beginning to be dampened down
           and ultimately squashed.

Terkel: Is that available to American readers?

Vansina: Yes it is.

Terkel: Publisher?

Vansina: Oxford University Press.

Terkel: Oxford University Press. O.k. Thank you very much
           gentlemen and, in absentia, Alice Harris and Dennis
           Tedlock; Jan Vansina, and Saul Benison and Ron
           Grele. I suppose, as a last word, the anonymous being
           heard from is what it is really about, in a way. And I
           guess enlightenment, illumination for all of us, the
           questioners and the answerers. Thank you very much.

The preceding conversation was recorded over station WFMT Chicago, and transcribed with only minor editorial changes.

Learning to Listen:
Oral History As Poetry
Dennis Tedlock

GUIDE TO DELIVERY:

A line change indicates a short pause, about ½ to 1 second; a double space between lines, marked by . , indicates a long pause, about 2 seconds;
bold type is loud;
light type is soft;
split-level lines indicate a chant-like delivery, with each level at a separate pitch;
long dashes indicate lengthened vowels, short ones at the ends of lines an interrupted delivery;
repeated consonants are lengthened;
other instructions are in *(parenthesized italics).*

Poetry is oral **history**
and oral **history**
is **poetry**.
.

First of all, historical information
and the **ideas** of history just spoken of by Mr. Grele
are found not only in
the relatively casual
conversational narratives of the interview situation
but also in forms of oral discourse which are
traditionally classified
as **poetry**--
songs and chants, for example.
Second
conversational narratives **themselves**
traditionally classified as **prose**
turn out, when listened to **closely**
to have poetical qualities of their **own**.
.

Here are two texts from the Zuni Indians of New Mexico
which demonstrate the **first** point.
On the surface both of these examples
would appear to contain nothing of historical value.
The first example is the text of a song first performed by

masked kachina dancers just this past summer.
It goes like this:
    •

"Rejoice! holy bundles, sacred bundles, because of your
    wise thoughts
there in the east your Moon Mother spoke, gave her word
when we went over there with the dragonfly, entered upon
    her road.
Rejoice! you will be granted many blessings, flowing silt,"
the two stars are saying this to all the sacred bundles
    here. [1]
    •

At one level this text is typical of Zuni rain songs.
The songs mention silt
because in desert country one of the main signs of
good recent rains is the presence of
fresh silt deposits all over the landscape.
The sacred bundles mentioned are the very powerful
    fetishes in the keeping of Zuni priests.
On another level the song is an **allegory:**
the sacred bundles
are **Houston Control**
the dragonfly is a **rocketship**
the silt is the alluvial deposits recently hypothesized for the
    moon's surface
and the two stars, who were reporting the silt to the sacred
    bundles
are the **astronauts.**
    •

At another level the song is saying that the Zunis have
    always had a way to the Moon Mother
through the
sacred bundles and the priestly prayers that go with them
and that the idea of
travelling to the moon is not
really something entirely **new** to them.
It's simply that the Zuni priests are capable of making
    spiritual journeys to the moon

rather than **mechanical** ones.
The song is an attempt by them to come to terms
with an historical event
and at the same time reassert
tradition.
I would suggest that oral historians working in the larger
   American society might find similarly important clues
to the meaning events have for people
in contemporary song texts.
   •

Now this next example comes from the Zuni story of
the creation.
It belongs to a genre that
we, looking on from the outside
would unquestionably label as myth
partly simply because the events described in it seem
   implausible to us.
Some of the lines, as you will hear
are in chant form.
The Zuni priests have just asked the Ahayuuta
the twin war gods
to look for the middle of the earth:
"Very well indeed.
I'm **going**," the twins said.
They came this way until they **came to Zuni.**
When they came here to the present village, they summoned
   the water-strider.
When they sum_{**moned him**}

he entered upon their roads.
There they spoke to him: **"Now**
this very day
we have summoned you here.
   •
You
must bend over here.
You must stretch out your arms and legs.
By the posi_{**tion**}

of your heart
The Middle Place will then become known."
That's what they said. "Indeed.
Is this your reason for summoning me?"
"Yes, this is why we have summoned you.
Now then, stretch yourself **out.**
By the position of your heart
  will be known
it
where the Middle Place is," that's what
the Ahayuuta told him.
"Very well."
Bending over toward the east
he stretched out, stretched out all his legs.
When they were **all out flat**
     when the ar
                    ms
le
  gs
stretched
a — — — —ll   round to the o
                 A   **ceans**
his heart rested
         site   **Middle**
at the   named the   **Place.**
•

They stood there:
"Very well, here is the middle
here is the middle of the **earth.**"[2]
•

The water-strider is that insect (*hold out hand with fingers
  spread but bent downwards*) that floats on the surface
  of ponds.
On the face of it this passage would seem
to be describing a

water-strider **so** gigantic
that its legs
can span an entire continent.
This is far into the realm of what we ourselves would call
   imaginary or mythic
but it is in fact a description of an actual experience.
Whenever the Zuni priests have something important to
   divine
they go into retreat to seek a vision.
In this case they are guided in that vision by the Ahayuuta
and one of them impersonates a water-strider by stretching
   out his arms (*stretch arms out horizontally to the sides*)
in the four directions, two at a time.
When the priest does this he **is** the water-strider and his
   arms **do** reach all the way to the oceans:
that is his experience.[3]
It is simply that the narrator does not specify which events
   are visionary ones.
•

Now the point that texts like this
rain song
and this section of a creation story
can refer to historical events
or ideas of history is not new to
Professor Vansina and other oral historians
who have worked in nonliterate societies.[4]
But what I would suggest **here** is that
oral historians working in literate societies should also pay
   attention to such texts.
People do not reveal their ideas of history only when they
   are conversing with an interviewer.
It's hard to imagine an oral history of the youth of the
   sixties, for example
without some reference to their songs
and to the wild stories that went around then.
•

Clearly
highly metaphorical or poetical speech events

can be
a source of history.
This brings me to my other major point which is that the relatively casual
conversational narratives
which are the more **ordinary** business of the oral historian
are **themselves** highly poetical
and cannot be properly understood from prose transcripts.
The **meaning** of **spoken** narrative
is not only carried by the sheer words as transcribed by alphabetic writing
but by the placement of **silences**
by **tones** of **voice**
by whispers and **shouts.**
In ancient Greece
written narratives
were still composed with oral delivery in mind.
Herodotus
for example
gave public recitations of his Histories
among other places at the Olympic Games.[5]
Right up through the Middle Ages written narratives
still retained their oral form, they were full of repetitions
formulaic phrases, the things that characterize oral performance.[6]
The punctuation and spacing that were used then came
much closer to representing actual
features of oral delivery than does the punctuation we use today[7]
and the manuscripts were accompanied by a tradition
of oral performance
carried on by professionals
who knew how to make the words **sound** right.
And not only professional performers but
other literate individuals
always read aloud
even in private.

The only recorded exception in all the time before the
    Renaissance
was St. Jerome.
His ability to read silently greatly disturbed St. Augustine
who had never seen anyone else do it
but even St. Jerome moved his lips,[8] it seems.
.

It was not until the Renaissance that there began to develop
    the kind of prose narrative we know today[9]
the kind that is
read silently and has lost many of its oral features.
Today's prose is no longer in the care of professional
    performers who know
how to turn it back into the oral
nor is it accompanied by performance notations
and so it is an **extremely** poor medium for the
    transcription of tape-recorded discourse
even the most ordinary conversation.
.

We must question whether **hundreds** of **reels** of oral
    history **tape**
ought to be converted into **thousands** of **pages** of
    prose typescript
after which the tapes are all too often **erased.**
To use a **visual** analogy, such a procedure is as absurd
as preferring to
make pencil sketches from photographs of historical events
and then destroy the photographs.
Nobody, whether in a
literate society or not **speaks** in **prose**
unless he is
unless perhaps he is
reading aloud
from **written** prose
and in the flattest possible voice.[10]
The **worst** thing about written prose is that there is no
    silence in it.
.

•
Even in an extended well-rehearsed discourse
the speaker of any language spends forty to fifty percent of
      his time being silent. [11]
The punctuation we use today is not an accurate guide
to these silences
though it is true that
people reading aloud usually stop at each period.
But in oral discourse a person may go right on from one
      sentence to another without pausing, or else he may
      pause in a place
where there would ordinarily be no punctuation in writing.
Here is an example of pausing from a Zuni narrative:
•

"You'll get to the dance in plenty of time," that's what
her children told her. "Then that's the way it will be,"
      she said, and she left. It was getting **so** hot. [12]
•

In the second of those two lines there were two
      complete sentences
and a part of third sentence, all delivered without a pause.
In this next passage there are eight different pauses
and no fewer than five of them occur where there would
      be no
punctuation
in a written version:
•

They brought him back, and when they
tried to unmask him
the mask
was stuck
to his face.
He was changing over.
•

When they unmasked the young man, some of his
flesh peeled off. [13]
•

Sometimes pauses
reveal great hesitation and doubt on the part of the speaker
as in this passage:

•
Well
there were about
a hundred and
hundred annnnn
hundred and six Zunis
signed up for it.[14]

•

But frequent pauses like these
don't always indicate hesitation, sometimes
pauses
are used

•

to create suspense
or to set off a series of elements that are in parallel
    construction
as in this next passage.
This passage
also illustrates the use of tone of voice.
The speaker is telling of a time when
B.I.A. officers
had to capture Zuni children in order to get them in school:

•

And I didn't see the **policeman** that came around.
Finally he came up behind me—
(*low and gravelly*) he caught me and dragged me down to the
    school.

•

Then in the **noontime**
I came home
as a **blue**bird:
had a blue shirt on
corduroy pants on
corduroy cap on:
a new boy. [15]

•

Besides pausing prose also fails to convey the way in which
    speakers may range all the way from a whisper
up to a shout.
We have italics and exclamation points of course

but we have been taught and taught and taught that any but
   the most sparing use of such devices
is unbecoming to written composition.
And we have no device at all that is suitable for
marking an especially quiet voice.
Here is a passage in which a speaker alternates between a
   normal speaking voice and a near whisper.
Beyond the first line he repeats everything he says twice
in terms of alphabetic writing that is
but when we restore the changes in amplitude to this
   passage we discover
that in fact he never says the same thing twice in the same
   way:
   •

At that moment his mother
embraced, embraced him.
His uncle got angry, his uncle got angry.
He beat
his kinswoman
he beat his kinswoman.[16]
   •

In this next passage
the speaker alternates between
a normal voice and something approaching a shout.
In the realm of tone of voice
he makes use in a couple of places of a sharpening or
tensing of the voice
and in one line he uses
a gentle or kind tone, although as you will hear in context
   this turns out to be ironic.
He is talking about the head of the Zuni Tribal Government:
   •

Look, **how many trips has the Governor made to
   Washington!**
He's got a **good**   **name**

(*sharply*) on **account of**
these B.I.A. guys like John Gray

and John Taylor
(*kindly*) he's got a good **record**, he's made a good
   effort
in **Washington**
but what about his people?
His people don't know anything.
When he sits in his office like we are in here
we don't know what's going on over there
right on the other side of the creek in the (*sharply*) Zuni
   village. [17]
   .

In this next example a speaker makes use of stress
hard stress on individual words rather than making entire
   lines loud.
He also makes use in a couple of lines here of a staccato
   delivery
where the stresses on words are evenly spaced
to give a constant beat:
   .

That was the **hardest** job because
up there in Kansas
the weather is too **hot**
even around
nine o'clock, ten, twelve o'clock
bo————y that's hot.
(*staccato*) The heat comes up to your **face**
and the heat comes on your **back**——
(*throaty*) gosh!
And you're pressing on
on the hot ground with your **bare hand**
your **knees**—
we almost gave up on it. [18]
   .

Now in this next case, patterns of amplitude, including a
   marked falling off of the voice in many lines
combine
with pausing
with tone of voice
and a general softness of articulation

to give the entire episode a strong
sustained emotional flavor.
The passage concerns a time
in the 1880's when
the U.S. Army was sent to Zuni to prevent the execution of a
    man accused of witchcraft.
They brought cannons with them and camped
on the opposite side of the river from the village
facing it.
It was the winter solstice, a time when the
medicine societies were in retreat to say prayers and
    meditate:
    •

(*with a sad tone throughout*)
Because a person's life
                        was being threatened

    •

the soldiers came.
The villagers were not happy, because the village might be
    destroyed.
The medicine societies were in retreat.
Their food was brought to them, but "Yes, I'll eat," that's
    not what the society members were thinking
(*falling off*)   because the village might be destroyed.
They were not happy.
This is the way it w$_{a_s}$

with the societies in retreat.
Now in **our** society
the one who was our
father
was a small boy.
When the food was brought no one ate.
(*gently, with a boy's voice*) "Let me eat—
I'll eat so I'll be good and full when I die."
That's what

(*falling off*) the one who was our
father said.
A small boy doesn't understand
so that's the way he talked
while he sat there eating. [19]
•
So far we've been talking about words and the way words
    are delivered
but the sounds in an oral performance include some
which are not
verbal
as in this next passage
which speaks of a long famine:
•
After four years
•
(*sighing*) there was really
nothing. [20]
•
Now this next passage needs a cigarette—
(*while taking and lighting a cigarette*) a good performer can
    use a cigarette in a way that effectively punctuates
    his pauses
and can add to the suspense and mystery of a passage.
This is a story about a Zuni named Pelhna, the strongest
    Zuni who ever lived, who was famed for (*puffing on
    cigarette*)
robbing and killing white men.
Here a Mexican is going to Gallup
to sell his cows (*puffing*)
and Pelhna is thinking about ambushing him on his way
    back:
•
They drove the cows to Gallup
they passed through Zuni.
They went to that short cut
where
Whitewater is, you know. (*a double puff*)

•
Well he saw them driving the cows through there so
   (*double puff*)
•
he decided he wanted to **check** on them
so
two days after the
cows passed
he went **north** (*double puff*)
•
on that **road**
where he could meet that Mexican again. Probably when he
   sold his cows, why he might come around **this** way.
Well
before old man Pelhna got to Whitewater he decided not to
   go too far
that's outside the reservation so (*double puff*)
•
he came back.
And he waited right where this (*single puff*)
Vanderwagen's ranch is right now
and that's the closest and narrowest **spot** there. [21]
•
The cigarette is something like an instrumental
   accompaniment in that episode.
Here is another example of instrumentation:
•
He's not looking outside.
He tells the people to go ahead and work it out
but (*rapping table at each accent*) he's right inside his
   office. [22]
•
And then of course some of the motions made by a speaker
   are direct illustrations of what he is saying.
Here are a couple of passages in which gesture is in fact
   essential to the understanding of the
exact meaning.
First:
•
They brought a bowl

about so (*indicates a one-foot diameter with hands*), not a
big bowl, and put the flour in there. [23]
•

And here is the other example:
•

He hid and
peeped over
the little hill:
one guy's cooking and two guys are talking to each other
you know.

First he aimed it	(*closes left eye and holds up both*
and decided	*forefingers, some distance apart, out*
how he could	*in front of the right eye, at arm's*
kill	*length, shifting them back and forth until,*
two	*on the word "two," both fingers are in a*
one shot.	*line with the right eye*) [24]

•

Sometimes
a narrator makes use of the immediate circumstances in
which he's performing:
•

I know one man named Kaskala, he used to live down below
where that Chauncey's wall is (*points out the window,
down to the bottom of the hill, to the southwest, in
Upper Nutria, New Mexico*).
Well back of it there used to be houses around there. [25]
•

There was a use of place. A·narrator may also make use of
the immediate time, time of day or time of year:
•

And we got to Zuni about this time I think.
Oxen go slow, you know. [26]
•

Here the transcript must be annotated
to show that the narration took place
around the time it was getting dark.

.
In its main features the system of notation
I've used here
in the passages recited here is a very simple one.
I use a line change as in poetry for a short pause
a double space, that is a strophe break
for longer pauses
boldface type
for words or lines that are loud
light type
for words or lines that are soft
and parenthecized italics, as in a play
for a good many other features
such as voice qualities and gestures.
This system of notation catches I think at least the main
outlines of specifically oral features
and displays them graphically
and at a glance, without resort to
a complicated inventory of technical symbols
such as is used by researchers in paralinguistics. [27]
Professor Vansina has rightly said
that one cannot properly understand a text
without understanding its form, [28] and I submit that the oral
    features I've been talking about are part and parcel of
    that form.
Once the importance of these features is accepted
then
it is clear
that tape recordings are infinitely preferable
to texts taken down in dictation.
Dictation hopelessly distorts delivery
especially in the case of a narrative that does not have
    fixed wording.
The transcription of tapes
should
if at all possible be done by the interviewer himself
and it should be done while the interview is
still fresh in his mind
so that he can provide such details as might not be clear

from the tape alone
such as gestures.
Far from being a mere clerical task
the act of transcription is **itself** of analytical value
when it is pursued with attention to oral qualities.
There is no better way to find out just exactly what it is that
    you've got on that tape.
The finished transcription shows at a glance
the structure
of the narrative
and its delivery
and even provides a much quicker guide to its content
than densely packed prose.
No visual transcription can of course be complete
so it is still absolutely essential that the original tape be
    saved.
The transcript provides a ready index to the tape in case
    there is need to refer back to it.

If anthropologists, folklorists, linguists, and oral historians
are interested in the full meaning
of the spoken word
then they must stop treating oral narratives
as if they were reading prose
when in fact they are listening to dramatic poetry.

The preceding text was set in sans-serif typography because of the range and flexibility of weights and variations that are available in this type design. The typeface, Helios, was used with Helios Light, Helios Semi-bold and italic variations.

1. Translated from a recording made in the field by Dennis and Barbara Tedlock (1972), XXII.
2. Dennis Tedlock, *Finding the Center: Narrative Poetry of the Zuni Indians* (New York: Dial, 1972), 278-80. A translation.
3. See Ruth L. Bunzel's version of this same episode in her "Zuni Origin Myths," *47th Annual Report of the Bureau of American Ethnology* (1932), 601-2; and my own "In Search of the Miraculous at Zuni," in *World Anthropology* (The Hague: Mouton, in press); the latter includes a discussion of Zuni divination.
4. Jan Vansina, *Oral Tradition: A Study in Historical Methodology* (Chicago: Aldine, 1965), 143-54.
5. Ruth Cosby, "Oral Delivery in the Middle Ages," *Speculum* 11 (1936), 88.
6. Ibid, 102-8.
7. Robert D. Stevick, "Scribal Notation of Prosodic Features in *The Parker Chronicle*, Anno 894 [893] ," *Journal of English Linguistics* 1 (1967), 57-66; and Sizzo de Rachewiltz, personal communication.
8. Sizzo de Rachewiltz, personal communication.
9. Charles Sears Baldwin, *Renaissance Literary Theory and Practice* (New York: Columbia University Press, 1939), 14.
10. For a lengthy development of the argument that spoken narratives are poetry, see Dennis Tedlock, "On the Translation of Style in Oral Narrative," in *Toward New Perspectives in Folklore*, ed. Americo Paredes and Richard Bauman (Austin: University of Texas Press, 1972), 114-33. The idea that written prose has no oral counterpart is related to the argument of sociolinguists that the rules given by an ordinary grammar do not describe the full range of competencies necessary to speaking a language properly; see Dell Hymes, "The Contribution of Folklore to Sociolinguistic Research," in the above anthology, 42-50, for example.

11. For a discussion of pausing, see Frieda Goldman-Eisler, "Continuity of Speech Utterance, Its Determinants and Its Significance," *Language and Speech* 4 (1961), 220-31; and "The Distribution of Pause Durations in Speech," Ibid., 232-37. For the psychological meaning of pauses and other delivery features, see G.F. Mahl, "Exploring Emotional States by Content Analysis," in *Trends in Content Analysis*, ed. I. Pool (Urbana: University of Illinois Press, 1959), 89-130; and R.E. Pittenger, C.F. Hockett, and J.J. Danehy, *The First Five Minutes* (Ithaca: Martineau, 1960).

12. *Finding the Center*, 71. A translation.

13. Ibid., 220. A translation.

14. Dennis and Barbara Tedlock, field tapes (1971), A.

15. Ibid., A.

16. *Finding the Center*, 27. A translation.

17. Field tapes (1971), C.

18. Ibid., A.

19. Dennis Tedlock, field tapes (1965), 8. A translation.

20. *Finding the Center*, 38. A translation.

21. Field tapes (1965), 5.

22. Field tapes (1971), C.

23. Dennis Tedlock, "When the Old Timers Went Deer Hunting," *Alcheringa* 3 (1971), 81.

24. Field tapes (1965), 5.

25. "When the Old Timers Went Deer Hunting," 79.

26. Field tapes (1971), C.

27. See Pittenger et al. and George L. Trager, "Paralanguage," in *Language in Culture and Society*, ed. Dell Hymes (New York: Harper & Row, 1964), 274-79.

28. Vansina, 65.

Movement Without Aim: Methodological and Theoretical Problems in Oral History
by Ronald J. Grele

During the past ten years the collection of oral testimony as an ancillary technique of historical study has expanded rapidly. Both in terms of number of persons interviewed and number of projects established, the growth of what is rather loosely called "oral history" has been steadily accelerating.[1] So too has its reputation, if the report of the American Historical Association committee on the state of the AHA and its recommendations are taken as an example of opinion in the profession at large.[2] Despite this growth and the evidence that more and more historians are using the oral history interview in their own work, there has been little serious discussion of oral history by historians. The dominant tendency has been to be overly enthusiastic in public print, and deeply suspicious in private conversation. Neither attitude speaks directly to the issues which should be raised by the use of oral interviewing for historical purposes.

Examples of the historian's enthusiasm for oral history abound. Typical of this reaction were the reviews of Studs Terkel's *Hard Times* and Professor T. Harry Williams' biography of Huey Long.[3] The praise of such works, while in many ways justified, also contains a lack of perspective because, as Michael Frisch notes in the most thoughtful review of *Hard Times* that I have found, ". . . oral history is of such self-evident importance and interest that it has proven difficult for people to take it seriously." By this Frisch means

> . . . that those interested in history, culture and politics have responded so intuitively to recent work in oral history that they have not generally stopped to think about what it is, on levels beyond the obvious, that makes it so worth pursuing.[4]

Despite this uncritical acceptance of the results of the use of oral testimony, there is evidence of skepticism about and doubt and distrust of oral history among professional historians—those paid to write and teach history. Surfacing only occasionally, these doubts are institutionalized within the profession in the organization and conventions of our practice. Few history departments either teach or encourage field work in oral interviewing or oral history. Few departments are willing to accept either the financial or intellectual responsibilities of oral history projects. More telling is the fact that while the collection and editing of manuscripts or personal correspondence has long been considered a legitimate task both for Ph. D. candidates and established scholars, no history department that I know of would grant a doctorate to one of its students in return for the submission of a set of thoroughly documented and well-conducted oral histories, and few historians would receive wide applause for the publication of carefully edited interviews such as is regularly done in other disciplines. In short, what the profession is saying is that oral history is not a respected practice of history.

This attitude is neither new nor unique. In a period of declining job opportunities, historians have taken a very limited view of their professional domain. "Had Clio's inspiration been sufficient, we would have now but one social scientific discipline. It's name would be history." [5] This has not, however, been the case. Historians have allowed the training of librarians, archivists, and bibliographers to pass by default to others. And so it has been with oral history—snubbed by the profession, oral historians have, for the most part, turned to librarians and archivists for support and sustenance. They, in turn, have been much more hospitable,[6] thus of course reinforcing the suspicions of most historians who, with the best intentions in the world, cannot conceive of librarians and archivists as significant initiators of serious scholarship. [7]

Some of the professional historians' doubts about oral history do surface occasionally when historians are called upon to evaluate such works as the interviews of historians conducted by Professors Garraty and Cantor. [8] These criticisms are however usually too gentlemanly and rarely ask questions about the methodological limits of oral history, even where one would expect it. Professors Cantor and Garraty, in their interviews, have shown little regard for the interviewing techniques developed by other disciplines such as anthropology, sociology, folklore, or even of industrial relations. They and others do tend to ask the same ill prepared and badly formulated questions with surprising regularity. As for *Hard Times*, one must question the editing techniques used by Terkel, his cryptic questions and the nature of the historical memories of his informants. As Terkel himself notes, his work is not history but memory, and he is searching not for fact, but the truth behind the fact. Such distinctions raise serious theoretical problems which have not, in the main, been addressed by professional historians. There are also major questions to be raised about such works as that of Professor Williams, which rely so heavily upon documents which will be unavailable for alternative readings by other scholars for years to come.

To be fair, it must be noted that among a few historians, serious concern about these issues has been raised. William Cutler of Temple University has been particularly articulate in warning oral historians about the vagaries of memory and in questioning some of our basic assumptions about the effect of cultural milieu and other influences on the validity of oral testimony.[9] Charles Morrissey, Gould Colman and Saul Benison have continually accented the need for scholarly standards for oral history and have raised other serious methodological questions.[10]

Despite these warnings and the public approval given to them, oral history has in a large part remained cursed, in the words of Gershon Legman's critique of folklore, with an ". . . endless doodling with insignificant forms and [an] ignorance of meaning to the people who transmit material."[11] The quality of oral history interviews varies too widely, as even a cursory examination of the now available Columbia University Oral History Office materials reveals (although this harsh criticism must be tempered by a reminder that Columbia is one of the few oral history projects which has attempted to make its interviews widely available). Few oral historians are forced to submit their work to public criticism. Many interviewers are poorly trained and far too many are willing to settle for journalistic standards of usefulness. In many projects, much too little time is devoted to the research necessary to prepare for an interview. Oral historians are still prone to rush out and ask how it happened without spending the arduous months plowing through related written materials. Worse yet, their sponsors often encourage this attitude and practice. There is much room for speculation about the reliability of the products of such activities.

In this situation, the professional historian has had little to offer in the way of constructive criticism. Eight years ago, Donald Swain noted the "need for . . . greater attention to the problems of oral history on the part of practicing historians." [12] Little has been done to answer that need. As noted earlier, historians have not raised the pertinent historiographical questions about oral history interviews when dealing with major works using the technique. In most cases, they have simply turned their responsibilities over to others and hoped for the best, and when they have offered criticism or comment, their remarks have usually been informed by a myopic paper or book fetishism, inadequate definitions of their own standards of judgement, and a hostility towards and reluctance to understand other social science disciplines. [13]

Generally the criticisms that have so far been leveled at oral history can be classified into three categories; interviewing, research standards for preparation, and questions of historical methodology. The oral historian should be able to deal with the first set of these criticisms rather easily, for there is an already adequate bibliography and an already existent body of knowledge concerning interviewing and questioning techniques available to those interested. [14] While much of the literature may not prepare the interviewer for the almost confessional nature and the various other responses engendered in the open interview, as Richard Sennett and Jonathan Cobb note, [15] there is no reason why an interviewer, if well prepared, cannot gain control over these techniques.

The second category of problems, those centering on research standards, can be met most forcibly simply by insisting that the highest standards of research and training be expected of oral historians. These are problems faced by all historians and the same canons of practice should apply. Sources should be checked, documentation should be provided, evidence must be weighed carefully. In this sense, oral history interviewing does not represent any major deviation from the methodology of other forms of historical research. There is no other solution to this problem, ". . . except in the exercise of that personal judgement which the historian has to apply to any source of information." [16] To insure such practice, those historians called upon to review works based on oral histories should insist on a review of the interviews used for documentation.

Questions of method cannot be dismissed so easily. As the most cogent critics have noted, there are real and serious issues to be faced by the practitioners of oral history. Many of these issues are not, however, those specifically noted by historians. When historians claim that oral history interviewees are not statistically representative of the population at large or any particular segment of it, [17] they raise a false issue and thereby obscure a much deeper problem. Interviewees are selected, not because they represent some abstract statistical norm, but because they typify historical processes. Thus, the questions to be asked concern the historian's concept of a historical process (i.e.: his own conception of history) and the relevance of the information garnered to that particular process. The real issues are historiographical, not statistical.

Another erroneous caveat of the profession concerns the primacy of written testimony to oral testimony. Oral history, runs the typical argument, ". . . cannot rank with an authentic diary, with a contemporary stock report, or with an eyewitness account transcribed on the day of the event." But, we are told, ". . . it is probably to be ranked above contemporary hearsay evidence.".[18] Not only does this criticism ignore the problems of accuracy faced by historians who use written testimony; it ignores a growing literature on the analysis of oral testimony for historical purposes. [19] The usefulness of any source depends upon the information one is looking for, or the questions one seeks to answer. It is quite possible to argue, as Ruth Finnegan has, that oral testimony or "literature" has its own characteristics and is not to be understood by the application of literary standards of judgment. [20] In some cases, oral testimony can be more full and accurate than written testimony. For, as Plato noted in regard to works of art, and by extension written documents, "You would think they were speaking as if they were intelligent, but if you ask them about what they are saying and want to learn [more], they just go on saying one and the same thing forever." [21] Thus criticisms of oral testimony often miss their mark because they fail to realize that to seriously critique any form, it is necessary to understand precisely what it is one is about to evaluate.

The same qualifications must be applied to those criticisms which question the accuracy of memory or the intrusion of subjective or social biases. [22] It all depends upon the questions one is seeking to answer. A linguist searching for the linguistic range, context and style of the language of ethnic Americans, is interested in a different kind of accuracy than that of a historian. [23] So too health researchers or those interested in sexual behavior. [24] Obviously, the careful interviewer does try, as Cutler suggests, to overcome these problems, yet it should be understood that not all the historical uses of information are covered by the conventional questions of historians. [25]

Important as many of these questions may be, they are still simply questions of method and depend in large part upon a theoretical frame of reference for their meaning and for their answers, and it is at this level that the lack of serious analysis of oral history interviews has had its most deleterious effects. The sad condition of our theoretical knowledge about oral history, and the lack of serious efforts to think through exactly what an oral interview is or should be, how it is to be analyzed, or for what purposes, has resulted in a situation of endless activity without goal or meaning. As a result, oral history has not become a tool for a serious analysis of the culture. It has continued as a movement without aim, with all the attendant problems of such a situation.

The two most significant debates over the nature of oral history are those articulated by Cutler and Benison, and Staughton Lynd and Jesse Lemisch. Since all four have at least tried to grapple with the larger theoretical and historiographical questions raised by interviewing, it is proper here to note the issues they raise. In the first case, Cutler argues that an oral history interview as it exists in final form—a transcript—is "raw material similar to any other source." [26] Benison, however, has argued that an oral history is an autobiographical memoir and, duly noting the creative role of the historian-interviewer, sees it as "a first interpretation, filtered through a particular individual experience at a particular moment of time." It is, he argues, a first ordering, "a beginning of interpretation although not an end." [27] In the second debate, Lynd has argued that oral history is history itself, in the form of an articulating consciousness. Impressed with the very real opportunities offered by oral history for the history of the "inarticulate," and by the dynamic of the interview situation, he has called for a new, radical use for oral history. In answer, Lemisch takes a more traditional view of an oral history interview as a limited document upon which is constructed a new historical synthesis. [28]

Neither of these discussions has, however, resulted in any serious reformulation of the thinking about oral history among oral historians themselves or others in the profession. Both discussions also center upon a number of questionable assumptions which so far have not been challenged. Cutler and Lemisch, in their view of oral history interviews as sources and documents, seem to have confused these interviews, which are a form of oral testimony, with written manuscript sources. Unlike these traditional sources, oral history interviews are constructed, for better or for worse, by the active intervention of the historian.

They are a collective creation and inevitably carry within themselves a pre-existent historical ordering, selection and interpretation. Unlike letters, records, archival materials or other manuscript sources, they are created after the fact, by historians—thus they are very singular documents indeed.

On the other hand, while Benison and Lynd recognize the active role of the historian-interviewer, their analyses suffer from differing, albeit equally limited frames of reference. Benison, as articulate and creative as is his analysis of oral history, is still reluctant to see the interviews as end products complete unto themselves. [29] Still bound by the book fetishism of historical study, Benison does not tell us why the written narrative of a historian with proper footnotes to his interview ranks higher in accuracy or interpretation than the interviews themselves. It may be that, even admitting the excellence of the biography of Huey Long, or the sometimes useful commentary in *The Hidden Injuries of Class* and other works using oral histories, in the long run the interviews themselves will prove much more useful to scholars than the texts grafted upon them.

This is, of course, the most useful of Lynd's insights but unfortunately, by stressing the consciousness-raising potential of the interview, he seems to have confused the moment of presentation with the material presented, and history as process with history as study, discipline or cognitive action. In addition, there would seem to be wide theoretical gaps between interviewing, consciousness and "praxis" which, for a Marxist especially, have to be articulated more precisely.

For all of these reasons, these debates and discussions, while worthwhile and refreshing, have not begun to yield the kind of theoretical introspection which oral history needs. Such introspection must begin with the object at hand—the interview as an end product—what it is and what it should be, for it is only in this framework that we can begin to discuss what kinds of information we are getting, what is it that structures an interview, and how it should be conducted. To initiate a tentative discussion of these points is the aim of the rest of this chapter.

The first question which must be asked, before we can begin the kind of analysis oral history needs, concerns the nature of the end product which is created by the oral historian and his subject—the interview. For reasons already noted, the final product of oral history is not a monograph or historical narrative based upon interviews as sources. The interviews may be used for such work, but all the prideful boasting about how many historians use our work for their own publications should not obscure the fact that the focus of oral history is to record as complete an interview as possible—an interview which contains, within itself, its own system of structures, not a system derived from the narrow conventions of written history.

If this is the case, and I strongly believe it is, we must then try to define rather precisely what the form of the completed interview is. For reasons which Professor Tedlock has already explained, the final form of the interview is not a transcript, no matter how beautifully typed or indexed. Neither is it, except in the most limited of mechanical aspects, a tape, for the tape is simply a reproduction of the verbal (or visual and verbal, if videotape is used) aspects of a particular set of structures or patterns, behind which exists some human relationship.

Given the active participation of the historian-interviewer, even if that participation consists of only a series of gestures or grunts, and given the logical form imposed by all verbal communication, the interview can only be described as a conversational narrative: conversational because of the relationship of interviewer and interviewee, and narrative because of the form of exposition—the telling of a tale. [30]

These narratives, while some may be constructed as chronological tales of personal remembrances of events, are not autobiographies, biographies or memories. [31] The recorded conversations of oral history, it must be repeated, are joint activities, organized and informed by the historical perspectives of both participants and therefore, as Professor Jan Vansina pointed out to me in an earlier conversation in regard to Alex Haley's *Autobiography of Malcolm X,* they are not really autobiographies. No matter what the construction of the narrative, the product we create is a conversational narrative and can only be understood by understanding the various relationships contained within this structure.[32]

The relationships in an oral history interview (conversational narrative) are of three types or sets, one internal and two external.[33] The first unites each element, word or sign to all of the others in the interview. It relates the words to one another to create a whole. It is the linguistic, grammatical, and literary structure of the interview, and while mainly the object so far of a formal linguistic analysis, if read properly, this relationship provides one of the most exciting methods of analysis possible in oral history.[34]

The second set of relationships is that which is created by the interaction of the interviewer and interviewee. Again, as psychologists, sociologists and especially those, like Erving Goffman, who are interested in small group interaction have shown, these relations are also highly structured, and if analyzed properly can add wide dimensions to our understanding of exactly what kind of communication is taking place within the interview and what meaning is being conveyed.[35] Contained within this relationship are those aspects of the interview which can be classified as performance. Since the interview is not created as a literary product is created, alone and as a result of reflective action, it cannot be divorced from the circumstances of its creation, which of necessity is one of audience participation and face to face confrontation.[36] To analyze an oral interview properly as a conversational narrative, we must combine an analysis of the social and psychological relationships between the participants, and their appropriateness to the occasion, with our historical analysis.

The third set of relationships present in the interview is more abstract, less studied, and therefore more elusive to define, although of far more importance to us as historians. When we interview someone, he not only speaks to himself and to the interviewer, but he also speaks through the interviewer to the

larger community and its history as he views it. This is a
dialogue, the exact nature of which is difficult to define. There
are seemingly two relationships contained in one—that between
the informant and the historian, and that between the informant
and his own historical consciousness.

The first of these relations is in large measure engendered by
the historian, for it is his curiosity, not that of the historical actor,
which both the questions and the explanations seek to justify. In
most cases the informant has acted as if his views of historical
processes were a given reality in his world, and he has not
thought them out until faced with the necessity to do so by the
interview. [37] The relation that thus emerges is both relative and
equivalent. It is relative in that the informant's view of history
(its use, its structure, a system of cause, etc.) are developed only
in relation to the historian's view of that process, while the
historian's organization of his questions (the structure of the interview) is in turn developed in response to the answers of the
interviewee. Each view is thus a standard of reference for the
other. The relationship is also equivalent in the sense that when it
is finally articulated, the questions, asked and unasked, and the
answers given, form an historical view equal to and independent
of that of the historian. [38]

The second relation, that of the informant to what he or she
views as the history of the community, is probably the most
clearly articulated aspect of the interview and also the most
difficult to grasp, for it is only one part of a much broader
cultural vision and cognitive structure, and demands a very
special type of reading to analyse. To read the narrative
properly, to discover this relation and the cultural vision which
informs it, we must give the interview the same kind of reading
which Jacques Lacan has given to Freud or which Louis
Althusser has given to Marx,[39] a method of reading Althusser
terms "symptomatic."

While few of us or our interviewees, will create narratives or
analyses as rich, as complex, or as theoretically sophisticated as
those of Freud or Marx, our interviews, as I have tried to show, are

far more complex than we usually assume. If read properly, they do reveal to us hidden levels of discourse—the search for which is the aim of symptomatic reading.[40] If read (or really listened to) again and again, not just for facts and comments, but also, as Althusser suggests, for insights and oversights, for the combination of vision and nonvision, and especially for answers to questions which were never asked, we should be able to isolate and describe the problematic which informs the particular interview.

It is at the level of this problematic—the theoretical or ideological context within which words and phrases, and the presence or absence of certain problems and concepts is found [41] —that we find the synthesis of all of the various structural relationships of the interview, as well as the particular relation of the individual to his vision of history. What we are here discussing is not simply a Weltanschauung, but a structural field in which men live their history and which guides their practice or action. Within this problematic, a view of history plays a key role, and provides for the oral historian a crucial tool of both creation and analysis.

In one of the most profound and important essays in American historiography, Warren Susman has brilliantly outlined how, "[t]he idea of history itself, special kinds of historical studies and various attitudes towards history always play—whether intelligently conceived or not—a major role within a culture." What we call a "worldview" [substitute problematic], Susman argues, "always contains a more or less specific view of the nature of history," and "attitudes toward the past frequently become facts of profound consequences for the culture itself." [42]

Noting that "the idea of history itself belongs to a special kind of social and cultural organization," what we usually call "contract societies", in which the social order must be explained, rationalized or reasonably ordered, Susman argues that "it is history which can [most] reasonably explain the origin, the nature and the function of various institutions and their interaction. History seems able to point the direction in which a dynamic society is moving. It brings order out of the disordered array of the consequences of change itself." [43]

To history, over which no one person or group has a monopoly, Susman contrasts societies in which myth predominates, status societies, where the "world view" is dominated by deeply believed myths whose articulation is usually the prerogative of a special class of people, usually priests. [44] Myth, with its utopian vision, its sacerdotal nature, its elements of authority in answer to ignorance, doubt or disbelief, functions as a cohesive element in a society, in contrast to history which, because it explains the past in order to offer ways to change the future and serves as the basis of political philosophy, becomes an ideological tool to alter the social order. Thus while actual consequences follow from each view of the world, it is history, in its most ideological form, which offers a plan for social action. [45]

As Susman notes, the historical vision of the past does not replace a mythic vision; rather, in historical societies they exist in dialectical tension with one another and by combination and interaction, they produce a variety of historical visions. These, as Susman demonstrates in American historiography, can become the basis for a morphology of historical thought; [46] a morphology which in turn becomes an accurate gauge of the tendencies of social integration or differentiation in the culture itself, and an index of the potency or impotency of the institutions of that society to further the cultural vision of the masses of people in the society.

All of this is important to the historian, and especially to the oral historian because this analysis allows us to focus our interviews upon the crucial element of the cognitive thought of the member of the culture with whom we are particularly concerned. We can thus use the idea of history and its relation to myth and ideology as the central aim of our interviews to grasp the deeper problematic of the interviewee. To do this, however, we must first recognize the crucial role played by ideologies in modern society. and develop a methodology for the analysis of the structure and function of ideology.[46A]

An ideology is more than simply a political program. As discussed by Susman and defined by Althusser, it is ideology which structures the consciousness of individuals and their conceptions of their relations to the conditions of existence, and which governs their actions and practices through an array of apparatuses such as the family, the church, trade unions, systems of communication as well as modes of conduct and behavior. It is the basic conceptualization of the relations of a class-based society.[47] It is therefore crucial to an understanding of the dynamics of the culture—learned patterns of behavior.

The key to the understanding of the function of ideology lies in the concept of "hegemony" as developed by Antonio Gramsci[48] for it is through hegemony — the "spontaneous loyalty that any dominant social group obtains from the masses by virtue of its intellectual prestige and its supposedly superior function in the world of production"[49] —that ideology attains its importance as a mechanism of class rule and finds expression in popular beliefs.[50] With a broad definition of ideology, and a proper understanding of the theory of hegemony, its limits, and the roles played by a view of historical change in the development of an ideology, the oral historian should be able to synthesize his analyses of the three sets of relations contained in the interview, for the socio or paralinguistic structure, patterns of behavior and theory of history are all united within the concept of ideology.

Earlier in this volume (Chapter II) Alice Kessler Harris noted her experiences in interviewing women who had migrated to the United States, and the contradiction between their actions within their families and their discussion of changing family patterns. Buried beneath this contradiction is a deeper structure of historical cognition which proclaims the necessity of progress in history and the participation of the immigrant in that progress. Thus history and myth have been synthesized into a dynamic view of life which if analyzed with care can explain many, if not most, of the tensions of immigrant life in America. In cases such as this, by concentrating our interviews on a series of questions aimed at the articulation by the interviewee of his views of historical change, causality, the evolution of institutions, and his view of the way in which the past has been ordered and rationalized, and upon which the future predicted, we can begin to explain the particular ideological context of the interview. We can also understand how and to what degree our informants have accepted the hegemonic view of the culture—in this case the idea of progress.

Such a use of the idea of history to gain an understanding of ideology and thus an understanding of the dynamics of the history of the culture is, of course, not limited to oral history. The special methods of oral history do, however, make such a procedure especially useful in structuring and analyzing our interviews.

Oral history, almost alone among the various practices of historiography is heavily dependent upon fieldwork, which means that not only can we come back again and again to our sources and ask them to tell us more, but we can also explore the varieties of historical visions in far greater detail and amid radically changing historical conditions. Indeed, just as in the case mentioned above, it is the interviewing experience itself which can reveal the contradiction between ideology, myth and reality. By careful observation and understanding of this experience we can add a depth to our historical understanding which is never revealed in the written record.

Also, alone among our peers our documents exist in the realm of sound and vision as well as printed record. If carefully prepared and symptomatically read we should be able to bring to our historical study the powerful analytical tools of more advanced disciplines such as linguistics and anthropology. There would seem to be no theoretical reason why historical documents of this type cannot be subjected to the same types of analysis given to other interviews in other professions.

To do this, however, we need a larger and more general concept of historical cognition, because without some larger context within which to place the information we gather, and the various aspects of the interview—linguistic, performatory, and cognitive—which will synthesize these structures, we risk not only the possibility of misunderstanding what is happening in the interview, but also of misunderstanding what is being said and why. It is only the larger context which makes the information conveyed in an interview unambiguous.

Also, if we fail to see our interviewees as bearers of a culture and thus people with their own view of the past, be it formed as part of a hegemonic ideology, or in opposition to that ideology, or as some combination of myth and ideology, or even a secret history, we will, because the information must be structured, infuse our own vision of the past into the interview. Such a situation is exactly what we do not want to do. Our aim is to bring to conscious articulation the ideological problematic of the interviewee, to reveal the cultural context in which information is being conveyed, and to thus transform an individual story into a cultural narrative, and, thereby, to more fully understand what happened in the past. While this can only be done through the interplay of the various conceptions of the past held by both the interviewer and the interviewee, the particular present ideological conceptions of the interviewer should not structure that articulation. [51]

Concentration upon the interplay of ideology and various conceptions of history is also of special importance to the oral historian because such a methodology is what distinguishes him from other field workers who use interviews, such as psychologists, anthropologists and folklorists. As historians we are trained to understand and analyze the varieties of historical thought and their cultural context, and thus oral history interviewing is simply an extension of that training into the field. [52]

This view of the role of ideology in uniting the various structural elements of the oral history interview also provides oral historians with a method of dealing with the vexing problem of historical memory. Our problem, as anyone who has done extensive interviewing will readily admit, is not, except in odd cases, the problem of forgetfulness but rather the problem of being overwhelmed with reminiscences and memories flowing in uninterrupted and seemingly unrelated fashion. [53] If we view memory as one form or vehicle of historical cognition and if we examine our interviews carefully for a view of the problematic which informs these memories, we can begin to grasp the deeper structures which organize this seemingly unorganized flow of words, and then so direct our questioning and other responses to develop as full an interview as possible.

Finally, as field workers we should, in general, hold to the view that ". . . the methods of collecting which are to be most encouraged are those which will supply the greatest amount of reliable information," in the sense of providing a systematic view of the creative activities of mankind. [54]   That systematic view, in many cases, can only be developed by the oral historian because the past, as it has existed, has never asked the pertinent questions about its own systematic view of the world—i.e., its own ideology and its own myth.

Such a view of the role of oral history—the search for the ideological and mythic matrix of the cultural consciousness of the society through the development of the idea of history—should not be taken to imply that the oral historian is now free to ignore the written records of facts and events in order to fly with the winds of grand theory. Rather it should be a call for oral historians to realize the potential of their work, and to take it seriously enough to become even more rigorous in their use of materials. Both theory and rigorous practice are necessary if oral history is, in the words of Henry Glassie, to contribute to ". . . a revolution in diachronic theorizing and to the development of an understanding of what people really did in the past." [55]

Footnotes

1. The most current survey, Gary Shumway, *Oral History in the United States: A Directory* (New York: Columbia University Press, 1970), lists 230 projects. Since this compilation is already out of date the figure is probably closer to 450. The largest project in the nation, at Columbia, has interviewed, as of 1971, over 2500 people. *Oral History Report for 1970–71, Columbia University* (New York: Oral History Research Office, 1971).

2. American Historical Association, *Newsletter*, Vol. X, No. 5 (November, 1972), p. 21.

3. See especially Richard Rhodes' review of "Hard Times," *New York Times Book Review*, April 19, 1970, p. 1, and G.B. Tindall's review of "Huey Long," *American Historical Review*, Vol. 75 (October 1970), p. 1792.

4. Michael Frisch, "Oral History and Hard Times, A Review Essay", *Red Buffalo*, Numbers 2 and 3, n.d.

5. Henry Glassie, "A Folkloristic Thought On The Promise of Oral History," *Selections From The Fifth and Sixth National Colloquia On Oral History*, published by the Oral History Association, New York 1971, p. 54.

6. Owen W. Bombard, "A New Measure of Things Past" *American Archivist*, Vol. 18 (April 1955), p. 156. A. Ray Stephans, "Oral History and Archives," *Texas Librarian*, Vol. 29 (Fall, 1967), pp. 203-214. M.J. Zachert, "The Implication of Oral History For Librarians", *College and Research Libraries*, Vol. 29 (March, 1968), pp. 101-103. Some have even argued that oral history is too important to leave to historians: see Richard A. Bartlett, "Some Thoughts After The Third National Colloquium On Oral History," *The Journal Of Library History*, Vol. 4 (April 1969), pp. 169-172 and Doyce B. Nunis, Jr., "The Library and Oral History," *California Librarian*, Vol. 22 (July 1961), pp. 139-144.

7. In his commentary on this paper Professor Benison took me to task for seeming to agree with this low estimate of librarians and archivists. If this is the implication of this paragraph I wish to correct it. I do not hold this opinion of the work of either librarians or archivists, but I am convinced that one of the reasons for the low esteem in which historians hold oral history is its rather close identification with the archival profession. This sad situation is far more indicative of the false pretensions of historical study than of the talents of archivists.

8. See especially Peter Gay's discussion of Norman F. Cantor, *Perspectives on the European Past: Conversations With Historians,* In *American Historical Review,* Vol. 77, Number 5 (December 1972), pp. 1404-1405.

9. William W. Cutler III, "Accuracy in Oral Interviewing," *Historical Methods Newsletter,* No. 3 (June 1970), pp. 1-7.

10. Charles T. Morrissey, "On Oral History Interviewing," *Elite and Specialized Interviewing,* edited by Lewis Anthony Dexter (Evanston: Northwestern University Press, 1970), pp. 109-118. Gould Colman, "A Call for More Systematic Procedures," *American Archivist,* Vol. 28, No. 1 (January, 1965), pp. 79-83. Saul Benison, "Reflections on Oral History," *Ibid,* pp. 71-77.

11. As quoted in Kenneth S. Goldstein, *A Guide for Field Workers in Folklore* (London: Herbert Jenkins, 1964), fn. p. 6.

12. Donald C. Swain, "Problems for Practitioners of Oral History," *American Archivist,* Vol. 28, No. 1 (January, 1965), p. 64.

13. Professor Gay discusses *Conversations With Historians* as textbook supplement or rival *op. cit.,* p. 1404. Susanne Paul of the New York Women's Collective criticizes oral history as being "elitist" without defining that term, and without any realization that even interviews with members of the working class if done

from a certain ideological stance are "elitist." Remarks at the Sixth Annual Colloquia on Oral History. See also, "Is Oral History Really Worthwhile?" *Ideas In Conflict: A Colloquium on Certain Problems in Historical Society Work in the United States and Canada*, edited by Clifford Lord (Harrisburg, Pa., American Association for State and Local History, 1958).

14. See: Eleanor E. Maccoby and Nathan Maccoby. "The Interview: A Tool of Social Science," *The Handbook of Social Phychology*, edited by Gardner Lindzey (Cambridge Mass.: Addison-Wesley Publishing Company, 1954), Vol. I, pp. 449-487, and Goldstein, *op. cit.* An updated and annotated bibliography of relevant works can be found in William H. Banaka, *Training in Depth Interviewing* (New York: Harper and Row, 1970), pp. 162-189.

15. Richard Sennett and Jonathan Cobb, *The Hidden Injuries of Class* (New York: Alfred A. Knopf, 1972), p. 24.

16. Christopher Storm-Clark "The Miners, 1870-1970. A Test Case for Oral History," *Victorian Studies*, Vol. XV, No. 1 (September, 1971), p. 73. For an excellent discussion of the problem of accuracy in oral history in an actual field work situation, see pp. 69-74.

17. Cutler, *op. cit.*, pp. 6-7. Leonard Eaton, "Book Review, Two Chicago Architects and Their Clients," *Historical Methods Newsletter*, Vol. 5, No. 4 (September, 1972), p. 169.

18. Vaughn D. Bornet, "Oral History *Can* Be Worthwhile," *American Archivist*, Vol. 18 (July, 1955), p. 244.

19. The classic work in this field is Jan Vansina, *Oral Tradition: A Study in Historical Methodology*, translated by H.M. Wright (London: Routledge and Kegan Paul, 1965). See especially Section III. See also: Storm-Clark, *op. cit.*, p. 73.

20. Ruth Finnegan, *Oral Literature in Africa* (Oxford: The Clarendon Press, 1970), p. 1. See also: George Ewart-Evans, *Tools of Their Trade: An Oral History of Men at Work, c. 1900* (New York: Taplinger Publishing Co., 1970), p. 18.

21. As quoted in Finnegan, *op. cit.*, p. 11.

22. Cutler, *op. cit.*, pp. 1-2.

23. For an example of the concerns of socio-linguists see *Readings in the Sociology of Language,* edited by Joshua A. Fishman (The Hague: Mouton and Company, 1968). An example of an especially interesting use of interview materials is William Labov, "Phonological Correlates of Social Stratification," *American Anthropologist,* Vol. 66. part 2 (December, 1964), pp. 164-176.

24. Kent Marquis, "Effects of Social Reinforcement on Health Reporting in the Household Interview," *Sociometry,* Vol. 33, Number 2 (June 1970), pp. 203-215. Paul H. Gebhard, "Securing Sensitive Personal Information by Interviews," *Selections, op. cit.,* pp. 63-79.

25. Also, as noted by Saul Benison, "Oral History and Manuscript Collecting", *Isis,* Vol. 53 (March 1962), pp. 113-117, the collection of untruth is often as valuable as what passes for truth.

26. Cutler, *op. cit.*, p. 7.

27. Saul Benison, "Oral History: A Personal View," *Modern Methods in the History of Medicine,* edited by Edwin Clark (New York: Oxford U. Press, 1971), p. 291.

28. The Lynd-Lemisch debate took place at a meeting of the Radical Caucus of the American Historical Association at its annual meeting in New York in 1971. For a fuller exposition of Lynd's

views see: "Guerrilla History in Gary," *Liberation*, Vol. 14 (October 1969), pp. 17-20, and "Personal Histories of the Early CIO," *Radical America*, Vol. 5, No. 3 (May-June, 1971), pp. 50-51.

29. Benison, "A Personal View," p. 293. This interpretation originally appeared as a level-headed caveat to the reader of *Tom Rivers: Reflections on a Life in Medicine and Science* (Cambridge, The MIT Press, 1967), about the limits of oral testimony. As such it was a useful brake to the overenthusiastic response to oral history already mentioned. Its inclusion in "A Personal View" (see fn. 27), which is a discussion of the methods of oral history, raises it to a new and different level. In the context of the article it is no longer a simple caveat but a theoretical proposition. That this is no longer Benison's view or that I have perhaps misinterpreted his position can be seen by his comments in Chapter II of this book.

30. George N. Gordon, *The Languages of Communication: a Logical and Psychological Examination* (New York: Hastings House, 1969), pp. 111-127. Elizabeth Rumics, "Oral History: Defining the Term," *Wilson Library Bulletin*, Vol. 40 (March, 1966), pp. 602-605.

31. For more precise definitions of these terms see R. Pascal, *Design and Truth in Autobiography* (London: Routlege and Kegan Paul, 1960). "Oral History" as used here should not be taken to include "Oral traditions" as usually investigated in other disciplines. Our only concern here is with eye-witness or second hand hearsay evidence or testimony of those who have participated in or observed past events.

32. "Structure" : "a systematic whole of self-regulating transformations." Jean Piaget, *Structuralism*, translated and edited by Chaninah Maschler (New York: Basic Books Inc., 1970), p. 44.

33. From a reading of Roland Barthes, *Critical Essays*, translated by Richard Howard (Evanston, Northwestern University Press, 1972), pp. 51-58, 203-211.

34. See for example William Labov, *The Social Stratification of English in New York City* (Washington D.C.: Center for Applied Linguistics, 1966). One of the most exciting attempts to use linguistic analysis for cultural history, which also attempts a needed historiographical reconstruction in labor history, is, Robert P. Baker, "Labor History, Social Science and the Concept of the Working Class," *Labor History* (Winter, 1973), pp. 95-105. See also Francis Berry, *The Physical Voice of Poetry* (Oxford: Oxford Press, 1962). For a brief but cogent discussion of linguistic theory and its relations to contextual meaning see Dan I. Slobin, *Psycholinguistics* (Glenview, Illinois: Scott, Foresman and Company, 1971).

35. Alfred Benjamin, *The Helping Interview* (Boston: Houghton Mifflin & Company, 1969). Erving Goffman, *Relations in Public: Microstudies of the Public Order* (New York: Basic Books Inc., 1971).

36. Finnegan, *op. cit.*, pp. 2, 9-10.

37. Hugh Stretton, *The Political Sciences* (New York: Basic Books Inc., 1969), pp. 14-15. See also: Ronald Blythe, *Akenfield: Portrait of an English Village* (New York: Pantheon, 1969), p. 20.

38. One is reminded of Collingwood's observation that you ". . . cannot find out what a man means by simply studying his spoken or written statements, even though he has spoken or written with perfect command of language and perfectly truthful intentions. In order to find out his meaning, you must also know what the question was (a question in his own mind and presumed by him to be yours) to which the thing he has said or written was meant

as an answer." R.G. Collingwood, *An Autobiography* (Oxford: Oxford Press, 1951), p. 31.

39. Jacques Lacan, *The Language of the Self: The Function of Language in Psychoanalysis,* edited and translated by Anthony Wilden (Baltimore: Johns Hopkins Press, 1968). Louis Althusser and Etienne Balibar, *Reading Capital,* translated by Ben Brewster (New York, Pantheon, 1970).

40. Althusser, *op. cit.,* pp. 16-17, 316.

41. *Ibid.*

42. Warren I. Susman, "History and the American Intellectual: Uses of A Usable Past," *American Quarterly,* Vol. 16, Part 2 (Summer, 1964) p. 243.

43. *Ibid.,* p. 244. For two interesting examples of this function of history see the Introduction to this volume by Alice Kessler Harris.

44. *Ibid.,* p. 244. See the discussion of the role of the myth among the Fon and Ashanti in Finnegan *op. cit.,* p. 365. See also W.R. Bascom, "The Forms of Folklore: Prose Narratives," *Journal of American Folklore,* Vol. 78 (1965), p. 4.

45. Susman notes, fn. p. 245, his particular usage of the terms "myth," "utopia," "history" and "ideology", but it is really the term "ideology", as derived from Ben Halpern "Myth and Ideology in Modern Usage," *History and Theory,* Vol. I (1961), pp. 129-49, which is used idiosyncratically. Ideology here is used to mean an analysis of a social structure, and a plan of action deriving from that analysis, which posits a socio-politico form in which one and only one class of people (no matter how defined) carries the burden of all culture. See also Althusser, *op. cit.,* p. 314. An ideology in this sense becomes the crucial form of con-

sciousness which becomes institutionalized in various apparatuses to insure the continuance or furtherance of the reproduction of the conditions of production. Althusser, *Lenin and Philosophy and Other Essays*, translated by Ben Brewster (New York: Monthly Review Press, 1971), pp. 127-186.

Myth, as used by Halpern, Susman and herein, does not mean something "incorrect" or "erroneous," nor is it simply a tale or a narrative, but rather a means of cognition by which human experience is interpreted and understood. In his commentary on this paper Professor Vansina argued that this was a highly romantic definition of "myth," rarely found in supposedly "mythic" societies. There are two reasons, I believe, for this criticism. In the original version of this paper I did not stress adequately enough the dialectical interplay of myth and history. These are not separate modes of thought but are, in effect, more often contained as antagonistic elements in any particular interpretation. Secondly, Professor Vansina speaks here out of his experience in Africa where, due partly to his own work, we have found out that what were supposedly "mythic" societies do indeed have very strong and real historical traditions.

An interesting example of an elite vision of history becoming myth can be found in James W. Wilkie, *Elitelore* (Latin American Studies, Volume 22, 1973).

46. That this view of the tension between myth and history may have wider implications is seen in the remarkably similar distinction drawn by Claude Levi-Strauss, *The Savage Mind* (Chicago: Chicago University Press, 1966), pp. 231-234. In many respects it is this distinction which lies at the heart of the debate of Levi-Strauss and Sartre, pp. 245-269. Susman's view of this tension is not, however, as static as that of Levi-Strauss. See also Finnegan, *op cit.*, p. 362 and J.C. Bottom, "Some Malay Historical Sources," *An Introduction to Indonesian Historiography*, edited by Soedjatmoko, Mohamad Ali, G.L. Resink and George McT. Kahin (Ithica: Cornell University Press, 1965), pp. 156-193, esp. p. 182.

46 A. We are here only concerned with modern societies, for in a very real sense all oral history is recent history.

47. Althusser, *Lenin and Philosophy*, pp. 143-161.

48. Antonio Gramsci, *The Modern Prince and Other Essays* (N.Y.: International Publishers, 1959).

49. John Cammett, *Antonio Gramsci and the Origins of Italian Communism* (Stanford: Stanford University Press, 1967), pp. 204-206.

50. Aileen S. Kraditor, "American Radical Historians and Their Heritage," *Past and Present*, Number 56 (August 1972), p. 139.

51. It is exactly this lack of context which mars such works as *Huey Long*. See R.C. Sherill's review in *The Nation*, November 3, 1000, p. 000. An even stranger case of intrusion is that of Sennett and Cobb in *The Hidden Injuries of Class*. Fully aware of the work of both Althusser and Gramsci, but unaware of the role of a view of history in the construction of an ideology and seeking to avoid the cultural consequences of their interviews, they are forced, when presented with the contradiction of members of the working class both sharing in and being oppressed by a hegemonic ideology, into a narrowly behavioral view of their informants as people without any objective definitions of themselves or their society, thereby affirming, in their own work, the validity of the hegemonic ideology.

52. This is not to imply that the analysis of ideology cannot be united with the formal analysis of culture as used in other disciplines. See especially Maurice Godelier, "Systeme, Structure et Contradiction dans 'Le Capital'," *Les Temps Moderns*, Vol. 22 (November, 1966) pp. 828-865. See also Piaget, *op. cit.*, pp. 120-134 and the remarkable tour de force of Anthony Wilden in *The Language of The Self*, pp. 302-311.

53. Cutler, *op. cit.*, pp. 2-4 cites evidence of forgetfulness, but the studies upon which this judgment is based, as well as others in the field of memory, are so narrowly "experimental" or behavioral that they tell us little about the actual functioning of historical memory. For example, see the reports in *Memory and Attention: An Introduction to Human Information Processing*, edited by Donald A. Norman (New York, John Wiley and Sons, 1968). For a more complex discussion of oral history and memory see Frisch, *op. cit.*, pp. 288-231.

54. Goldstein, *op. cit.*, p. 5.

55. Glassie, *op. cit.*, p. 57.

A Surmisable Variety:
Interdisciplinarity and Oral Testimony

Happy Hooligan in his rusted green automobile
Came plowing down the course, just to make sure every-
   thing was O.K.,
Only by that time we were in another chapter and con-
   fused
About how to receive this latest piece of information.
Was it information? Weren't we rather acting this out
For someone else's benefit, thoughts in a mind
With room enough to spare for our little problems (so they
   began to seem),
Our daily quandary about food and rent and bills to be
   paid.

John Ashbery, *Soonest Mended*

"Ah well! It means much the same thing," said the
Duchess, digging her sharp little chin into Alice's shoulder
as she added "and the moral of *that* is—'Take care of the
sense, and the sounds will take care of themselves.'"

Lewis Carrol, *Alice in Wonderland*

If ever the queen had reason to chop off the head of the
poor old Duchess, or at least to curb her tongue, this little
moralism should have provided the moment; for as every field
worker who has conducted interviews or collected oral testimony, even on the narrowest of questions, has sooner or later
realized, the Duchess's dictum is simply wrong. The variety
of information conveyed by spoken language, the manner in
which it is conveyed and the affective relationships between
the interviewer and subject make it impossible to take care of
the meaning and let the sounds take care of themselves; indeed
there may not even be any sense unless we try to make sense
of the sounds themselves. Even then, when we do try to make

sense out of what has been said to us we have recurring doubts
and fears about how to receive information which is being
given to us and what *is* and is not information, and what is
the context in which it is being conveyed and how that context
influences what is being conveyed, and in what sense do *we*
fully understand what is being said. In addition, the range
of information descending upon us, the answers to questions
never asked, the hidden levels of discourse behind the slightest
pause or connective, the cognitive or ideological links between
pieces of information, produce a gnawing feeling that we may,
perhaps, be in another chapter and confused.

Still, because we do try to explain what it is we are doing and what it is we are collecting, and because we' do try
to understand the meaning of what is being said, despite our
doubts and confusions, we are led inevitably to synthetic levels
of analysis and discussion. In this situation our daily quandary
then becomes the perennial question of trying to work out
manageable and lasting relationships between our own work
and training and the work and training of those in other disciplines. In short, the practice of collecting and using oral data
produces its own impetus toward interdisciplinarity. Because
we cannot fully understand or exploit the materials we are
dealing with if we remain within the narrow conventions and
methods of our own fields of specialization, we reach out with
much uncertainty for some more or less sophisticated cooperation with other field workers. We become interdisciplinary
in spite of ourselves. To write at length once again about the
need for interdisciplinary approaches and cooperation in any
field, let alone in a journal devoted to American Studies, may
seem a thankless task, one which simply adds to an already
overgrown and unused bibliography of unread tomes. It may
indeed even contribute to what Stanley Bailis in an earlier article in this series has termed the "incoherency" and "Babel"
produced by the ad hoc use of different disciplines.[1] There are,
however, beyond the obvious necessities of field work and the
fact that we do it anyway, solid reasons why, at this particular

moment, interdisciplinary uses of oral interviewing and oral testimony should be discussed and even attempted.

Some of these reasons, indeed the most significant, have their origins in the internal developments now occurring within two of the core disciplines dealing with oral testimony: linguistics and anthropology. Others stem from the exciting possibilities for intellectual integration offered by fairly flexible subdisciplines such as psycholinguistics, sociolinguistics, ethnohistory and ethnomethodology studies whose very existence is an indication of interdisciplinarity. Within still older and more traditional disciplines new and increasingly attractive methodologies or practices, such as oral history, English as a second language and the linguistic study of poetics, have led to a new awareness of the voice as a medium through which information is conveyed. Lastly, the academic revolution of the 1960s, a declining job market and a concern for cultural analysis in the broadest sense have stimulated teachers and students to investigate the possibilities of field work involving face-to-face contacts.

Within this concatenation of forces and pressures, theoretical reorientations, change of foci and interests, and new concerns, the most significant alterations for the purposes of our discussion have occurred within the field of linguistics. This is especially significant because linguistics is the key discipline in the analysis of the spoken word, the discipline which has developed the most elegant and powerful theories explaining and predicting language behavior and the discipline upon which some form of synthesis of the various disciplines can be based.[2] Also, the particular form of the debates and changes in linguistics make it more possible than ever before to initiate a preliminary interdisciplinary discussion.

While the debates within linguistics over theory and practice are far too complex and convoluted to detail in this essay, and are in any event probably of little interest to those outside the field itself, the consequences of the reorientation of the discipline would seem to have enormous implications for the analysis of oral materials and for our thinking about oral materials. In particular those debates within linguistics now raging over the usefulness of the traditional *langue/parole*[3] distinction and the validity of formal properties devoid of context would appear to offer the most fruitful area of investigation because they offer the most logical basis for interdisciplinary integration.

To bastardize, and in some very important respects to trivialize, these debates: to an outsider, what seems to be taking place is a rebellion among many scholars who, while they recognize the enormous contributions of Noam Chomsky and his theories of transformational and generative grammar, are becoming more and more critical of the formalism inherent in his concern with the potential competence of speakers of the language rather than the actual performance of these speakers. In this rebellion and attack upon the formalism of linguistics as it has emerged over the past decade, those who have mounted serious objections, such as Robin and George Lakoff, Ronald Langacker, William Labov, Robert Stockwell, M. A. K. Halliday and others, have not attacked the basic validity of studies of grammar but rather have expressed a concern with the nonformal questions of context and meaning and their relation to formal theories, concerns at one time labeled semantic. For a number of technical reasons this new concern does not, in any way, resemble the old semantics but is an attempt to build upon structural models, new models which will explain the full range of the role of language in the culture.[4] What is of most importance for us here is that this concern with the nonformal aspects of language has led these linguists to investigate and reach out to other disciplines. As expressed by Robin Lakoff, " . . . we must extend our vision beyond what is normally considered 'linguistics' proper, and erase some of the boundaries that have been imposed upon our domain: We must become engaged in research that we might be tempted to call 'psychology,' or 'psychiatry,' or 'literary criticism'—anything in fact—but linguistics. Yet if we are going to be serious linguists, we must agree that our field is part of theirs (and vice versa)."[5]

While probably few professional linguists would go as far as Lakoff in urging a merger of their concerns with those of others, if these newer voices in the field who are concerned with such questions as the nature of the human conceptual apparatus, the study of personality, the study of social relations revealed by and inherent in language, the language of politics, art, minorities, and the methods of linking the style of language to the style of life—if they represent an important tendency in linguistics, as they obviously do, then the basis of a true dialogue with students in other disciplines seems obvious to even an untutored observer.

The mutuality of interest and concern over method between linguists and others is nowhere more obvious than in the field of anthropology. Intimately linked since the birth of both disciplines, this interest has been clearly marked in such intellectual events as the formulation of the Sapir-Whorf hypothesis, a joint collaboration of an anthropologist and a linguist, and the restructuring of anthropology called for by Lévi-Strauss in his use of constructs drawn directly from the theories of linguists.[6] It is also found in the discussion of kinship terms, myth and other major topics of analysis in anthropology.

Increasingly, however, this interaction is becoming closer and more refined on both the theoretical and operational levels, and as anthropologists begin to concern themselves with the formal problems of cognition, synchronic structure and the basic theories of linguists they have infused the study of linguistics with an ethnographic perspective.[7] The results have in turn spawned subdisciplines such as psycho- and sociolinguistics, and other areas of investigation such as nonverbal communication, body language and other forms of what has come to be called paralanguage.

While it would simply be too time-consuming and confusing to describe in detail the internal gestation of these subdisciplines which have developed their own theories and methods and their own bibliography,[8] it is worthy of note that in many cases it is these newer areas of study which have provided the theoretical base for the concern among anthropologists to relate their own research and teaching to the problems of complex historical change. This in turn has led to a search for a method of synthesis which will integrate the diachronic concerns of historians and the synchronic models of anthropology.[9] While the form of this synthesis is unclear there is some evidence that a type of Marxist-structuralist perspective is emerging. Whether it does is not of immediate interest to us here; what is of interest is the impulse in anthropology. As Dell Hymes forcibly notes, "It is obvious in the dimension of human life central to anthropology—the cultural—to implicate historical processes. No attempt in anthropology can escape historical assumptions."[10] Interestingly enough, given the close relationships between the fields, one finds much the same concern and direction in folklore studies, a concern with urban historical societies and a concern with the historical dimension of their work—not a return to historical studies, but a new concern with a context which is historical.[11]

This discussion should not be taken to imply that serious problems do not remain before any kind of integration of these disciplines can become a reality.[12] However, as John W. Oller has noted, the mere fact of argumentation between disciplines over whose territory is whose is some indication of their interpenetration.[13] Allow us to suggest that as this interpenetration becomes more and more obvious, and as the concern with language as a key element of the culture continues to guides this interaction, at some point a common set of perspectives will begin to emerge. Even a cursory examination of the bibliographies of disciplines other than anthropology and linguistics—such as folklore,[14] literature (especially the concern with problems of grammar, prosody, minority languages or semiology or tagmemics)[15] and oral history[16]—indicates that at the least a community of interest exists among those whose work and practice is dependent upon knowledge of the contextual analysis of the spoken word. It is upon this common need and community of interest that an interdisciplinary study of oral interviewing and oral testimony can be built. Despite many problems, for a number of reasons and among a number of different academic disciplines a collective approach to interviewing and the analysis of oral testimony seems possible. For the remainder of this essay, we would like to sketch out some of the details of that approach and suggest a few lines of investigation incorporating these disciplines.

The approach we want to discuss is primarily a field work approach which seeks through recorded interviews to preserve spoken conversations capable of being analyzed by the use of a number of disciplinary perspectives. Such a field work approach would encompass all fields of investigation using the interview as a basic source except law, journalism or the more therapeutic branches of psychology. Law and journalism have been eliminated from this discussion for two reasons: the adversary relation between investigator and subject is so at odds with the cooperative nature of field work in other, more academic studies that the same models of interviewing cannot be applied to those fields; secondly, in both professions the use of materials collected through the interviewing process is governed by a legal structure which, if it does not demand, at least tolerates a potentially detrimental use of those materials.[17] We have also excluded from this discussion many branches of psychology because, although there is a sense in which interviewing is a therapeutic experience for those being interviewed, it should not be undertaken for therapy by anyone not trained explicitly to handle the problems which can emerge during the process, especially not by professors and students acting as amateur therapists. These limitations aside, we can discuss the collective use of the interview in field work in two ways: first, as an introduction to an interdisciplinary approach to interviewing; and secondly, as a set of materials capable of being analyzed from an interdisciplinary perspective; in other words, as an experience and as a study.

An almost unanimous consensus exists among writers of field work manuals and handbooks that the first stage of the interview experience is a period of intensive research into the culture one proposes to study; this means in essence consulting what work has already been done and simply plowing through what written sources already exist. We suggest that in addition to an intensive investigation of the people one is to talk to, these field manuals be among the first sources consulted by the interviewer, for a training in methods is equally a part of one's research design.[18] Aside from these manuals, such introductory research should allow for the widest possible search for sources in the language, geography, history, politics, folklore and society of the region and its people. If students are properly directed, such research procedures could provide a basic introduction to interdisciplinary study as well as an introduction to archival practices, forms of library reference services, bibliographical materials and the various forms of implicit and explicit languages used by disciplines other than one's own.[19] If we are to truly create an interdisciplinary approach, we must first devise a proper cooperative approach to our preliminary investigations.[20]

As in research preparation, the interview process should be used as an introduction to interdisciplinary work, discovering the real differences in technique employed by others yet concentrating upon the common elements in the literature and the experience itself. While much of the literature on interviewing will not prepare the field worker for the almost confessional nature of some interviews and the theoretical problems posed by the affective relations engendered by interviewing, it does provide a basic grounding from which one can discuss the nature of questioning and the nature of respondent's answers.[21] A particularly effective discussion of interviewing problems and practices would, we think, be engendered by a reading of the methodological notes of participant-observers in light of the

tradition in most disciplines of the interviewer as outside objective observer or even a stranger.[22]

It is, however, in the analysis of the interview as a recorded
document that the truly exciting possibilities for interdisciplinary work rests. Because we strongly believe this to be the
case and because the following suggestions for analysis represent a fairly idiosyncratic view of the interview, we would like
to preface further discussion with a few very tardy remarks
concerning what is meant here by an interview.

When we talk about an interview we mean essentially
a tape-recorded question-and-answer session conducted in an
unstructured manner allowing for spontaneous discourse and
in which the relations between interviewer and subject are
more or less harmonious, at least to the extent that both have
agreed upon the ground rules covering the conversation. This
definition is limited for very particular reasons. It is limited
to audio tape because film or video tape presents a major
theoretical problem in analysis. While an audio tape is all
inclusive within its range—recording all sound—film or video
tape is severely focused, limited to only what is chosen by
the film technician for presentation. This film, because it
concentrates upon one gesture, face, artifact, etc., infuses the
sound with new and ofttimes bizarre meaning, and therefore
defies analysis in the form which we want to pursue. In
addition, there is strong evidence to suggest that the viewer,
not the interviewer or subject, infuses meaning into filmed
presentations,[23] thus increasing the interrelationships within
the interview situation by an exponential factor.

This definition of an interview is also limited to spontaneous or informal speech genres.[24] It does not cover more
formal types of speech such as rhetoric, read speech, solilo-
quies, oratory, poetic readings or formalized story telling. It
does, however, include proverbs, folk tales, recitation of ge-
nealogies, etc., which, while they are fixed-form genres, often
arise by free-form association as methods of explanation. Also
excluded are interviews which exist as notes or other written

documents for they contain none of the performance aspects or oral dialogue or "literature" as described by Ruth Finnegan.[25] Lastly, although by implication our analysis covers interviews conducted for rather narrow or highly focused research purposes, our attention is directed primarily at interviewing situations seeking to go beyond mere verification of facts or simple recitations of events outside of their full context.

Within these limits there are even further clarifications necessary before a full analysis of oral interviews can be suggested. As noted most forcefully by Aaron V. Cicourel, every interview, since it is a social situation which is never repeated, is unique. Therefore any analysis must search for and concentrate upon the invariants of the interview situation.[26] It is only by concentrating upon these invariants that we can link each item or segment of the interview directly to its proper set of variables, or, in plainer terms, link each item with its proper structural matrix.

In an earlier essay published elsewhere we have argued that oral history interviews, and by implication all interviews, are a set of three structures, one internal and two external, each containing within itself a set of self-regulating relationships.[27] Based upon a reading of Piaget and Barthes,[28] we have described these structures as linguistic, performatory and cognitive and have argued that each must be analyzed on its own terms before we can understand what it is that is occurring during the interview.

In brief, the linguistic structure of the interview is that set of relationships which emerges between each sound, word or sign to create the grammatical or literary form of the interview. The performatory structure of the interview has its base in the dialectical relationship between the interviewer and the subject and the social, psychological and cultural biases, habits, perceptions and codes each brings to the interview. In this relationship, because of the nature of the conversation, the interviewer (and sometimes, although rarely, the subject) is transformed into an audience. The cognitive structure contains

those relations which emerge within the interview between
the subject and the information which is being conveyed.
This information is structured by the interviewee and thus
transformed into a dialogue between the subject and his culture
at large for which the interviewer serves as representative.
Descriptively, these sets of relationships are quite close to
what John L. Fischer had called the conative, affective and
cognitive functions of oral interviewing.[29] The term "structure"
is used here to allow us to concentrate upon the coded, regular
and predictable nature of these relations rather than their
manipulation, and to view them not only as analytical devices
but also as relations which have their base in some form of a
material reality.

If we view the interview in this framework and begin
our analysis with the linguistic structure of the interview,
our investigation could first concentrate upon several types of
analysis. These range from the most formal distinctions based
upon generative grammar to the broader types of analysis
done so successfully in sociolinguistics by Labov and others.[30]
We could then consider the questions and propositions of
psycholinguistics concerning pauses, breathing, etc., and their
meaning for the interview.[31] From such a beginning we could
then move on to the kinds of historical linguistic propositions
raised recently by Nancy Struever.[32]

In the process of a linguistic analysis of the interview, folkloristic and literary analysis could be integrated, thus raising a
different set of questions about the nature of the information
being conveyed. Folkloristic techniques, for example, would
concentrate upon the search for motifs, folktales, urban folk
images, etc., and the distinction between folk and historical
representation.[33] We could, perhaps, even use the distinction
made by Henry Glassie between folk and popular artifacts to
understand the language of the interview.[34] While some of
this analysis would be foreign to those trained in other disciplines (such as historians), such an analysis could be used to
bring these outsiders to the realization that the representation

of reality is as significant an event in the culture as the reality itself.

The literary analysis of the interview could move from linguistic analysis to encompass the claim of Dennis Tedlock that all oral dialogue is poetic in form.[35] We could combine Tedlock's analysis with Finnegan's excellent discussion of oral presentation as literature,[36] to discuss the forms of speaking contained in the interview in terms of their literary forms, prosody, or other formal constructions. The variety of possible combinations and permutations of such an analysis can be barely hinted at here in this short essay, but there is no reason why, if this is done with care, such activity could not provide some of the most exciting possibilities for understanding the nature of the interview.[37]

Equally exciting and important interdisciplinary connections can be made in the analysis of the interview as performance. Relying heavily upon the work of such students of small group interaction and face-to-face encounters as Erving Goffman,[38] our analysis could move quite logically to a discussion of the methodological questions concerning interviewing raised by Harold Garfinkel and Cicourel about the validity and reliability of the information being conveyed, given the affective form in which it is being conveyed.[39] We could also integrate Garfinkel's ethical concerns about raising to a conscious level commonsense propositions about life which people have operated with in an unconscious manner for years into a discussion of the role of the interview in raising consciousness and the support of this process urged upon us by Staughton Lynd.[40] In addition, if we talk about audience, there is no logical reason why we cannot begin to investigate those questions which are normally pursued by drama critics or those interested in the social history or social context of the arts. Without prolonging this discussion of the performatory structure of the interview, if carefully conceived and prudently conducted, we could use the concepts and tools developed by ethnomethod-

ologists to integrate our discussion of the linguistic form of the
interview and our discussion of performance.

The importance of current work in ethnomethodology is
that it reveals to us the underlying codes and rules which
govern the affective relationships in social situations, such as
interviews. But Cicourel has pointed out, these questions lead
to unavoidable problems as to whether or not the validity
of the information is determined by subjective factors such
as trust, or whether or not the goals of research must be
sacrificed for the maintenance of the good will engendered
during the interview.[41] If our analysis is not directed to some
form of a more general level of synthesis we risk entrance into
a *cul de sac* from which we could not possibly emerge. The
problems raised by ethnomethodology can only be resolved
by a more synthetic view of the interview which encompasses
a consideration of the cognitive propositions being expressed,
for it is within the cognitive structure that the objective and
rational features of a dialogue are to be found.

This third set of relationships present in the interview
is more abstract, less studied, and therefore more elusive to
define. When we interview someone, he or she not only speaks
to himself or herself and to the interviewer, but they also speak
through the interviewer to the larger community and its history
and cultural vision (paradigm?) as they view it. This is a
dialogue, the exact nature of which is difficult to define. There
are seemingly two relations contained in one—that between the
informant and the interviewer, and that between the informant
and his own historical consciousness.

The first of these relations is in large measure engendered
by the interviewer, for it is his curiosity, not that of the
historical actor, which both the questions and the explanations
seek to satisfy. In most cases, the informant has acted as if
his views of the world were a given reality, and he has not
thought them out until faced with the necessity to do so by the
interview. Essentially what occurs as a result of this interaction
is that the interviewer by his questioning forces the subject to

take the commonplace and, as Garfinkel has noted, "make it anthropologically strange,"[42] a process which Collingwood has claimed is indeed part and parcel of the historical method and which Michel Foucault has exploited so brilliantly.[43] When this is done in an interview the relation that emerges is both relative and equivalent. It is relative in that the informant's view of history and culture (its use, its structure, a system of cause, his role in it and his relations with others) are developed only in relation to the interviewer's view of that participation, while the interviewer's organization of his questions (the structure of the interview) is in turn developed in response to the answers of the interviewee. Each view is thus a standard of reference for the other. The relationship is also equivalent in the sense that when it is finally articulated, the questions, asked and unasked, and the answers given form a world view equal to and quite independent of that of the questioner, since that world view has its origins not in the interviewer's questions but in the subject's own role in the world of production.

The second relation—that of the informant to what he or she views as the vision of the community—is probably the most clearly articulated aspect of the interview, and also the most difficult to grasp, for it is only one part of a much broader cultural vision and cognitive structure and demands a very special type of reading to analyze. To read the narrative properly to discover this relation and the cultural vision which informs it, we must give the interview the same kind of reading which Jacques Lacan has given to Freud or Louis Althusser has given to Marx,[44] a method of reading Althusser terms "symptomatic."

While few of us, or our interviewees, will create narratives or analyses as rich, as complex or as theoretically sophisticated as those of Freud or Marx, our interviews as we have tried to show are more complex than we usually assume. If read properly, they do reveal to us hidden levels of discourse— the search for which is the aim of symptomatic reading.[45] If read (or really listened to) again and again, not just for facts or comments, but also, as Althusser suggests, for insights and oversights, and the combination of vision and nonvision, and especially for answers to questions which were never asked, we should be able to isolate and describe the problematic which informs the particualr interview we are analyzing.

It is at this deeper structural level of the ideological or theoretical context within which words or phrases and the presence and absence of certain problems and concepts are found that we discover the synthesis of the various structural relationships of the interview as well as the particular vision of the relationship of the individual to his history and culture. What we are here discussing is not simply a *Weltanschauung*, but a structural field in which men live in history and which guides their practices and actions. Within this vision the dialectical tension between myth and historical vision plays a key role and provides for the analyst a crucial tool by which he can understand the dynamic of the interview.

In a much discussed addendum on the nature of cognition, Lévi-Strauss has attacked Sartre for his view of the relationship between dialectical and analytical thought.[46] In the process of that attack he raised fundamental questions about the relationship between history as a cognitive mode, and myth. While his distinctions have been rather bitterly attacked by historians, few of his critics have come to grips with just what that relationship is.[47] As Ben Halpern and Warren Susman have tried to show, myth and history are not mutually exclusive ways of viewing the world, nor are they simply one version of each other (myth simply a form of historical thought or history just one form of myth) but rather they are alternate ways of interpreting the culture which, while they exist in dialectial antagonism, can often be synthesized into a number of differing visions.[48] Susman in particular has brilliantly outlined how the use of the idea of history has been interwoven with the myth of Christ over the course of American history to produce a number of complex and potent intellectual structures

that have formed the basic ideological vision of those who pro-
pounded any particular synthesis of the two.

There is simply not enough space here in which to develop
in detail the refined definitions of myth, history and ideology
which form the basis of the analysis of Susman and Halpern,
but we should note some of the consequences that they draw
from their studies. Myth, both would claim, is essentially
a conservative, cohesive force in a culture;[49] its ritual, its
appeal to authority, its claims for sacerdotal sanctity and its
suprarational aspects demand that those in a culture rise above
divisions and participate in the dominant ethos of the culture.[50]
Ideology, on the other hand, because it always includes a vision
of history and seeks to mobilize the past to direct the future,
is a dynamic force in the culture and most often exists in
conflict with other ideologies devised by other classes or groups
in the society. It is ideology, therefore, which becomes the
basic expression of a world vision in a class-based society—the
type of social system which we are particularly interested in
investigating. This is the case because,

> Ideology—regarded diachronically and synchronically—
> assumes the most efficient possible form of expression,
> given the historical circumstances; whether magical, myth-
> ical, religious, philosophical, scientific, or artistic. Ideol-
> ogy can express the tasks set by history correctly or falsely
> (or defectively), adequately or inadequately (or unsatisfac-
> torily), meaningfully or unmeaningfully (or distortedly),
> from the point of view of the objectively necessary strat-
> egy. This depends on its structure in relation to its his-
> torical function and the historical data. In other words it
> is ideology . . . through which man as a historical subject
> visualizes his position in the historical universe.[51]

In addition, in those cultures where the historical vision
plays this role, there is usually one form of such a vision,
because it is the form of the dominant class, which either

becomes or tries to become the hegemonic ideology. Because
it may at any one moment of time face other equally potent
views of the world, the nature of this conflict becomes an index
of the stability or bitterness of class relations in the culture.[52]
Such a tension therefore becomes the crucial focus of the study
of ideology around which we can organize our analysis of our
interviews to fully comprehend the meaning of what is being
said to us, and the role of the interviewee in the culture.

This brief outline simply hints at the complexity of the
problems and the questions raised by the analysis of oral data.
What we are suggesting is that the interviews, if properly structured and properly understood within the context of the creation, can "show the dynamics remaining central to the way
people live with their history over time . . . and encourage us
to stand somewhat outside of cultural forms in order to observe
their workings and permit us to track the elusive beasts of consciousness and culture in a way impossible to do within . . . ."[53]
We can do this because the interviewing situation forces the
subject to make historical and cultural connections between
pieces of information, and these connections contain the expression of cultural values or public philosophy, no matter how
crudely articulated. If we are to begin to ask the significant
questions about the nature of culture, it is this expression of
the deeper ideological values of the people in the culture that
we must focus upon and analyze. Because of its seemingly
spontaneous internal generation and the nature of the relations contained within the interview, we can use the interview
to study this tension and the structure of its exposition. This
tension then becomes the synthesis of the varying structures
of the interview, because the way something is said and the
context within which it is said are simply expressions of this
deeper tension and indeed are often determined by this cognitive structure.

Another dimension of this cognitive tension could be
explored within this framework from the perspective of the
discipline of psychology. In fact, it could easily be argued that

it is obvious that we cannot understand the affective, cognitive
and (despite the claims of some linguists), linguistic structure of
such conversations without some form of psychological analysis.
In this case, although we are entering strange territory, it is our
impression that the work being done by Jerome Bruner and
his students on the nature of cognition and cognitive growth
would provide the most productive integration of psychology
and the other disciplines concerned with the problems we have
mentioned here.   This would seem to be the case because
Bruner's approach, based as it is upon the structuralism of
Piaget and others and a concern with language and upon
forms of cognition, addresses itself to these problems in a more
extensive fashion than either psychohistory or more narrowly
behavioristic studies.[54]

A vexing psychological problem in interviewing that has
faced almost every field worker and therefore must be mentioned is that of memory.   While many studies of memory
would seem to indicate that subjects forget events and facts
quite rapidly after their occurrence,[55] commonsense derived
from the interviewing situation seems to tell us differently, as
do a few studies now being conducted on the nature of long-
term memory which suggest that retrieval, not retention, is the
problem.[56] In this situation what we need, as any interviewer
who has been overwhelmed by the flood of memory engendered in the interviewing situation will attest, is a study of the
structure of memory in order to understand the connections
between our questions and the subject's responses.   Beyond
this immediate problem, however, there is no reason why the
methods and insights of field workers using their training as
psychologists, such as Robert Coles,[57] could not be employed
to add a deeper dimension to our discussion of language, affect and cognition and thereby aid us in our search for the
invariants of field work in oral interviewing.

The major portion of our discussion so far has centered
upon the larger theoretical and methodological problems of
an interdisciplinary approach to oral materials. Before closing

this discussion we would like to move for a moment to a much more mundane but in the long run equally important, level of discussion, and talk briefly about technical and ethical questions as a basis for interdisciplinary cooperation. In the first case, if a truly interdisciplinary approach is to be undertaken, field workers in each discipline must familiarize themselves with the technical needs of those in other fields. On the most practical level, such questions as the quality of sound recordings must be considered, for what is needed in a recording used by a linguist is a far higher degree of quality than that produced currently by other field workers, such as oral historians. To work collectively we must also produce materials that can be used by the widest range of investigators. More importantly we must learn what kinds of information each of us needs in order to begin the kinds of investigation we want to pursue, and while the bibliography in this article might help, there is no substitute for face-to-face dialogue. Perhaps this is the place to begin our interdisciplinary approach.

A more troublesome problem is that of ethics. Despite the rage expressed by Gershon Legman[58] about the exploitation of subjects in folklore studies and despite the statement on professional ethics issued by the Oral History Association,[59] there is much evidence that scholars in every field under discussion have continued to exploit others, for fame, money or in the name of science. In general what we have done is to depend upon the positivistic ethic of the natural sciences and assume that our subjects were similar to the phenomena investigated by natural scientists. We have also assumed that we are objective observers endowed by a higher calling and deeper sense of mission to produce something called knowledge. We must amend that conception by a realization of our responsibilities to our subjects and their lives and personalities. If humanely conceived, there is no reason why an interdisciplinary code of ethics would impose great restrictions upon any of us, and in all probability it might help all of us in the field.[60]

To return from this digression: What we have attempted to do here is to sketch out a possible method of collection and analysis of oral materials which will allow us to grasp the invariants of the interview situation and to understand the structure of those invariants. While there is much that is doubtful about the particular directions suggested in this essay, and the theoretical and ideological issues raised may leave more questions than answers, we hope we have stimulated workers in a wide array of disciplines to an awareness of the possibilities of such a study of oral testimony and interviewing. Perhaps we may yet rescue the Duchess from the chopping block and make some sense of both words and meanings.

> To make a totality surmisable requires much variety,
> The recreating spirit enjoys the joy of creation.
> All seems ordered to him, since he ordered it.
> So much that does not fit he leaves out and calls it "little"
> Or else history is formed. Before one's eyes
> The situations succeed one another. Only a few constantly
> Recurring laws regulate the proceeding.
> Such images are useful as long as they serve us. Not longer.
>
>   Bertolt Brecht

Footnotes

1. Stanley Bailis, "The Social Sciences in American Studies: An Integrative Conception," *American Quarterly*, 26 (Aug. 1974), 202, 204.

2. The reason for the central role of linguistics is fairly obvious. "It is the language which is the vehicle of personality, society, and culture." Denis G. Hayes, "Linguistics as a Focus for Intellectual Integration," *Georgetown University Round Table on Language and Linguistics* (hereafter GURT), 1974, pp. 165-178.

3. Langue/parole is another form of saying competence/performance. All this distinction means is that "the behavior of actual speech events differs significantly from theoretical predictions and idealizations." Yorick Wilks, "One Small Head—Models and Theories in Linguistics," *Foundations of Language*, 2 (Jan. 1974), 75-95.

4. Robin Lakoff, "Pluralism in Linguistics," GURT, pp. 59-82; George Lakoff "Humanistic Linguistics," GURT, pp. 103-17; Ronald Langacker, "Remarks on Introduction to Linguistics," GURT, pp. 23-31; William Labov, "The Study of Language in Its Social Context," *Studium Generale*, 25 (1970), pp. 30-87; *Linguistic Change and Generative Theory*, Robert Stockwell and Ronald K. S. Macaulay, eds., (Bloomington, Ind.: Univ. of Indiana Press, 1972), pp. 1-8 especially. For an example of the range of questions being asked by linguists, see the essays in "Language as a Human Problem," *Daedalus*, 102 (Summer 1973). A popular but often superficial discussion of linguistics is Peter Farb, *Word Play: What Happens When People Talk* (New York: Knopf, 1974). The bibliography, pp. 335-50, is useful. For an outsider's view of these debates and their consequences, see Stanley E. Fish, "How Ordinary is Ordinary Language?" *New Literary History*, 5 (Autumn 1973), 15-34.

5. Robin Lakoff, *op. cit.* For a quite similar view from a somewhat different perspectcive, see John Gumperz and Dell Hymes, "The Ethnography of Communications," *American Anthropologist: Special Publications*, 61, part 2 (1964), 55-69.

6. Benjamin L. Whorf, *Language, Thought and Reality* (Cambridge, Mass.: MIT Press, 1956). See also Harry Hoijer, ed., *Language in Culture: Conference on the Interrelations of Language and Other Aspects of Culture* (Chicago: Univ. of Chicago Press, 1954). On Lévi-Strauss, see "Structural Analysis in Linguistics and Anthropology" in *Language in Culture and Society: A Reader in Linguistics and Anthropology*, Dell Hymes, ed. (New York: Harper and Row, 1964), pp. 40-53. The clearest statement of Lévi-Strauss's claim can be found in *Structural Anthropology* (New York: Basic Books, 1963).

7. On the variety of these theoretical concerns and problems, see "Transcultural Studies in Cognition," A. Kimball Romney and Roy G. D'Andrade, eds., *American Anthropologist*, 66 (June 1964), especially: Dell Hymes, "Directions in (Ethno-) Linguistic Theory," 6-56; William C. Sturdevant, "Studies in Ethno-Science," 990-131; and Part V, Discussion and Summary, 230-53. See also Kenneth L. Pike, "Towards a Theory of Structure of Human Behavior," in Hymes *Language and Culture*, pp. 54-62; Karl V. Teeter, "Linguistics and Anthropology," *Daedalus, op. cit.*, pp. 87-98; and Joel Sherzer, "On Linguistics and Other Disciplines: A Perspective from Anthropology," GURT, pp. 131-42. That this perspective has more than academic consequences can be seen in the discussion in Ladislav Matejka, "On the First Russian Prolegomena to Semiotics," Appendix I, *Marxism and the Philosophy of Language*, by V. N. Volosinov, trans. by Ladislav Matejka and I. R. Titunik (New York: Seminar Press, 1973), pp. 161-74.

8. See for example: Joshua A. Fishman, ed., *Readings in the Sociology of Language* (The Hague: Mouton, 1968); Dan I. Slobin, *Psycholinguistics* (Glenview, Ill.: Scott Foresman, 1971); George L. Trager, "Paralanguage," in *Studies in Linguisitics*, 13 (Spring 1958), 1-12; Frieda Goldman-Eisler, *Psycholinguistics: Experiments in Spontaneous Speech* (New York: Academic Press, 1968); Ray L. Birdwhistel, *Kinesics and Context: Essays on Body Motion Communication* (Philadelphia: Univ. of Pennsylvania Press, 1970); and William Bright, ed., *Sociolinguistics* (The Hague: Mouton, 1966).

9. See for example the essays in Dell Hyme, ed., *Reinventing Anthropology* (New York: Pantheon, 1969), especially Kurt H. Wolff, "This is the Time for Radical Anthropology," pp. 99-118. For examples of this newer form of study, see Joseph J. Jorgensen and Marcello Truzzi, eds., *Anthropology and American Life* (Englewood Cliffs, N.J.: Prentice-Hall, 1974). The bibliography, pp. 517-24, is especially useful for those interested in the latest work on American culture being done by anthropologists

10. Hymes, "Introduction," *Reinventing Anthropology*, *op. cit.*, p. 13.

11. Alan Dundes, *The Study of Folklore* (Englewood Cliffs, N.J. Prentice-Hall, 1965). The Urban Experience and Folk Tradition," *Journal of American Folklore*, 83 (April-June 1970), whole issue. On the relationship between folklore and other social science disciplines, see John L. Fischer, "The Sociopsychological Analysis of Folktales," *Current Anthropology*, 4 (June 1963), 235-95.

12. Kenneth C. Wylie, "The Uses and Misuses of Ethnohistory," *Journal of Interdisciplinary History*, 3 (Spring 1973), 707-20;

WIlliam C. Sturdevant, "Anthropology, History and Ethnohistory," *Ethnohistory*, 13 (1966), 1-51.

13. John W. Oller, Jr., "Towards a Supradisciplinary Graduate Program," GURT, p. 120.

14. See for example such basic works as: Richard M. Dorson, *Folklore and Folklife: An Introduction* (Chicago: Univ. of Chicago Press, 1972), and Bruce Jackson, ed., *Folkore and Society* (Hatboro, Penn.: Folklore Associates, 1966). On the debate among folklorists over literary or behavioralist approaches, see: Kenneth Laine Kitner, "The Role of Hypothesis in Folkore," *Journal of American Folklore*, 86 (Oct-Dec. 1973), 113-30, and Anne Cohen and Norm Cohen, "Notes and Queries," *ibid.*, 87 (April-June 1974), 156-59. On examples of the uses of linguistics, see Arewa E. Ogo, "Proverb Usage in a Natural Context and Oral Literary Criticism," *ibid.*, 83 (Oct.-Dec. 1970), 430-37. See also Dundes, *op. cit.*, and Melville Jacobs, *The Content and Style of an Oral Literature* (New York: V. King Fund, 1959). For a discussion of the relation between history and folklore methods, see William L. Montell, *The Saga of Coe Ridge: A Study in Oral History* (Nashville, Tenn.: Univ. of Tennessee Press, 1970), Introduction.

15. Where does one begin to list works integrating linguistics and literature? Perhaps the most widely consulted guide to linguistics in literary study is John Lyons, *Introduction to Theoretical Linguistics* (New York: Cambridge Univ. Press, 1968). More difficult works are: Seymour Chatman and Samuel R. Levin, eds., *Essays on Language and Literature* (Boston: Houghton Mifflin, 1967), and Samuel R. Levin, *Linguistic Structure in Poetry* (The Hague: Mouton, 1969). Somewhat more readable is Don Geiger, *The Dramatic Impulse in Modern Poetry* (Baton Rouge, La.: Louisiana State Univ. Press, 1967). For a

view at odds with Lyons, see Michael A .K. Halliday, "Linguistics and English Studies," in A. L. McIntosh and M. A. K. Halliday, eds., *Patterns of Language* (Bloomington, Ind.: Univ. Of Indiana Press, 1971), pp. 25, 51, and "The Context of Linguistics," GURT, pp. 179-97. A discussion of conflicts between the two can be found in Fish, *op. cit.*, pp. 41-48. On semiotics, see Roland Barthes, *Elements of Semiology*, trans. Annette Laver and Colin Smith (New York: Hill and Wang, 1968). Tagmemic theory is developed in Kenneth L. Pike, *Language in Relation to a Unified Theory of the Structure of Human Behavior* (The Hague: Mouton, 1967). For an example of its use, see William O. Hendricks, "On the Notion Beyond the Sentence," *Linguistics*, No. 37 (1967), 12-52. An interesting example of the use of linguistics in literature is Richard M. Ohmann, *Shaw: The Style and The Man* (Middletown, Conn.: Wesleyan Univ. Press, 1962). An interesting discussion of linguistic models in literature is George Steiner, "Whorf, Chomsky and the Student of Literature," *New Literary History*, 4 (Autumn 1972), 15-34. For a brief overview of the role of structuralism in this mutuality of concerns, see Jonathan Culler, "Structure of Ideology and the Ideology of Structure." *New Literary History*, 5 (Spring 1973), 471-82. A handy bibliography on black English can be found in J. L. Dillard, *Black English: Its History and Usage in the United States* (New York: Random House, 1972), pp. 315-47. See also the essays in Jack L. Daniel, ed., *Black Communication: Dimensions of Research and Instruction* (New York: Speech Communication Association, 1974).

16. There are really no essays in oral history which discuss language in historical interviewing, although the problems and promises are often mentioned. See for example, Ronald J. Grele, ed., *Envelopes of Sound: Six Practitioners Discuss the Method, Theory and Practice of Oral History* (Chicago: Precedent, 1975), and Saul Benison, "Oral History and Manuscript Collecting," *Isis*, 53 (March 1962), 113-27. An excellent discus-

sion of the potential impact of linguistics on historical study
is Nancy S. Struever, "The Study of Language and the Study
of History," *Journal of Interdisciplinary History*, 2 (Winter
1974), 401-15. Struever, following Barthes, describes history
primarily as a language skill. For a brief introduction to the
concerns of oral historians, see Norman Hoyle, "Oral History,"
Library Trends (July 1972), 60-81, and the symposium on oral
history in *The American Archivist*, 28 (Jan. 1965). One of the
most self-conscious oral histories which raises many of the issues
discussed in this essay is Martin Duberman, *Black Mountain:
An Exploration in Community* (New York: Doubleday, 1973).
The classic analysis of oral testimony for historical purposes is
Jan Vansina, *Oral Tradition: A Study in Historical Methodology* (London: Routledge and Kegan Paul, 1961). For other
works, see Manfred Wasserman, *Bibliography on Oral History*
(New York: Oral History Association, 1971).

17. Not all journalistic interviewing fits this mold. In particular,
the interviews found in *Playboy* and *Rolling Stone* are very
often profound cultural commentaries. In both instances,
however, the interviews are printed in full and not quoted
selectively for the purposes of the documentation of someone
else's story line.

18. The classic statement of field work in anthropology, Bronislaw
Malinowski, "On the Methods and Aims of Ethnographic Fieldwork," which originally appeared in his book, *Argonauts of the
Western Pacific*, pp. 4-25, has been reprinted in Alan Dundes,
ed., *Every Man His Way: Readings in Cultural Anthropology*
(Englewood Cliffs, N.J.: Prentice-Hall, 1968), pp. 119-37. The
standard work in folklore is Kenneth S. Goldstein, *A Guide
for Fieldworkers in Folklore* (Hatboro, Pa.: Folkore Associates,
1964), and in linguistics, William J. Samarin, *Field Linguistics:
A Guide to Linguistic Field Work* (New York: Holt, Rinehart and Winston, 1967). There is no manual in oral history

but William Moss, *Oral History Program Manual* (New York: Praeger, 1974), and Willa K. Baum, *Oral History for the Local Historical Society* (Nashville, Tenn.: American Association for State and Local History, 2nd ed. 1971), are useful. The classic statement of sociological field methods is W. I. Thomas and Florian Znaniecki, "Methodological Note," in *The Polish Peasant in Europe and America* (New York: Knopf, 1927), Vol. 1, pp. 1-87. See also Buford H. Junker, *Field Work: An Introduction to the Social Sciences* (Chicago: Univ. of Chicago Press, 1960), and Thomas Rhys Williams, *Field Methods in the Study of Culture* (New York: Holt, Rinehart and Winston, 1967). For an ofttimes hilarious account of field work experience, see Eleanor Smith Bowen, *Return to Laughter* (London: Gollancz, 1954).

19. A point made most clearly by Howard J. Ehrlich, "Notes from a Radical Social Scientist," *Radical Sociology*, J. David Colfax and Jack L. Roach, eds. (New York: Basic Books, 1971), pp. 200-01.

20. Research prior to interviewing is, in many cases, commonplace, yet varies in depth and focus from discipline to discipline. No folklorist or anthropologist would go into the field without some investigation into dialect manuals or linguistic atlases. Most historians and some sociologists, however, have never consulted such works as Hans Kurath, *A Word Geography of the Eastern United States* (New York: AMS Press, 1973), or Gordon Wood, *Vocabulary Change: A Study in Regional Words in Eight Southern States* (Carbondale: Southern Ill. Univ. Press, 1971). In anthropology, archival materials are used loosely only as background; see Zachary Gussow and George S. Tracy, "The Use of Archival Materials in the Analysis and Interpretations of Field Data," *American Anthropologist*, 73 (June 1971), 695-709. Linguists, on the other hand, have usually felt it quite unnecessary to research the social contexts of their field

interviews, the assumption being that their theories would stand or fall on formal grounds alone; see Robin Lakoff, *op. cit.*, p. 60. For those interested in a humorous account of what happens when untrained and uninformed field workers are sent into the community, see James E. Myer, "Unleashing the Untrained: Some Observations on Student Ethnographers," *Human Organization*, 29 (Summer 1968), 155-59. As will become apparent to the reader, we are convinced that the single most important starting point is C. Wright Mills, *The Sociological Imagination* (New York: Oxford Univ. Press, 1959).

21. There are several handbooks on interviewing available. The most useful we have found are William H. Banaka, *Training in Depth Interviewing* (New York: Harper and Row, 1970); Alfred Benjamin, *The Helping Interview* (Boston: Houghton, Mifflin, 1969); and Lewis Anthony Dexter, *Elite and Specialized Interviewing* (Evanston, Ill.: Northwestern Univ. Press, 1970). For more detailed discussions, see Eleanor E. Maccoby and Nathan Maccoby, "The Interview: A Tool of Social Science," in *The Handbook of Social Psychology*, Gardner Lindzey, ed. (Cambridge, Mass.: Addison-Wesley, 1958), Vol. 1, pp. 449-87. A somewhat less useful discussion by R. L. Kahn and C. F. Cannell in the revised edition of the *Handbook*, Vol. II, pp. 526-95, is more behavioral in its accent. See also Harry Stack Sullivan, *The Psychiatric Interview* (New York: W. W. Norton, 1954); R. E. Pittenger, C. F. Hockett and J. J. Danehy, *The First Five Minutes* (Ithaca, N.Y.: Martineau, 1960); and N. A. McQuown, ed., *Natural History of an Interview* (New York: Grune and Stratton, 1969). In oral history consult Moss, *op. cit.*, as well as *The Proceedings* of the National Colloquia of the Oral History Association, 1964-72. Some of the major theoretical problems which will be discussed below are pointed out in Harold Garfinkel, *Studies in Ethnomethodology* (Englewood Cliffs, N.J.: Prentice-Hall, 1967).

Perhaps the most important discussion of interviewing methods and problems published recently is Aaron V. Cicourel, *Method and Measurement in Sociology* (New York: Free Press, 1964), pp. 73-104. A classic example of field workers discovering the full range of affective relations in an interview can be found in Richard Sennett and Jonathan Cobb, *The Hidden Injuries of Class* (New York: Knopf, 1972), p. 24. An extensive bibliography on interviewing can be found in Raymond L. Gordon, *Interviewing: Strategy, Techniques and Tactics* (Homewood, Ill.: Dorsey Press, 1969), pp. 367-80. Every student should also consult Karl Marx, *A Workers' Inquiry* (repr. Freedom Information Service, Tougaloo, Miss., 1973).

22. See for example the discussion in William F. Whyte, *Street Corner Society: The Social Structure of an Italian Slum* (Chicago: Univ. of Chicago Press, 1955), pp. 279-358, and especially his discussion of his activities in organizing his interview respondents to march on City Hall, pp. 337-41. See also Herbert J. Gans, *The Urban Villagers: Group and Class in the Life of Italian Americans* (New York: The Free Press, 1962), pp. 336-50. On the objective observer, see Malinowski, *op. cit.*, Thomas and Znaniecki, *op. cit.* On the stranger as interviewer see "Notes on the Stranger," *The Sociology of George Simmel*, Kurt H. Wolff, trans. and ed. (Glencoe, Ill.: The Free Press, 1950). Some other works in sociology discussing the problems of field work are: Gerhard E. Lenski and John C. Leggett, "Caste, Class and Deference in the Research Interview," *American Journal of Sociology*, 65 (1969), 463-67; S. M. Miller, "The Participant-Observer and Over Rapport," *American Journal of Sociology* 48 (1952), 97-99; and Robert K. Merton, *The Focused Interview: A Manual of Problems and Procedures* (New York: The Free Press, 1956).

23. E. H. Gombrich, "The Visual Image," *Scientific American* (Sept. 1972), 82-96.

24. This limitation should not be taken to suggest that the concerns of those working in the various fields of speech communication are not to be integrated into our approach. Any brief glance at the literature on speech, on oral communication and on the relation of speaker and audience should make the connection clear. For an introduction to these concerns, see George N. Gordon, *The Languages of Communication: A Logical and Psychological Examination* (New York: Hastings House, 1969). See also R. J. Kibler and L. L. Barker, eds., *Conceptual Frontiers in Speech Communications* (New York: Speech Communications Association, 1974). The SCA publishes a *Bibliographic Annual in Speech Communication* listing latest works in the field and also a table of contents and index of the major journals from their founding to 1969; see Ronald J. Matlon and Irene R. Matlon, eds., *Table of Contents and Index* (New York: SCA, 1971).

25. Ruth Finnegan, *Oral Literature in Africa* (Oxford: Clarendon Press, 1970). For a much more narrowly focused discussion, useful despite its severe limitations, see James W. Gibson, Charles R. Gruner, Robert J. Kibler and Francis J. Kelly, "A Quantitative Examination of Differences and Similarities in Written and Spoken Messages," *Speech Monographs*, 33 (Nov. 1966), 444-51.

26. Cicourel, *op. cit.*, pp. 80-81.

27. Ronald Grele, "Movement Without Aim: Methodological and Theoretical Problems in Oral History," *Envelopes of Sound*, pp. 127-54.

28. Jean Piaget, *Structuralism* (New York: Basic Books, 1970), pp. 40-44; Roland Barthes, *Critical Essays* (Evanston, Ill.: Northwestern Univ. Press, 1972), pp. 51-58.

29. Fischer, *op. cit.*, pp. 255-58.

30. See for example, William Labov, *The Social Stratification of English in New York City* (Washington, D.C.: Center for Applied Linguistics, 1966). "The Internal Evolution of Linguistic Rules," *Linguistic Change*, pp. 101-17, and "Contraction, Deletion and Inherent Variability of the English Copula," *Language*, 45 (Dec. 1969), 715-62. Perhaps the most famous and controversial essay in sociolinguistics is Basil Bernstein, "Elaborated and Restricted Codes: Their Social Origins and Some Consequences," *American Anthropologist*, 66 (Dec. 1964), 55-69. For an attack on Bernstein, see the journal *Language and Class*, ed. by Harold Rosen (London, 1974). See also Frederick Williams and Rita Naremore, "On the Functional Analysis of Social Class Differences in Modes of Speech," *Speech Monographs*, 36 (June, 1969), 77-102. The influence of Bernstein's thesis is most clearly seen in its heavy quotation in Martin Deutsch, *The Disadvantaged Child: Selected Papers of Martin Deutsch and Associates* (New York: Basic Books, 1967). The assumption here, of course, is that the supposed free variation of language is not free, "but is correlated with systematic social differences." John Bright, "The Dimensions of Sociolinguistics," *Sociolinguistics*, p. 11.

31. Goldman-Eisler, *op. cit.*, pp. 4-12.

32. Struever, *op. cit.* See also *The Language of History in the Renaissance: Rhetoric and Historical Consciousness in Florentine Humanism* (Princeton: Princeton Univ. Press, 1970).

33. See for example, Don Handelman and Bruce Kapferer, "Forms of Joking Activity: A Comparative Approach," *American Anthropologist*, 74 (June 1972), 484-517; or Bela Gunda, "American Hungarian Folk Tradition," *Journal of American Folklore*,

83 (Oct.-Dec. 1970), 406-16. One of the most interesting attempts to move folklore in the direction of this kind of analysis
is Bruce E. Nickerson, "Is There a Folk in the Factory?" *Journal of American Folklore*, 87 (Apr.-June 1974), 133-39. The
classic reference in folklore is Stith Thompson, *Index to Folk
Literature*, 6 vols. (Bloomington, Ind.: Univ. of Indiana Press,
1955-58). See especially Vol. I, pp. 9-27 for an explanation of
the process of selection and the system of classification.

34. Henry Glassie, "Artifacts: Folk, Popular, Imaginary and Real,"
    in Marshall Fishwick and Ray B. Browne, eds., *Icons of Pop-
    ular Culture* (Bowling Green, Ohio: Bowling Green Univ.,
    Popular Press, 1970), pp. 103-22. If Glassie's analytic cat-
    egories of culture (progressive-elite, popular-normative, and
    folk-conservative) have any meaning, then they should find
    expression in spontaneous language.

35. Dennis Tedlock, "Oral History as Poetry," *Envelopes of Sound*,
    pp. 90-127. See also his "On the Translation of Style in
    Oral Narrative," *Journal of American Folklore*, 84 (Jan.-March
    1971), 114-33; and Dell Hymes, "Some North Pacific Coast
    Poems: A Problem in Anthropological Philology," *American
    Anthropologist*, 67 (April, 1965), 316-41. Along these lines,
    see Francis Berry, *The Physical Voice of Poetry* (New York:
    Oxford Univ. Press, 1962). For a decidedly different view of
    poetry as a special language rather than ordinary language,
    see Levin, *Linguistic Structures, op. cit.*, pp. 11-18.

36. Finnegan, *op. cit.*, pp. 1-11.

37. One thought along these lines would be to use Bernstein's
    conception of working class language as specific, transcribe
    interviews with workers as poetry, and then seek to ascertain

whether or not this form of specificity is a poetic use of language.

38. See for example Erving Goffman, *Relations in Public: Microstudies of the Public Order* (New York: Basic Books, 1971). The importance of the work of Goffman and his students to the kind of analysis we are proposing lies in its fundamental proposition that the ordinary acts of social intercourse are as rule-governed as the use of language. It is therefore possible to integrate these studies with the linguistic studies already mentioned.

39. Cicourel, *op. cit.*, pp. 99-100; Garfinkel, *op. cit.*, pp. 3-4. See also Garfinkel's questions addressed to Labov in *Sociolinguistics*, p. 110.

40. Staughton Lynd, "Guerrilla History in Gary," *Liberation*, 14 (Oct., 1964), 17-20; and Staughton Lynd and Alice Lynd, *Rank and File: Personal Histories of Working Class Organizers* (Boston: Beacon Press, 1973). On the role of consciousness in oral history and its relation to historical memory, see the excellent discussion in Michael Frisch, "Oral History and *Hard Times*," *Red Buffalo*, Numbers 1 and 2, n.d., pp. 217-31. We should not, however, confuse the moment of presentation with the historical process itself. Bringing events to consciousness and consciousness raising may be two quite different cognitive processes.

41. Cicourel, *op. cit.*, pp. 99-100. Or as put by Garfinkel, "recognizable sense, or fact, or methodic character, or impersonality, or objectivity of accounts are not independent of the socially organized occasions of their use. Their rational features consist of what members do with, what they 'make of,' the accounts in the socially organized occasions of their use."

42. Garfinkel, *op. cit.*

43. R. G. Collingwood, *An Autobiography* (Oxford: Oxford Univ. Press, 1951), pp. 31-39; Michael Foucault, *The Order of Things: An Archaeology of the Human Sciences* (New York: Vintage Books, 1970). An excellent example of this process is "A Dialogue Underground," *New York Review of Books*, March 11, 25, April 8, 1971.

44. Jacques Lacan, *The Language of the Self: The Function of Language in Psychoanalysis*, ed. and trans. Anthony Wilden (Baltimore: Johns Hopkins Univ. Press, 1968); Louis Althusser and Etienne Balibar, *Reading Capital*, trans. Ben Brewer (New York: Pantheon, 1970).

45. Althusser, *op. cit.*, pp. 16-17, 316.

46. Claude Lévi-Strauss, *The Savage Mind* (Chicago: Univ. of Chicago Press, 1966), pp. 245-69. See also pp. 231-34.

47. See for example, T. O. Beidelman, "Lévi-Strauss and History," *Journal of Interdisciplinary History*, 1 (Spring, 1971), 511-25. A far more complex discussion is Lawrence Rosen, "Language, History, and the Logic of Inquiry in Lévi-Strauss and Sartre," *History and Theory*, 10 (1971), 269-94.

48. Ben Halpern, "Myth and Ideology in Modern Usage," *History and Theory* Vol. 1 (1961), 129-49. Warren I. Susman, "History and the American Intellectual: Uses of a Usable Past," *American Quarterly*, 26 (Summer 1964), 241. For an exciting presentation and discussion of how views of history become fundamental ways of viewing the world, see Kenneth Burke, *Attitudes Toward History*, rev. 2nd ed. (Boston: Beacon Press,

1961). An interesting example of a particular synthesis of myth and history can be found in James W. Wilkie, *Elitelore* (Los Angeles: UCLA Latin American Center, 1973).

49. A point also made by Fischer, *op. cit.*, p. 242.

50. Myth as used here does not mean something incorrect, nor is it simply a tale or narrative, but rather a fundamental form of cognition by which human experience is interpreted. For an interesting discussion of the role of myth among the Fon and Ashanti, see Finnegan, *op. cit.*, p. 365. For a view of the tension between myth and history, see Mircea Eliade, *Myth and Reality* (New York: Harper and Row, 1963), Chapter IX. The short bibliography, pp. 203-04, has been most useful for this essay. See also Claude Lévi-Strauss, "The Structural Study of Myth," *Journal of American Folklore*, 68 (1955), 428-44.

51. Wilhelm Girnus, "On the Problem of Ideology and Literature," *New Literary History*, 4 (Spring, 1973), 485.

52. An ideology in this sense becomes the crucial form of consciousness in historical societies and is institutionalized in the various apparatuses of the culture in order to insure the continuance or further reproduction of the conditions of production. Althusser, *Lenin and Philosophy and Other Essays*, trans. Ben Brewster (New York: Monthly Review Press, 1971), pp. 127-86. On hegemonic ideologies, see Antonio Gramsci, *The Modern Prince and Other Essays* (New York: International Publishers, 1959). An interesting attempt to trace the latent ideologies within the culture is Robert Lane, *Political Ideology: Why the American Common Man Believes What He Does* (New York: Free Press, 1967).

53. Frisch, *op. cit.*, pp. 229-230.

54. See for example, Jerome S. Bruner, Rose R. Oliver and Patricia M. Greenfield, *Studies in Cognitive Growth* (New York: John Wiley, 1966), and Jerome S. Bruner, Jacqueline J. Goodnow and Austin G. A. Goodnow, *A Study of Thinking* (New York: John Wiley, 1956). See Romney and D'Andrade, *op. cit.*, for another perspective on the relation of linguistic, anthropological and psychological studies of cognition. See also N. D. Sundberg and L. E. Tyler, *Clinical Psychology: An Introduction to Research and Practice* (New York: Appleton Century Crofts, 1962), and R. Schrank, "Conceptual Dependency," *Cognitive Psychology*, 3 (1972), 47-64. A basic introduction to behavioralist approaches to these questions can be found in the essays and bibliography in Wilbur Schramm, ed., *The Science of Human Communication: New Directions and New Findings in Communications Research* (New York: Basic Books, 1963). The final word on psychohistory, in our opinion, is Robert Coles, "How Good is Psycho-history," *New York Review of Books*, 20 (Feb. 22, March 8, 1973). But see also William Saffady, "Manuscripts and Psycho-history," *American Archivist*, 37 (Oct. 1970), 28-37. For a different view of the relation of history and psychology, see Leonard Doob, *Becoming More Civilized* (New Haven: Yale Univ. Press, 1960), Chapter I, pp. 1-19.

55. This seems to be the conclusion of the studies in Donald A. Norman, ed., *Memory and Attention: An Introduction to Human Information Processing* (New York: John Wiley, 1968). See also William W. Cutler II, "Accuracy in Oral Interviewing," *Historical Methods Newsletter*, No. 3 (June, 1970), pp. 1-17.

56. Harry P. Bahrick, Phyllis O. Bahrick and Roy P. Wittlinger, "Those Unforgettable High School Days," *Psychology Today*, 8 (Dec. 1974), 50-56.

57. Robert Coles, *Children of Crisis*, 3 vols. (Boston: Little, Brown, 1967-73). In "Political Children," *New York Review of Books*, 22 (Feb. 20, 1975); Coles explicates the close relation between ideology and psychology as it emerges in his interviews.

58. Gershon Legman, *The Horn Book* (New Hyde Park, N.Y.: University Books, 1964), pp. 505-21.

59. Reprinted in Baum, *op. cit.*, pp. 46-47.

60. These notes represent the various fields under discussion at the time of the writing of this article. Obviously, while I do not think that I would change the focus of the article, recent work in oral history, linguistics, folklore—and especially anthropology, psychohistory, and ethnography—would more directly speak to the issues raised.

Can Anyone Over Thirty Be Trusted?
A Friendly Critique of Oral History

It has been thirty years since Allan Nevins began the first formal oral history project at Columbia University, and the birthday celebration of that project is probably as good a time as any to ask what has been the value of our efforts to use oral testimony to enrich the study of history and what are the problems now confronting us. It is as good a time as any because unlike the situation a few years ago we seem to be enjoying the respectability which comes with age, as well as the gnawing doubts which come with middle age.

That the oral history movement has grown and is now accepted seems beyond doubt. By last count there were some 500 projects in operation and probably the same number contemplated, already finished or in the process of formation. The Oral History Association now boasts over 1000 members, and a few years ago the Association captioned its annual colloquium as "Oral History Comes of Age." Increasingly within the academic community new courses are being announced in catalogs, and more traditonal scholars are praising our work and efforts. Two years ago, Beloit College awarded a baccalaureate degree in "oral history."

In short we have reached our middle years stronger and more accepted in the community than we have ever been. But just like millions of individuals who have passed the invisible markers of age which our culture sets before us this celebration comes with certain doubts. After thirty years are we to be trusted? What are our achievements and how can we assess them? I think that we have accomplished much, but many of our successes have brought with them some very real problems which we as oral historians must now confront. In middle age we can no longer argue that we do not have the time or cannot spare the manpower to deal with the larger historiographical questions raised by our work. Nor can we any longer ignore these problems, because to do so may bring our very achievements into suspicion. We need to assess our position and to highlight some of the problems which that position calls upon for solution.

We have accumulated an enormous amount of data. A brief look at the Meckler-McMullin directory,[1] admittedly incomplete, can give some indication of the mountain of material already collected, the thousands of people interviewed, some for the eighth or ninth time, and the quantity of paper transcripts derived from oral history tapes. Libraries are bulging with used and unused collections, presidential archives are jammed with interviews, and many local historical agencies are generating oral testimonies each day. In the meantime, historians in the academy are encouraging more and more of their students and fellow faculty members to collect even more oral histories. As a result, there now seems to be no possible way to count these piles of tapes and transcripts, to catalog them, and to monitor their use. Moreover, there seems to be no possible way to evaluate this material according to the usual standards of the profession. One of the ironies of the growth of oral history is that it has taken place during a period of time when written sources are being increasingly created and made available to scholars, and it in turn is aiding in the creation of even more paper.

We are faced with two related problems. First, from a records management perspective we must seek to gain some control over this data. Second, but more important, we must try to evaluate the data in terms of its usefulness for the profession, a goal which depends upon the successful solution of the first problem. To solve the first problem we must begin to take seriously Cullum Davis's[2] argument that interviewing is only the first step of the oral history process and that processing and making our materials available are equally important. Along these lines what we need are a series of catalogs and indexes of oral history material. The Meckler-McMullin volume is a step in the right direction, and so are the various catalogs of individual projects, most notable the series produced by the Columbia University Oral History Research Office. Smaller, less well financed projects, however, simply do not have the time, money or staff to compile such listings; neither do graduate students who conduct interviews as part of their dissertation research. In such situations granting agencies and universities and other sponsors must be made to insist that some part of their funds be given for program planning, as grants allocated for processing interviews, or for developing catalogs or indexes.   Another alternative is to work out consortium arrangements such as those devised by Columbia in order to achieve the national listing we need.   Although technically oral histories are now supposedly listed in the National Union Catalog of Manuscript Collections, much remains outside its purview, and all of us must work to somehow get a handle on what is being produced before we are simply innundated and before it is too late.

The second problem, that of evaluation, goes deeper than merely money or staff, and unfortunately is a problem which the profession at large seems unwilling to help us with. While this may sound like a very unflattering conclusion, one simply has to read through the reviews of works which have used or are based upon oral interviews—reviews which have appeared in both professional and popular journals—to verify the correctness of the claim. I can remember no review which asked the pertinent questions about sources. Who did the interviews? Where are they held? Are they open and available to others interested in checking the validity of the information? Were the questions biased or intrusive? What is the quality of the interview? Were they quoted correctly or were statements taken out of context? All of these are questions which reviewers usually raise when dealing with manuscript sources and works based upon their use. Yet for some reason when it comes to interviews we find a high degree of willingness to suspend disbelief among trained historians. Most do not insist upon a review of the interviews or some guarantee from authors of even the existence of such interviews.

Some of us have tried to interest the profession at large in serving this evaluative function. The Evaluation Committee of the Oral History Association is a case in point.   At other times others of us have asked historians using collections to which we have contributed to evaluate those contributions. To date my own experience with such requests has been unsuccessful, and I assume that the same holds true for others. The only evaluation now taking place occurs when insisted upon by granting agencies such as the National Endowment for the Humanities or at such times when foundations such as Rockefeller have sent writers out into the field to survey what has been done with their money.

Barbara Tuchman has complained that in many cases oral historians are collecting trivia and giving what should have been forgotten a new life by recording it and passing it on to others as history.[3] Are we, like Lincoln Kirstein's ballet dancer, giving our all to oral history and it is proving to be too much? In order to answer such questions we in the business must begin to conduct our own evaluations, such as Charles Morrissey has recently done for the wine industry project of the University of California Regional Oral History Office.[4] We must also attempt to make such reviews and evaluations available to a larger public if we are to serve that public. There is nothing wrong with peer review. In fact most of us would welcome such review if only some more or less manageable form could be devised. The normal review of the profession is not working in the case of oral history, and new and more innovative methods must be found.

We have opened new areas of American life and history to investigation and brought into the writing of history groups of people heretofore ignored by the profession. Partly this is luck. Oral history came into its own at a particularly fortunate moment of time during the upheavals of the 1960s. As a result of the growing tensions over war and racism in American culture, and the growing consciousness of the dispossessed, oral history was seized upon as one way to recreate the history of those who had been ignored in the past. Thus oral history was endowed with an enormously important and exciting mission—at last, through the medium of the voices of the people themselves history would recognize the lives and contributions to the culture of blacks, Chicanos, women, workers and members of once considered outcast groups.

On the one hand this thrust has given us such powerful documents as *All God's Dangers* and *Hillbilly Women*.[5] Unfortunately it has also given us a pile of racist or sentimental trash. We have ennobled some and demeaned others, sometimes at the same time. Interviews and works based upon them with no sense of the dialectical relationships between ethnic groups and class identification in the United States have sometimes moved from the careful analysis of the tensions of life in industrial society into a celebration of survival, and then beyond that to a set of concepts arguing with greater and greater frequency that one group and one group alone has the set of values, the honesty, the dignity and the trust to bear the burdens of the culture and of history. At other times, in many tapes which I have reviewed we get instead the sentimentalism of the popular front, a failure in its own time and imposition in ours.

Partly this has occurred through our own enthusiasm. We have, at times, lost our perspective by assuming that because someone says something it automatically contains a truth beyond those of established historians who have written in the past. I hold no brief with the historical establishment, not being a member of that charmed circle—not even a sympathizer I suspect—but it is not the case that all studies of the past done in the past are in error. Nor is it true that oral histories of the dispossessed are *ipso facto* free of the biases of the larger culture. One simply has to compare Henry Shapiro's[6] sensitive and evocative work on what our American culture has defined as Appalachia and the carefully documented oral histories in *Our Appalachia*[7] to see how the larger culture impinges upon the imaginations of those in a region which by all accounts seems to have been more isolated from the mainstream than most.

One of the features of the so called "new social history" which has intrigued me is that despite the promise of oral history it is not in the area of recent history that the most innovative and perceptive works have been written and published. Most of the best of this work concentrates upon the period from 1830 to 1890 and relies not at all upon oral testimony. I think it is time that we ask seriously if this fact reflects the biases of the profession, the usefulness of the data we produce, or perhaps the fact that the most interesting period for social historians is that period when classes were in the process of formation rather than the present, when those classes are already formed.

In any case I think it is important to admit that there are problems with how we have brought into history those who had heretofore been excluded and how useful those efforts have been. We must also begin to explain to others what we mean by "community history" and what we mean by community. It is not enough to expand our horizons. We must concern ourselves with how we populate that land beyond the horizon and, if we believe that the old models have no relevance, then we must devise new models around which our view of that territory will be organized.

We have made the study of history more exciting. I don't think that there is any doubt that oral history fieldwork is exciting and that this excitement leads to a new appreciation of the study of the past. For myself, I like the fact that my work brings me face to face with people in their homes, offices, or social halls in as most direct a manner as possible for an outsider. I am excited by the continued unfolding of new perspectives on the past, by new ways of seeing old issues and by new ways of framing questions about experience. I think this feeling exists among other fieldworkers, and I have seen it expressed by students when, at times, an off-the-cuff remark or a particular way of phrasing an issue has captured a historical insight much as a great teacher does.

But two very dangerous tendencies have their roots in this excitement. The first is the tendency within the historical profession to view oral history as another panacea, a quick and painless way to revive sagging enrollments and flagging interest in history. That history seems to be facing a crisis most would say is beyond doubt. Unfortunately, one of the reactions to this crisis is a search for that one gimmick—the one film strip, the one machine, or the one video cassette program—which will revive the profession. In this situation oral history is oftentimes tolerated because it increases the number of students signing up as history majors, not because it is honestly believed that anyone can learn anything from such fieldwork. Instead of looking for short cuts to difficult questions about why anyone should study history, what we mean by history, and how we teach it, we as historians should begin to address these real problems. Oral history, psychohistory, melodrama in the classroom will not save the day. In fact, if the careful methodology of the traditional canons of historical practice is not taught and followed oral history shall soon be reduced to collecting trivia, justifying the charges of critics.

The second tendency is equally defeating but has two facets: one involving the trustworthiness of our products and the other our concept of ourselves. The excitement of fieldwork, the genuine friendliness of the people we interview, and the involvement we feel in their lives very often lead to distortion. We begin to ask questions which we know our respondents are going to want to answer, and they begin to give us answers which they know we are going to want to hear. On both sides of the microphone, to ease the social situation, to maintain empathy and rapport, we avoid the hard questions and the unsettling answers. At times we become too much like journalists and their sources—compromised. History without biases and passions is probably impossible and if attainable would be as dull as dishwater. But in doing our fieldwork we must overcome the natural tendencies of social intercourse and remember that we are historians and we are interested in the

fullest exposition of the passions of the past, not in gathering
material which is acceptable to the present. The past we seek
to grasp was formed without us; the past we collect should be
equally free of our presence.

In addition the closeness of relationships in oral history
fieldwork has, at times, produced an equally disquieting attitude. At times, a student, or other interviewer, after some time
in the field comes to believe that he or she is part of the social
milieu which is under investigation. This is just not the case.
For example, when I worked for the John F. Kennedy Library
Oral History Project, no amount of interviewing or day-to-day
contact with those who knew John Kennedy, or fantasizing on
my part, would have ever made me a part of that world or that
class. The same held true on the Ford Foundation Project—I
was a recorder of the history of the institution, not a part of it
or the class it represents. But the same holds true for projects in
working class history. In this case it is false proletarianization
to assume that because one interviews miners, auto workers or
ghetto blacks one becomes a "worker" or a member of a dispossessed community. More than studying a class, living among
members of that class, or even accepting the views of that class
is involved in class position and class identification. It is a distortion of one's history and culture to assume otherwise. We
may share political perspectives with those we interview but
in most cases, not their lives.

We have produced some of the most innovative and exciting histories of the last two decades. When I say this I am
thinking of such works as *All God's Dangers*, Peter Friedlander's *Making of a UAW Local*, *Black Mountain* by Martin
Duberman, *Hannah's Daughters*, *Hillbilly Women*, *Our Appalachia*, *Huey Long* or the works of Studs Terkel.[8] Yet it is
only in *Black Mountain* that we find the kind of methodological introspection that we so need, and it is only in Friedlander's
work that anyone has come close to beginning the theoretical
dialogue that oral history demands. In this case I think it is instructive to compare oral history with works in quantification.

In the latter case historians and statisticians have developed and used models of the most rigorous elegance and sophistication and have asked the most mundane of questions. In oral history we have used the simplest and most naive theory and method to ask the most significant questions about human and class relationships in the past. For the most part we have been satisfied with comments such as those of Studs Terkel in *Hard Times* when he writes, "This is a memory book not a history." Yet, as Michael Frisch notes, Terkel is far more aware of the problem posed than his critics and reviewers have been.[9]

Because we have not generally paid attention to these questions we are now faced with the problem of how to evaluate oral history when we have no conception of what standards are or ought to be. Such considerations are far more important than even our rhetoric assumes them to be. For example, how are we to evaluate a proposed project which seeks to capture the consciousness of change rather than simply document such change? Can we say with certainty that this is something which oral history can do? Do we know how to do it? Is there a theoretical body of information to which we can turn? What methods of collection should be used to gather such information? Will the returns on the investment be as rich as a more practical or mundane project? How can we judge this question, or any of these questions, when for the most part we are operating by the seats of our pants?

The path open to us in some respects is clear. What we oral historians, who are concerned about these questions, must do now is to pick up on the discussion in Friedlander's Introduction and begin to ask questions about the linguistic and cognitive structure of historical memory and dialogue. Beyond that we have to search for some view of the role of history in the culture in general and among different populations in particular. For this task we shall have to reach out to folklorists and anthropologists or others who use fieldwork interviews. Especially will we have to familiarize ourselves with the literature in psychology which discusses memory, its formation, maintenance and its role in human life.

In all of this there are several problems unique to oral history which must be kept in mind, for all of them bear directly upon any theoretical formulations which we may or may not derive from our experiences. First, the documents we produce are not the product of the age we are investigating; they are the products of the here and now. As Frisch has correctly noted about *Hard Times*, it is not a set of documents of the Thirties, but it is data about what the Sixties remembers of or thinks of life in the Thirties. As such it cannot avoid being influenced by memory and how the experience of the Depression was explained by members of the culture during the 1940s and 1950s. Any discussion of oral history must take cognizance of the facts of its creation now, and of how the now informs the discussion of the then. In short how history lives as a field of experience and expression.

Secondly we must realize that in many cases our interviewing forces people to make their lives anthropologically strange. We ask people to justify actions and ideas which they in the course of their lives never dreamed needed justification. We thus force people into history in very unique ways. To understand this phenomenon and the effects it has on the materials we collect and what special opportunities for analysis it presents us should be one of our main priorities, especially if we are, as we say we are, concerned about consciousness.

Also we must be aware of the individualizing or alienating tendency of oral history; how it by its nature asks people to personalize events and experiences. Oral history, based as it is on a one to one personal dialogue, often reinforces the tendency in American historiography to see institutions and social forces as secondary to human will. If we are not careful we can distort the past in much more subtle ways than through our own biases and will come to view that past as simply one more version of Protestant individualism.

We live in an age fascinated with standards, their maintenance, their destruction or their alteration. In oral history this
may simply be a reflection of the fact that we have moved into
middle age and now wish to somehow control the actions and
activities of those who are adolescents in the field and who are
building upon what we have already done. Perhaps it is simply a reflection of our new-found respectability. In any case,
no matter what the motivation, the call for standards can best
be met by sitting back and honestly assessing what it is that
we have done, what are the problems with the work which we
have produced, how do we now establish some forum for discussion of that evaluation, doing it, and then moving forward
into our forties with a bit more confidence.

Footnotes

1. Alan Meckler and Ruth McMullin, *Oral History Collections* (New York: R. R. Bowker, 1975).

2. Cullum Davis, Kathryn Back, and Kay MacLean, *Oral History: From Tape to Type* (Chicago: American Library Association, 1977).

3. Barbara Tuchman, "Distinguishing the Significant from the Insignificant," *Radcliffe Quarterly* 56 (October 1972), 9-10.

4. Charles T. Morrissey, "Oral History and the California Wine Industry: A Review Essay," *Agricultural History* 61 (July 1977), 590-96.

5. Theodore Rosengarten, *All God's Dangers* (New York: Knopf, 1974); Kathy Kahn, *Hillbilly Women* (Garden City, N.Y.: Doubleday, 1973).

6. Henry D. Shapiro, *Appalachia On Our Mind* (Chapel Hill: University of North Carolina Press, 1978).

7. Laurel Schakelford and William Weinberg, *Our Appalachia* (New York: Hill and Wang, 1978).

8. Rosengarten, *op. cit.*; Peter Friedlander, *The Making of a UAW Local* (Pittsburgh: University of Pittsburgh Press, 1975); Martin Duberman, *Black Mountain: An Exploration in Community* (Garden City, N.Y.: Doubleday, 1976); Helen Gallagher, *Hannah's Daughters* (Garden City, N.Y.: Doubleday, 1976); Kahn, *op. cit.*; Schakelford and Weinberg, *op. cit.*; Harry Williams, *Huey Long* (New York: Random House, 1973).

9. Studs Terkel, *Hard Times: An Oral History of the Depression* (New York: Pantheon, 1970); Michael Frisch, "Oral History and *Hard Times*," *Red Buffalo*, n.d., pp. 217-231.

**Listen to Their Voices: Two Case Studies in the
Interpretation of Oral History Interviews**

I

Most works of historical analysis which use oral history interviews have accented, quite correctly, the documentary aspects of those interviews. When used carefully and creatively in this manner interviews have been able to shed new light on once obscure historical processes. They have presented us with a new and different kind of evidence about the behavior of people in the past; evidence which has often forced us to re-evaluate our conceptions of that past. They have also provided a rich source for the documentation of the ambiance and context which surrounded events, and particularly the context of the lives of people who would not have otherwise been noted by historians.

All of this has been work that has enriched our under-standing of our past. However, aside from Michael Frisch's remarkable review essay on *Hard Times* and the recent work of Peter Friedlander,[1] historians have not yet tried to analyze and grasp the underlying structure of consciousness which both governs and informs oral history interviews. Although many oral historians have discussed the necessity of undertaking such an analysis, few have tried. This essay is an attempt to begin the task using two of the interviews collected for the New York City College Oral History Research Project.

The theoretical and methodological basis of the method employed here has been outlined elsewhere in some detail.[2] Briefly, what this essay attempts to do is seek the particular vision of history articulated in an interview, outline its struc-ture, and speculate upon the consequences of such a vision and structure and how it helps us to understand the people we are interviewing and their historical point of view. Hopefully this will allow us to understand how the interview functions as an historical narrative and what the deeper meaning of that narrative is.

In formal terms the type of analysis outlined here is paradigmatic, in that it seeks to isolate a pattern around which the segments of the narrative can be grouped according to a logical formulation of the problem stated in the interview. The analysis is phenomenological, rational and logical; it seeks to order the complexity of the information being presented, by discovering the assumed structure of that presentation.

The City College Oral History Project, directed by Professors Virginia Yans and Herbert Gutman, was established under a grant from the National Endowment for the Humanities. The goal of the Project was to document the history of various segments of working class New York City. To this end interviewers were trained and sent into the field with a fairly precise and fairly well defined set of questions based upon the research interests of the group. Unlike archival projects or more established oral history projects, we did not seek to collect autobiographical narratives, but rather to establish a collection of information—a data bank—on certain limited topics.

For this reason not all of the interviews in the City College collection lend themselves to the kind of analysis proposed here, and the two chosen have been selected for very specific reasons. Both of these interviews contain within themselves a more or less fully developed narrative structure. Unlike many of our interviews, they are more than simply a set of responses to a varied set of questions which were asked in line with specific research interests. Both contain lengthy and *seemingly* extraneous narrative sections which allow us to view the historical perspectives which lie beyond specific responses. In addition, the people interviewed, while not extraordinary story-tellers, are capable of complex inventions and historical speculation about their testimony and its meaning. Also, both are Jewish and thus we can be somewhat more comparative than had we selected interviews from a wider variety of ethnic or minority respondents.[3]

Most importantly these two interviews have been selected because they contain internal evidence that the interviewees had thought about their interviews and the form of those interviews. We therefore know more about the creation of these interviews than of others and can accept them as conscious attempts to tell a tale.

Both interviewees, Mel Dubin and Bella Pincus,[4] had been contacted about an interview at least two weeks prior to the interview and both had obviously thought about the interview, what they would say, and in what form they would say it. Bella had already told her tale off-tape to another interviewer some weeks prior to taping and states so in her interview:

Was you here when they interviewed? All the students? Was you here?

Yes.

When I told the story from the strike?[5]

More straightforward is the interview with Mel Dubin which opens as he is formulating his narrative and outlining the method by which he will proceed:

I'll tell you as I go along. I'll talk as if I'm telling a story. You know what I mean?[6]

Such facts of creation are important because they provide evidence of the initiative of the interviewee in formulating the structure of the interview. It can, of course, be argued that every interview is so constructed, but it is not often that we have such clear evidence of that initiative.

Given the obvious intentions and the rather forceful personalities of both Mel and Bella, it is not surprising that both interviews are more than simply question and answer sessions. Each interviewee has a tendency to return again and again to the main thrust of his or her story, despite the sometimes strained efforts of the interviewers to control the situation and to divert them to other questions of more interest to the project.

Ironically, it is this failure of the interviewers to manipulate the interviews which makes the analysis which we seek to pursue possible.

As already stated, the focus of our initial inquiry here is the historical presentation contained in the interviews and its formal structure, around which we shall try to group other elements of the narrative. In the interview with Mel Dubin the structure of historical presentation is fairly clear and obvious. It is in form a chronological narrative of his life, his working career, and his career in the International Ladies Garment Workers Union. This narrative contains, however, at least four different historical strands; his own autobiography, the history of the organization and success of the ILGWU, a history of the garment industry, and a brief history of the City of New York.

The autobiographical narrative is clear and uncomplicated. Including a discussion of the work processes of a cutter, it is the most fully developed aspect of the interview. Born in 1894 on the Lower East Side of New York, the son of immigrant Jews, Mel Dubin was one of seven children. His family, all of whom except his mother worked, was poor, and shortly after graduation from grammar school Mel went to work in the garment industry. Drafted during World War I, he returned to work in 1919 and eventually became a marker and a cutter, both highly skilled trades in the industry.[7] While still a young man he attended classes at the Rand School and studied with Algernon Lee, an experience which he claims helped him in his union work as a business agent of the ILGWU. During the 1920s he developed his skills as a cutter and became active in the Union as an organizer both in Manhattan and in Brooklyn. He eventually became a member of the Executive Board of the cutters' local branch, president of the Joint Board and in 1948 a paid ILGWU business agent.

He was also interested in politics and at one time (the late 1940s or early 1950s on the basis of the evidence) was selected by the Citizens Union and the Liberal Party as a candidate for election to the New York State Assembly. Now retired and a member of the Retired Officers Club of the Union, he is somewhat nostalgic about his past experience, says he misses the old faces, and takes a keen interest in the history of the ILGWU.

Closely interwoven with this autobiographical account is a series of vignettes about New York City, which when placed next to one another give a brief history of the City. Focusing upon various neighborhoods, which is the typical form taken by such descriptions in most of our tapes, Mel notes his early life on the Lower East Side, the hustle and bustle of the Garment District when he worked there, and concludes with a brief description of the affluence of the City during the prosperous days of that industry. Heavily nostalgic, each description gives us some insight into what will become the dominant themes of the interview.

The East Side, as Mel remembers it, was a poor but safe neighborhood, "where everybody and anybody was able to walk the streets without turning their head, without fear." It was an area where there was indeed crime but where "those gangsters would never bother anybody."[8] It was also a neighborhood of minimal anti-Semitism. While Mel does describe the poverty of the area, the burden of his description is an implied comparison with New York City today and is formally a series of contrasts between then and now, with then obviously better than now.

The same contrast between then and now is more explicit when Mel discusses the Garment District as he remembers it when he was a young man. Once a thriving section of the city filled with workers and restaurants, it is now, to Mel, deserted, the restaurants closed and its future bleak. "I don't know what is going to happen to Seventh Avenue," he at one point laments.

In this discussion of the Lower East Side and the Garment District, we can discern three themes which will be repeated again and again during the interview: the binary opposition of then and now, a view of now as a state of decline and end of a cycle, and lastly the isolation of the particular cause of that

decline. In this particular case New York is declining because
its prosperity was based upon "an industry that's coming to a
close, and just like Detroit and automobiles, when one fails so
must the other."[9] But the district is also closing down

> ... because those people who work there now in the
> industry bring their own lunches with them or they go
> to Chock Full o' Nuts and have a hot dog and a cup of
> coffee, or the Automat. Those restaurants prospered from
> us . . . . [10]

The same themes are articulated even more clearly in Mel's
discussion of the history of the Union. As Mel tells it, the
ILGWU was firmly established in 1910 after the great strike
of that year. After that date the history of the Union, to Mel,
is remarkably quiet, even and progressive. Led by a group of
outstanding leaders who built upon that strike, the Union was
able to continue to organize workers, sometimes against great
odds, secure better working conditions and better pay, and put
an end to the "real slavery" of the sweat shops.[11] Despite some
notice of difficulties in organization, Mel's account ignores
every strike except that of 1910, ignores the struggles of the
1930s and the bitter strife between socialists and communists
and left and right in the Union during that period. His
narration describes three decades of continual improvement
secured by the Union, by the movement of the industry
into better constructed shops and by the actions of "public
spirited citizens" in securing the enactment and enforcement
of various building codes. This is a remarkable example of
consensus historiography, as in Mel's view the Union and the
manufacturer's association in concert stabilize the industry.
    But to Mel, a high point was reached in the late 40s and
early 50s and the end of the tale is equally fascinating. It is a
tale of unrelieved woe since that time. The Union is declining,
losing members as shops move out of the City and as imports
undermine heretofore safe markets. Locals are disappearing

into one large administrative structure, and the will and fire of members is fading. Once again we are presented with a tale of rise and decline, but now we are able to date the cycles of this pattern with greater historical precision.

The same pattern is even more fully articulated in Mel's history of the garment industry. Once a great complex employing hundreds of thousands and paying substantial wages upon which the greatness of the City rested, the industry now is a mere shadow of itself and in a few years will leave the City completely, except for a few show rooms.

> The industry is shrinking for the reason that the stores, the fine stores like Altman's and Lord and Taylor and others who depend upon the fine garment, the expensive garment for their clientele—it's not very easy to get the garment today because the employers became old, passed off. The designers became old, passed off the scene. The workers, the help became old, died, retired.

> Immigrants to the United States from Italy which had a lot of hand-made, fine tailors and the Russian tailor—there's no immigration. The Jews are clamoring only to go to Israel. Very few come here. And they were the tailors that was taught, and handed down from family to family and they worked at home, made it by hand. And the same with the Italians.[12]

What Mel Dubin is really saying here is crucial to our understanding of the world view which governs his narrative. The decline of the industry has been caused by the end of an era of immigration, for it was these immigrants who created the industry, and they can never again be replaced. The industry upon which the City was built rested for its greatness upon this one generation of Jews and Italians, and now that they are passing from the scene the industry, the Union and the City are collapsing.

What has occurred at this point in the interview is a phenomenon familiar to every fieldworker: we have been given an answer to a question which has never been asked, and we must now supply the question. The surface question is obvious enough—what is the cause of the decline of the industry? But the answer given to that question contains within itself an even deeper question: what was the origin of the greatness of the industry—and therefore the origin of the historical proceses under investigation, here the rise and decline of the industry? And the answer is: the history, as related here, had its chronological and logical beginnings when Jews and Italians learned to sew and to pass that skill down from generation to generation. Somewhere in the deep recesses of the past, when Jews and Italians perfected these particular skills, Mel's history begins.

What we see created here is a mythic past out of which historical processes emerge, but a very special kind of myth, which functions in very particular ways to give a dynamic to the tale, and leads inevitably to certain very real conclusions about the nature of the world of the garment industry today. It is an etiological and charter myth. Etiological, because it fixes an origin and cause to a particular process or event; and charter, because it fixes something "in a tradition to establish its relevance and true entity . . . . " and provides "emotional support for an attitude or belief."[13]

That this view is not factually or historically correct— that the economy of New York City has never rested solely on one industry, that this view ignores the 59,000 garment workers counted by the United States Census of 1880 which was taken before Jews and Italians came to New York in large numbers[14]—is not the issue. The point of the myth is not historical in the sense of its factual content, but ideological, in that it uses a mythic past to ascribe to one group and that group alone the morals, the value system, the set of talents and abilities which make it possible for them to bear the burden of history. In this case a generation of Jews and Italians with a very special history and a very special mission migrated to the United States, created an industry, a Union, and a city (and along the way Mel Dubin).[15] Now that they are passing from the scene, the world which they created must pass with them.

In the narrative this myth of origins and charter is given a historical dynamic over time, and transformed into an explanation of the present upon which a rather bleak future is predicted. In this process these mythic elements become the basis of an ideological statement of potent force.[16] If we accept the basic assumptions of this view (either on an emotive or cognitive level) then it seems obvious that those who now stand to inherit the industry, the Union, and the City—blacks and Puerto Ricans—cannot bear the burden of history or of the culture. They are unqualified because they have not participated in the crucial mythico-historical experience of Minsk or Calabria. Neither do they possess the talents necessary to assume that burden, for they have not been taught these skills from generation to generation, and therefore cannot make the fine garment. Newcomers, in this view, cannot be the well from which renewal will spring, but are rather the symptoms of the decline of just about everything.

What do you have now? Twelve to thirteen million illegal aliens. So you can imagine . . . .

Today it's all Puerto Ricans and blacks. The contractors prefer Puerto Ricans because they can do anything they want with them.[17]

Explicitly in these statements and others, some of which we have already cited, and by implication, Mel ascribes to these groups of people the responsibility for crime in New York City. They also violate Union rules, in that they are poorly organized. In essence they simply cannot bear the great historical mission of the culture. Yet, because of the waning of migration from Italy and Russia, they now fill the industry. Thus the bleak future for Mel.

The interview with Mel Dubin, as a document containing evidence of the past of the garment industry, is primarily a discussion of work processes, and it does shed light on questions which are still somewhat vague. The power of the interview, however, lies in the imagination of Mel and how he uses that imagination to construct a history. It is at this deeper level of discourse, where myth becomes history and history becomes ideology, that we find the consciousness—false perhaps but consciousenss nonetheless—that informs the material which has been presented to us.

Through the examination of this historical narrative, we can begin to see the structure of the imagination which forms that narrative. We have isolated four distinct histories, all of which exhibit in one form or another the same pattern of rise and decline, and all of which are united by the basic mythic vision. Thus it is perfectly logical that certain omissions and distortions should appear in the narrative. With such a vision of progressive rise prior to the 1950s and decline afterwards, the 1920s and 30s must be integrated into that rather mechanical vision of progress. Also 1910 rather than 1930 must be seen as the crucial moment in the history of the Union, for it is then that this very special generation begins to articulate, in action, its mission in history. It is that action, after all, not the general strike of 1934, not Franklin D. Roosevelt, and not the Wagner Act which creates the Union.

There are other sections of the interview which can be examined closely to show us this pattern and its consequences. One of the most interesting is a by-play between Mel and his student interviewer which catches both in the contradictions of their ideologies, and shows us how historical events can be used to buttress those ideologies. In this excerpt Mel is asked when the Union was able to negotiate the end of Saturday work in the garment industry:

A: 1938, 40, 41.

Q: That late?

A: Yes, it was that late. Uh. It was a little earlier than that. I don't know.

What makes this dialogue ideological rather than simply an attempt at precise historical verification, is that prior to this moment we have been presented with no evidence upon which we would be able to base a judgment as to whether that victory was either early or late. Therefore that judgment depends entirely upon what each participant views as early or late. To the interviewer, who obviously believes that a more militant stance would have brought reform earlier, 1940 is late. To Mel, who views the accomplishments of the Union in a progressive evolutionary manner, it is difficult to admit that 1940 was late and so he pleads ignorance to protect that view. But then how few of us are really concerned with the pastness of the past?

II

Aside from its origins, the fact that both are Jewish, and a certain agreement on ideology, Bella Pincus's interview is quite unlike that conducted with Mel Dubin. It contains none of the chronology, the historical generalization, or clearly delineated structures. Yet it is equally fascinating in its own terms.

Born in 1893 or 1895 in a small village in Russian Poland, Bella came to the United States in 1911 at the age of seventeen (the seeming contradiction is explained by a vagueness over the year of birth and the month of arrival) to find a husband. Having learned to sew when she worked for nothing in a small shop in her village, Bella became a machine operator in the garment industry three weeks after her arrival. She lived first with an uncle, and then with a brother and his wife, until her marriage in 1918. After twelve years of married life, during which time she did not work, her husband died in an accident and she was left with four children. At this time she returned to work where she stayed until her retirement. Always a socialist, she was an active participant in the strikes and struggles of the Union, and at one time was arrested for her militancy on the picket line. Now retired, she was at the time of the interview involved in organizing the residents of the nursing home where she lives in order to secure reforms in the selection of meals. Her two children of whom she speaks attended City College and New York University; one is a teacher, the other a businessman.

The interview itself contains rich descriptions of life in a small Russian village at the turn of the century, the Lower East Side, work in garment factories in both Russia and the United States, and the family life of working class Jews. Her recollections are more unstructured and less formally ordered than those of Mel Dubin, and a much wider range of issues is touched upon in a briefer time span. This scattering is probably the result of the techniques of the interviewer, who was seeking specific answers to specific research questions, and had a tendency to break off the narrative flow in order to move on to another question, or to divert Bella from what he obviously believed to be tangential remarks. Despite this, Bella herself is such a dynamic woman that she ofttimes simply overpowers her questioner and completes her tale. It is in these sections that we are able to begin to grasp the deeper structure which informs her testimony.

In Mel Dubin's interview the basic binary opposition which appeared in the narrative was the contrast between then and now—a fairly common opposition in the interviews which we have conducted and probably quite common on other projects. In Bella's interview we find the same juxtaposition, but it is stated in a much more complex manner, and exhibits a fascinating set of mediating variables. The key to these

variations is found in her recollection of how she felt when
she viewed New York for the first time.

> The United States?   I was surprised.   The first thing
> surprised me right away when I saw the houses hadn't
> got no (peaked) roofs.   In Europe the house is fixed up
> with a roof and it's nice.   In the middle is like a chimney
> where they light a stove, you know, and the smoke comes
> out.   And here it was strange, and that was right away
> surprising and strange to me.
>
> And another thing surprised me when I saw lines with
> clothes in the street.   So I said to my uncle I says . . .
> (explanation of why she spoke in Yiddish).   So I says: "This
> is America?   The *Grete im Droysen* (the laundry out in
> the open) and . . . a house without a roof."   So he laughed.
>
> I remember in Europe when my mother made a wash she
> hung it in a—you climb a ladder in a house.   You call it
> like, let's say a penthouse.   But that was nothing.   Only
> things were kept there like sources   they used to keep
> it up there like a pantry.   And *there* she used to hang the
> clothes.   There we had like lines . . . Inside.   Nobody saw
> anything outside.   Nobody!   But here it struck me funny.
> And then, you know, such a little incident like that which
> I never saw before.
>
> Of certain foods that I never saw before which my aunt
> gave me to eat . . . .   (Here she relates a tale of her first
> banana and how she had difficulty in opening it and a
> fear of breaking it.)
>
> And then I saw certain things that you don't see now.   At
> that time, you know, when they used to collect the garbage
> there were street cleaners.   They used to clean the streets
> and put it in a barrel and when the garbage truck came

they used to put it in an open garbage truck. You don't
see it now. Nothing is open.

Another thing . . . a bus with two horses. And car fare was
only five cents. And on Fifth Avenue they had an open
coach, double coach. We used to ride. A double decker.
A double decker. We used to climb up. We didn't want
to be inside so we climbed up. And also on Lexington
Avenue ran a streetcar. It wasn't closed doors like now,
the buses, you open up the door . . . . We used to sit and
you saw everything that passed by, which you don't see
here anymore.[18]

In spite of interruptions by the interviewer and an aside on
Yiddish usage among young Jews, there is a remarkable con-
sistency of image and theme in this passage. When examined
closely, each element is based upon the opposition of open and
closed—in the sense of inside and outside—and each is a variation of this theme. The open roofs of the buildings of New
York, compared to the closed roofs of the village from which
she had emigrated; the American laundry flaunted shamelessly
and democratically in the open, contrasted with the closed pri-
vacy of Europe; the problem of opening a banana; the open
garbage trucks and streetcars in New York when she arrived,
contrasted to the closed vehicles of today.

As evidence of historical fact all of this is trivial and well-
known information. We know about the roofs and streetcars
and the laundry in New York, even the problem that immigrants had with bananas. This is not new information. What
makes the passage so fascinating is that over space and time,
Bella has reconstructed her past through this poetry as a series
of variations of the opposition between open and closed, to give
us the sense of openness she felt in her own life when she was
a young girl in New York, compared to her life in Russia, and
to her life now as an old and ill retired person.

Elsewhere in the interview the same opposition appears again and again. The closed dark shop of Russia is contrasted to the open and bright shops of New York, Russian weddings held outside are compared to American weddings held inside. And, of course, the main point and dramatic climax of her interview—her arrest and incarceration—is simply another variation on the same theme.

When viewed in this light that experience as related by Bella has several interesting sidelights. Jailed after she was arrested on the charge of spitting at a policeman, a charge which she still denies, Bella contrasts her attitude with that of her cellmate, an Italian girl arrested at the same time. Bella is optimistic because she knows she is in the right and that the Union will attempt to get her released. She is aware of the possibility of release from a closed universe. Her Italian compatriot is depressed and tearful over her shame and fear of jailing and Bella tries to comfort her to no avail. Again we have the contrast between open and closed, not only personalised but in a somewhat dialectic juxtaposition, for it is her union activity which has both brought her to jail and will also free her

To understand Bella and her historical narrative on its own terms we must try to fathom this structural opposition, and trace its implications as revealed in the rest of her testimony. On the most obvious level, Bella's comparisons and contrasts offer new evidence of the exhilaration and sense of freedom which must have been felt by millions of immigrants as they compared their lives in America with their closed lives in Europe. No matter how desperate the privations and how necessary the struggles, Bella remembers that sense of openness and possibility. We get some idea of this mixed reaction in her descriptions of factory work when she was a young girl:

The first day I was very much surprised. I didn't know where to look first. There were so many machines there, and dresses, and finishers, and examiners. Those that cut

around the collar, you know, on ladies' waists—we used
to make the waists—they used to go around the collar so
quick, quick, quick.

I said to my future sister-in-law, I says, "Everything looks
to me so comical. I don't know where to look first." She
said, "You'll get used to it. I got used to it. We all get used
to it."[19]

Without hearing the tape it is difficult to describe how this
last sentence introduces a sense of limit and finality into the
description. Said in a sing-song Jewish or New York accent and
inflection, it seems more a lamentation than a word of advice,
and definitely gives an impression of acceptance and fatalism.
      Yet Bella continues,

The Factory . . . amused me. I liked it. I liked it. I had
a lot of people to talk to, a lot of people to look at. They
used to make jokes. They used to sing Russian songs which
I knew all what they said, you know. I know Russian. And
it amused me, you know, all the Greenhorns!

Yet even here the contrasts and contradictions continue,
for Bella's world is a world wherein the same institutions and
events contain the qualities of open and closed. The factory
which she enjoyed was also a place where,

We had a poor life. We were like slaves and we didn't
want that and that's why we were striking.

We couldn't talk, you couldn't take a sh . . . —forgive the
expression—you couldn't go to the bathroom without the
forelady following you, you couldn't eat an apple in the
afternoon. Is that human?[20]

Thus while the factory impressed her as open and freer than her life in Russia, it was not a place where contradictions did not exist nor a place where struggle was no longer necessary.

On another level Bella's socialism is consistent with her view of the past as the arena for the opposition of open and closed, a past where the struggle is a constant attempt to free oneself. To Bella socialism is freedom of a very specific form.

> The Union? Well we were good fighters. We were true to the Union. We'd fight for our rights. And in general that's what it really means. Socialism means that we should have—we don't say that the rich people should give away everything that they have. But we should have a fair share, that we should make a fair living—not in luxury, but a living. Right? That's what means socialism.

Like her view of the shop and her definition of socialism Bella's historical world is a world of limits. There is no progress as there was in Mel Dubin's view, for at a certain level things never change and therefore neither does the struggle.

> If you have money, you have money. It's always the same. Ever since the world is it's rich and poor, and struggling and well off. That's how it is. Sure![21]

Despite the victory of the Union and the securing of better conditions in the last half of a century, in Bella's consciousness lies the deep underlying belief that some things do not change, that there is a constancy in history and that progress has, at any one time, its limits. Almost as if to punctuate this sense of limits, Bella tends to end her sentences and phrases with emphatic markers which signify the end of discussion, the limits to the dialogue. "That's the way it is." "That's the way it was." "And that's how we lived." Such phrases and expressions give a finality and a sense of closeness to the narrative itself so that form and content reinforce one another. These phrases, however, are not markers of desperation. The interview itself is fundamentally dramatic in form. Each element posits an eternal contrast between open and closed, and a constant struggle between freedom and slavery.

As expected, given this theme, Bella's interview contains many references to the special nature of the Jewish immigrants of her generation, and their special role in building the Union as part of their struggles against Tsarism. On the surface, her attitudes are somewhat similar to those of Mel Dubin, as she compares that generation to those who belong to the Union today:

> We were the ones who made the Union . . . the people who came from Russia, all the girls and boys. They were socialists, like fighters, because over there they were always fighting Tsarists and Tsarism. Everybody knows. That's really in history what was doing in Russia *mit* the cossacks and pogroms and all that. And we are really the fighters. We made the Union. They even say it now, that it's the people that died out and the people that retired are the Union people.

> What have they got there now? All these Puerto Ricans and the *Schwartza*. They're not Union people like we were. All right maybe they pay dues. Maybe? They have to pay dues but it doesn't have any more power like when we were there. They were really afraid of us. The bosses were really afraid of us because we were never forgetting. We were always on the working side for the people. And no matter what kind of worker you were we were all together.

> We put up a very strong union.

And:

We made the Union, all those European girls and boys made the Union. Otherwise there still wouldn't be no Union now. And they had very good leaders. Dubinsky was our president . . . . At that time it was very nice. It was all Jewish, you know.[22]

Although her ideological point here is quite similar to, if not the same in thrust as that made by Mel Dubin, there are several differences which must be noted. Most obvious is the fact that the special mission of this generation of Jews, in Bella's view, was not formed in some mythic past beyond the reaches of memory, but rather in a specific historical past—the events of Tsarism. As Bella says these "are really in history" and "true." Secondly what the Jews develop out of that experience, while special, is not a set of unique qualities. They develop very real human characteristics which allow them to secure and exercise power: they don't forget, they side with the working class, they build a strong union and make the bosses fearful. All of these qualities are capable of being attained by other oppressed peoples in other times or as a result of other historical circumstances and can be duplicated.

Another difference is in Bella's concept of power, which rests upon the organization of the masses. While Mel Dubin recognizes the necessity of organizing, and indeed was an organizer, in his interview he lays great stress upon electoral politics, the necessity of bureaucratic procedures which he learned at the Rand School, and the good will of "public spirited citizens." None of these elements of power impresses Bella. When asked about electoral politics, she recalls voting for Norman Thomas and "Alf Landon" (who she says ran as a Socialist candidate for Congress from New York and must obviously be Meyer London). Bella also notes that "around here it's always the same," for even if the Socialists won, the "people behind them would not allow them to do the right things for the people." To Bella power originates in people opening their world for themselves, not in elections and the good graces of officials.

III

Irving Howe has written brilliantly and perceptively about the special sense of history developed by this generation of Jews and the special sense of mission derived from that view of history. He has also argued quite persuasively that their socialism and their commitment to unionization was the result of this vision, and not simply one mode among many for the acculturation of that generation.[23] Yet Howe has failed to note the consequences which flow from these variations. It is therefore important and instructive to speculate upon the meaning of the two views which we have presented here.

Although their current ideological positions are, in at least one case, quite similar, Mel Dubin and Bella Pincus are very different people. Mel was born in this country, attended school here, was drafted into the American army, involved himself in the American electoral process, and worked in a more or less administrative position within a major American institutional environment. Bella is the product of Tsarist Russia, and many of her views remain those of that time and those experiences. She is far less assimilated into the dominant culture than Mel. She uses Yiddish as readily as English, and shifts from one to the other with ease. She remains a socialist in the same sense that she became a socialist as a young girl. Her allegiances are to the Yiddish theatre, Union struggles and her family, not to the institutions of the larger society.

What concerns us here is the relationship between these divergent experiences and the views of history which emerge when both Mel and Bella organize their lives into historical narratives, for each uses history in a very different manner to ground that narrative in the past. Thus each has viewed the world from a different problematic and while we would be hard pressed to argue that either vision is exactly typical of large numbers of American workers, when we try to relate these visions to the lives of the narrators certain larger themes do emerge.

We have, in essence, been presented with two different views of historical process: one a cyclical view of progress and decline, the other a more dramatic view of eternally contending binary oppositions. The first is a view which contains a vision of progress in history, the second a view of the past which poses a set of limits and unchanging verities. Such views, although stated in very original terms, are not idiosyncratic. Both are held by large numbers of people, and have been examined in detail elsewhere for their implications.[24] Aside from these implications, both views are heavily laden with ideological consequences. Despite the fact that they are different people, and the structures of the narratives are quite different, both Mel and Bella seem to end up arguing the same point—that the present problems of the Union and the City are the result of the fading away of an older generation and their replacement on the stage of history by black and Puerto Rican newcomers.

Yet the stage as it is perceived by each is different. To Mel the stage is a point in a process of rise and decline. To Bella it is an arena of dramatic conflict. And this difference does allow us to understand each and to begin our search for the underlying structure of the interviews and their histories as they have formulated them.

Before beginning that search, however, it is necessary to deal with at least one commonsensical consideration. Both Mel and Bella when they structure their histories begin with a basic contrast between then and now. While we can argue that this is the beginning of some sort of historical consciousness, it may also simply reflect the age of both people. It could be argued, and has been, that what we have here is the nostalgia of the elderly for the days of their youth. This may be, but any full exposition of this argument would have to

begin with considerations far beyond the limits of this paper—
considerations of the complex relationships between nostalgia
and consciousness which at this time cannot be delineated
with precision. In any case, what is here so intriguing is not
the dichotomy between then and now, but the manner of its
expression, the form it takes, and the capacity for generating
complex structures which each interview exhibits.

Also there are more interesting questions about origins to
be asked. Mel Dubin's view of history and its structural presentation seems to be heavily influenced by what professional
historians would term "liberal consensus historiography." Even
if we agree that he is simply an old man looking on his past
with nostalgia, it is significant that Mel held a progressive vision
of history in an age of progressivism and a vision of decline
in the age of Niehbuhr. It is also significant that in the 1970s,
the age of the Moynihan Report, this vision should have the
explicitly racist context that it does. There seems no doubt that
this historical presentation is ultimately and heavily influenced
by popular views of history. It is thus another index of Mel
Dubin's participation in the hegemonic ethos of his times.

But beyond this, the complexity of the vision exhibits a
competence at historical formulation which gives us a greater
insight into just how these popular conceptions can be transformed to answer the immediate and personal needs of historical explanation. For as E. J. Hobsbawm has noted, most often
a view of the past is "essentially the pattern for the present."[25]
It also shows us how the past becomes usable to someone who
has not necessarily thought about that past in historical terms.
It is the structure and form rather than the specifics which give
us this insight.

While on one level Bella's narrative would seem to be more
historical and less mythic than that of Mel ("It's in history,
and true"), it is really almost non-historical. In Bella's vision
there is no change over time. History is rather a series of
dramatic episodes, each repeating the other, and all exhibiting
the same moral lesson of struggle. In this sense her vision

is basically static and this stasis is used to give force and vigor to her own explanation of her own life. But again it is the structure of the history which reveals the complexity of the history itself. To Bella there is a limit to change over time, yet the special characteristic of her memory of the past is the very real historical experience of oppression, and the drama of history is the struggle between that oppression and freedom as that struggle reveals itself in historical events. If Mel Dubin's historical narrative is an index of his participation in the dominant culture, Bella's is an index of her isolation from that culture. Her view of her own life over time remains, in a sense, folkloristic or prehistorical. Even at that point where it could become historical—her socialism—it retains its basic static nature and, in effect, defines socialism in terms of its own structure, not that of socialist theoreticians—a phenomenon which we may find is generally observable among the American working class.

What we are presented with in these two interviews are two different ways in which ordinary garment workers structure their histories and the past itself. Obviously, these two examples do not exhaust the possibilities of such structuring. Frisch and Friedlander have both shown other ways in which it is possible to see such structuring. Frisch's major insight is to show us how Terkel's respondents in *Hard Times* divorce themselves from history by turning history into biography and thereby personalizing events.[26] To Friedlander the particular historical structure leads not to an ahistorical mythic explanation but to an ideological consciousness derived from praxis and capable of penetrating insight.[27] What we now need are more studies which would allow us to say with some precision what the limits to such structuring are, and how each relates to the other at particular moments of time and within the context of particular events.

Because we lack such studies, we do not yet have enough evidence to state with any clarity or precision what it is that accounts for the differences among the various ways in which the past is structured and used—how myth becomes history and history becomes myth, and how each is transformed into ideology. The rules however seem clear. Whether history is one form of myth, or a form of ideological thought—or something unto itself[28]—the peculiar relationship of the three is the matrix of the deep structure of historical cognition, which generates the complex surface structures which explain experience. What is also clear is that ideological utterance is a talent, skill or attribute widely shared in our culture, available equally to presidents and working class garment workers.

Also, what we can say on the basis of rather limited evidence is that the process of oral history interviewing, because it involves the structuring of memory and because meaningfulness influences the construction processes of memory, is actually a process in the construction of a usable past. In this manner, when used in this way, oral history can live up to the promise of "Everyman his own historian."

What also seems beyond doubt is that relatively obscure people do create their own history, and they do so within their own conceptions of its value and use in the culture. Mel Dubin and Bella Pincus were not formally instructed by the agencies of the larger culture on how they should view their world and their own lives and pasts. That they did so anyway and in such a complex fashion is some indication of the rich and vital culture out of which they emerged as personalities, and for which they have become bearers. The fact of the existence of such complex structures of historical memory is also an indication of the enormous amount of work we must do as social historians, if we are to begin to comprehend working class culture by transforming oral autobiographies into general historical statements, and as oral historians if we are to create the documents upon which that comprehension will be based.

Footnotes

1. Michael Frisch, "Oral History and *Hard Times*," *Red Buffalo*, Vols. 1 and 2, n.d., 217-231; Peter Friedlander, *The Emergence of a UAW Local: A Study in Class and Culture*, Pittsburgh, University of Pittsburgh Press, 1975.

2. Ronald Grele, "A Surmisable Variety: Interdisciplinarity and Oral Testimony," *American Quarterly* (August 1975), 275-295. See Ch. V.

3. For a brief discussion of this methodology, see Svata Pirkova-Jakobson, "Introduction," in V. Propp, *Morphology of the Folktale*, 2nd Edition, Austin, Texas, University of Texas Press, 1968, pp. xi-xii.

4. Real names have not been used in this essay. For those seeking to verify the quotations used in this essay the interviews are I-106, 107 and I-30 and 31 of the collection of the City College Oral History Research Project.

5. Interview with Bella Pincus (hereafter BP), Cassette 1, Side 1.

6. Interview with Mel Dubin (hereafter MD), Cassette 1, Side 1.

7. He calls himself a mechanic as do many of our interviewees. When asked to define this term he indicates that a mechanic is anyone with a skill. We have yet to come to terms with this word usage and its meaning. It may simply be a derivation of the Yiddish term *Macher* for operative.

8. MD, Cassette 1, Side 1.

9. MD, Cassette 2, Side 1.

10. *Ibid.*

11. "Real slavery" is a term used again and again by our garment worker interviewees, both Italian and Jewish. It refers in every case to more than just working conditions and includes a very specific sense of the loss of personal freedom. The study of this term and its usage would, I think, be an interesting example of how a theoretical proposition derived from a formal system becomes part of the consciousness of masses of people. In this case the Marxian notion of wage slavery, as used and redefined by the socialist press in America and the Socialist Party, filters into the Union rhetoric as struggles are undertaken and issues are defined by that struggle, and thus the term becomes part of the working everyday vocabulary of union members.

12. MD, Cassette 1, Side 1.

13. G. S. Kirk, *Myth: Its Meaning and Function in Ancient and Other Cultures*, Berkeley, University of California Press, 1975, pp. 257-258.

14. *United States Census, 1880.* This figure does not include workers in hosiery, hats, furs, knit goods, gloves, lace or corsets.

15. The interviewer is Italian American. Whether Mel would have included Italians had this not been the case can only be guessed.

16. This process has been outlined most clearly by Warren Susman, "History and the American Intellectual: Uses of a Usable Past," *American Quarterly*, 16 (Summer 1964), 211-245.

17. MD, Cassette 1, Side 2.

18. BP, Cassette 1, Side 2. The same tale is repeated on Cassette 2, Side 1.

19. BP, Cassette 1, Side 1.

20. BP, Cassette 2, Side 1.

21. BP, Cassette 2 Side 2.

22. BP, Cassette 2, Side 2.

23. Irving Howe, *World of Our Fathers*, New York, Harcourt Brace Jovanovich, 1976, pp. 1-33, 321-324.

24. See especially Kenneth Burke, *Attitudes Toward History*, 2nd ed., Boston, Beacon Press, 1961. See also J. P. Bury, *The Idea of Progress*, New York, Peter Smith, 1960; and E. H. Carr, *What is History?* New York, Random House, 1967.

25. E. J. Hobsbawm, "The Social Function of the Past: Some Questions," *Past and Present*, 55 (May 1972), p. 3.

26. Frisch, *op. cit.*

27. Friedlander, Ch. I.

28. Henry Glassie, "Meaningful Things and Appropriate Myths: The Artifact's Place in American Studies," *Prospects*, Vol. III: Edited by Jack Salzman, New York, Burt Franklin and Co., 1975, pp. 1-39.

**Private Memories and Public Presentation:
The Art of Oral History**

Conversations take on meaning within history. Even in those conversations which, on the surface, seem to function solely to cement a human bond: to establish a human relationship, to signify community identity, whether what is said is appropriate or true depends upon its placement in what we believe to be appropriate or true of the processes of change over time. In oral history interviews, as we speak together and as we listen, we wonder at the meaning of what we say and hear. Caught at the same moment in the creation of conversation and in reflection upon that creation, it is only later that we can reinterpret our initial interpretation. To do this we search for a method to connect "their stories" and "our stories," a process of reconstructing the past, requiring "a double vision that focuses at once on historians' modes of composition and [our] subjects' ways of conceiving the past."[1] We stand both within and without a complicated set of social and cultural relationships. We aid in the creation of life documents, yet we serve as critics of those documents. Often it is difficult to explain to ourselves and others what this experience is, its composition, its meaning, its value.

With the increasing popularity of oral history we who work in the field are called upon more and more to answer the question, "what is it that oral historians do and what is so special about it?" At meetings of historical organizations, in classes, in private conversations with colleagues, and in workshops the question is raised with a quiet regularity, and sometimes, impatience. We and our various publics have become less and less satisfied with the pat answer that we interview people about the events of the past, make the resultant documents (tapes or transcripts of tapes) available to others for research, or use them for our own historical reconstruction. Such a functional definition seems too limited when we apply it to our own fieldwork experiences; or when we find ourselves in agreement with those who have seen oral history as a unique opportunity to understand consciousness, to radically alter historical practice by bringing ordinary people into the study of history, to reshape the discipline, to create a public that is conscious of its own history, or to move beyond the limits and biases of the written record.[2]

The gap between new claims and traditional explanations has, in the past ten years, generated an exciting and sophisticated literature on oral history and a reaching out to other disciplines using fieldwork techniques.[3] This important work has begun to focus upon the oral history interview itself and to address the question of how we make a conversation historical, and to link explanatory theory with fieldwork practice. But literature in oral history has yet to become as fully self conscious as that in folklore or ethnography, where works of penetrating insight such as *Passing the Time in Ballymenone* by Henry Glassie and *The Ethnographic Interview*[4] by James P. Spradley have combined theory and practice into new formulations of the goals of those disciplines. For reasons which will be developed later, works such as these, however sophisticated, do not solve the problem of the historian, for while there is an area of mutual interdisciplinary concern there are also important differences. To think historically is a special mode of thought. However in much of our reflection on oral history we still rely upon rather traditional visions of what we do.

To relate theory and method in oral history our starting point must be the document we, as oral historians, produce: what it represents, its distinguishing characteristics, and the problems posed by its use. We can then move on to discuss how we overcome these problems or, where possible, redefine them in such a manner as to explain the historiographical issues involved. We will then be able to speculate upon the special promise of oral history and how we realize this promise in our work.

Most clearly our documents are representations of people themselves, of their lives. At the same time oral histories are only a portion of those lives. They contain within themselves a preselection. People live their lives and formulate a perception of themselves which may or may not correspond to our perception of them. The oral history may or may not reflect either of these views. In some cases our informants seriously distort, in some case we do, not because we or they lie, but because both of us know that the way the past is viewed has consequences for the way the present is structured, and because we have different reference points for our presentations of ourselves. Thus, what we decide to discuss and the manner in which it is discussed, the selection, observation and interpretation of the events of the past, is done within the context of how we have lived our own history and the meaning we have attached to that history. In some ways our documents are too rich. They tell us of what happened but they also tell us what people thought happened and how they have internalized and interpreted what happened. They tell us how individual personalities and social forces reconstruct memory to advance or hinder the development of particular ways of viewing the past.

The interview must be based upon interaction, but to interact *with* is not the same as to engage critically.[5] Thus, it is imperative that the oral historian move beyond a simple interactionist view of the interview. It may be true, as Alessandro Portelli has argued that oral histories are by their nature subjective because they depend so heavily upon the view of the past of those we interview, but we must meet the challenge offered by Luisa Passerini to take this fact and try to devise a "science of the subjective" which will allow us to develop new categories of explanation of historical processes.[6] In other words, we must devise methods to understand oral histories in their own terms and to read them for what they can tell us of the "cultural and psychological activities—of an individual and collective range—which can be embodied in language and behavior, as well as expressed in more 'spiritual' forms, such as speculative thought."[7] The past is not dead. It lives on in daily life and the people we interview are the embodiment of that fact and process. To grasp the intimate and complex relation between past and present has always been the goal of the historian. Oral histories offer us an entry into that phenomena, but only if we understand the markers along the path.

Many commentators have expressed reservations or objections to the use of the term "oral history." Yet, in some sense it does convey the distinguishing characteristics of the document as conversation and as commentary upon the past. Archivists and others are correct in arguing that the basic document, the one from which we should work, is the sound recording, not the transcript.[8] This is not necessarily unique to audio recorded oral histories since radio, film and video documents also exist in the realm of sound (when such documents become recorded conversations about the past which attempt some reconstruction and analysis of that past they become oral histories); but it does distinguish oral histories from other historical documents and makes clear that they can only be understood as conversational narratives. The whole of the following analysis is predicated upon this fact and is in many ways incomprehensible without bearing it in mind. Elsewhere I have argued that this means that an understanding of linguistics and communications is a necessary tool in the kit of the oral historian. Here, I wish to draw attention to the formal structure of such conversations in order to understand the recording, the aural text, as a historical document.

The most singular characteristic of an oral history, and by far its most significant for the historian as both creator and user, is its creation through the active intervention of the historian. Over the years many of us have noted this feature of oral histories, but it is necessary to reiterate it in order to rip the mask of objectivity from the process and to avoid a narrow and superficial view of the interview as solely a source of factual information about the past. An oral history, unlike an autobiography, and unlike oral traditions,[9] would not exist without the active intervention of the historian. It is a document created as a result of the interests, questions, values, ambitions, ideas and drive of the historian. The story, the tale, the explanation, of course, exist without the historian, but the record and its particular form exist only thorough the active agency of the historian interviewer. There is history as process and history as discipline. The first exists separately from the historian but as time passes what we know of history as process becomes increasingly, and in some cases, unfortunately, monopolistically, what history as discipline tell us. Nowhere is the old Beardian-Becker dictum, now updated by Frederic Jameson, that history is what the historians say it is, more apparent than in an oral history.[10] We have only to listen to our interviews to realize this fact.

Since we create our own documents, certain consequences follow and we must now introduce in new forms the four problems discussed earlier in this volume.[11] They are: the problem of the creation in the now of a document about the then, the problem of rapport in the interview, the problem of making life anthropologically strange, and the problem of the alienating and individualizing tendency of the interview situation.

The documents we produce are artifacts of the time of their creation, not the period under discussion. When we ask people to discuss, for example, a strike of 1900, and they do so, they speak from the perspective of today, as does our questioning. It is not that we or they consciously attempt to fashion the past to present concerns (although that does happen in some interviews) but it is inevitable that our questions and answers are infused with those concerns. Indeed it is the method whereby we increase our understanding of the past and like Socrates' slave, create new knowledge. Thus, it would be a poor interviewer today who did not ask about the role of women in that strike. This may or may not have been a question of the 1920s, or even the 1930s or the 1940s, or if it was, it was not a question which carried the same meaning it does today. But it is a question of great import to us now and we weigh the answer in light of what we now know and in light of what we now want to know. In that process we discover new knowledge about the past and renew the life of cultural debate.

Obviously, there are limits to such a method. It may be that women did not play a significant role in the strike, and no amount of concern on our part will create that role without distorting our history. But, within these limits, each generation writes its own history and this is to the good. It is the way culture expands, the way in which people reinterpret, reexplain old experiences, and integrate new issues into the past to make sense of their lives. "Manipulating truth," as Glassie explains, "is essential to the formation of mind." History thus becomes a fact of history.[12]

All histories, whether written or spoken, are discussions (texts) of both past and present. They tell of then, and of the now of their creation as well. Gibbon and Rostovtzeff have both told us much about Rome, but they have also told us much about the eighteenth century and the early twentieth century. They contain many truths about both times, the time under examination and the time from which the examination is undertaken. This dialectic allows us to build upon the past and make it relevant for today and for the future. In an oral history it is what gives the conversation its dynamic, creating the particular dialogue and the dialectical tension between past experience and present meaning.

This two-sidedness poses problems for analysis because at some level we *are* interested in knowing what happened in the past, and what is or is not fiction. Not that we hold to some abstract vision of the true, but we know that to understand the past we must know the questions the past asked of itself, and that what is true, what corresponds to everything else we know, allows us to use our history with more accuracy, freedom and creativity. In the interview we are forced into a self consciousness of ourselves and our informants and into a consideration of the interplay of history and its uses. We are forced, if we are to be critical historians, to confront memory and its meaning in culture.

The arguments over memory and its role in oral history have been particularly sterile. Most critics have concentrated upon the vagaries of individual memory and the factors, physiological and psychological, which impede recall. In most cases one would have to agree that Paul Thompson's *The Voice of the Past*,[13] which devotes extensive space to these questions, should have settled these arguments. Yet they crop up again and again and one wonders why, in the face of ever larger collections of ever more complex oral histories of ever more usefulness, the criticisms continue to be framed so narrowly and with such a distorted view of what oral historians do.

We are not testers of memory or recall. We do not go into the field to test how much an informant knows of an event or how good his or her recall is. Nor are we folklorists or anthropologists searching for history in tales or oral traditions and testing their integrity and validity over time.[14] This particular difference can be seen in who is referred to as the "oral historian." In folklore, and among some anthropologists, the oral historian is the person interviewed, the person who carries in his or her head the collective history of the community. From that person one seeks the history as it has been passed down from generation to generation because that history is an artifact of the thought of the culture which one seeks to understand. Among historians, the oral historian is the historian who records the conversation, the creator of the document. Thus we have a different task. Although we are deeply interested in the oral narratives collected by those in other disciplines and in the question of the role of traditional historical narratives in the culture, and indeed, collect them with relish and discover historical meaning in them, we go into an interview prepared to test and expand the histories. We want to know who saw the great deeds, how large was the crowd, who else was there, who decided what particulars of the battle. We want to know if other alternatives were considered or why they were not. Above all, we want to know what the events under discussion meant to those who recall them.

We are involved in a collective effort to recall specifics and attach meaning to them, and we go into the interview armed with documents, photos, citations from other sources, and other memory aids.

"I don't remember who else was there, so I can't recall the full debate," says our informant. "I have a roster of participants, perhaps if you glanced over it, it might help," says the historian. "Oh, yes, now I remember," she answers and the testimony continues. Or, we ask, "Can you give me another example?" or "Can you tell me more?" We sometimes destroy the story as story but expand the memory as history. We create a different kind of text, based to be sure upon the stories we have been told but elaborated upon under our questioning.[15]

In this construction, individual recall is not our basic problem, collective memory and collective amnesia is.[16] People experience events as individuals and as members of a particular culture at a particular time. They seek to preserve their self indentification and their social honor, and they often hold quite closely to the dominant myths and shibboleths of the social order. Thus we confront memory. Passerini and Annamarie Troeger, among others, have brilliantly explored how the memory of Fascism and Nazism, as lived through experiences, affects the lives of people today and how they choose to remember or forget aspects of the past in the reconstruction of that past.

An interesting, albeit unintended, example of the differences between testing recall and the formation of the memory of past events is found in the latest work of Elizabeth Loftus, *Memory*.[17] In the early sections of that work, Loftus examines a number of studies showing the fragility of recall. In most of these tests respondents were presented with scenes or images (automobile accidents, etc.) and then later asked to recall details of the presentation which they had often forgotten. But, these were not lived through experiences. If they had been tested on taking the test (the lived through experience) one wonders what recall would have been. In later sections of the book where Loftus discusses long term memory and where actual events in people's lives are discussed, these events are recalled but their nature, details, and meaning are altered, rearranged, exaggerated and reinterpreted in light of the intervening history or present concerns.

All history is selection and the basis of selection is our current concern. Our problem is quite similar to those who have tried to fathom why, in the *Education of Henry Adams*, the autobiographer chose not to mention his marriage and his wife. We live in a culture in which many have a vital stake in what is and is not remembered of the past, as Ophuls's film *The Sorrow and the Pity* shows us.[18] Vast ideological apparatuses conspire to impose upon us a "correct" vision of our history and in this way our memories are shaped, reawakened, dulled, distorted or forgotten. But it also the way they are sharpened, honed, kept alive, and used and argued about.[19]

Not only does the present impinge upon the memory of the past, but the past also impinges upon the present. Just as we can sometimes distort the questions the past asked of itself in order to answer today's questions, so also the questions the past asked of itself can live on and distort our current questions. Memories of past events, while often liberating in the sense that they point to alternative lessons and confront current ideologies, can at other times become a trap. In some cases they can freeze the present. They become nostalgia.[20] An obvious example of this is the peculiar way in which millions of Americans from Ronald Reagan to Studs Terkel's respondents have chosen to remember the Great Depression. The common litany of "We had it bad and we survived, not like those bums of today," the use of the experience of poverty as a cudgel with which to beat the poverty stricken of today, presents us with a fascinating and politically important example of how the past is used ideologically to freeze the present. Another example is the way many people discuss the intimate details of their lives in terms of the popular songs of their teenage years. In such cases problems are evaded, difficult decisions masked, both past and present fitted into sentiment, and analysis avoided as we move beyond that careful line between history and nostalgia.

To critically confront, as historians, both aspects of the relationship between past and present, it is necessary that we, in Gelya Frank's terms, not take the testimony we are given as self evident, but seek an interpretation beyond that contained within the testimony that is presented to us.[21] In the field we must test such testimony: to press for examples, to offer possible alternative interpretations, to demystify nostalgia. As fieldworkers we must be cognizant of the pain of memory, but as historians we must, if we are to be honest to our craft, explore in detail the contradictions inherent in such formulations of history.

As these examples show, our problems with memory are far more complex than problems of recall. How simple indeed would be our work if behavioral psychology were correct. All we would have to do is present evidence of the "truth" over and over to reinforce proper recall. We would not have to ask, as Terkel has, "Whose truth?"[22] Nor would we have to wonder about the role of history as an artifact of culture and politics.

Our second problem is equally complicated. When we interview people in an oral history interview, because we ask them to examine and give meaning to their pasts as well as to our concerns, we ask them to step outside themselves, to distance themselves from their experiences and to become, like us, both insider and outsider; to make their lives "anthropologically strange."

The term is Harold Garfinkle's, but the phenomena is familiar to anyone who has ever done field work.[23] Simply put, when we move into the field we ask people about their lives and behavior, their acts and thoughts, things which were never questioned before. Most people do not go through life constantly questioning what they do or consciously seeking and weighing their motivations. Perhaps when involved in shattering events they question themselves, but for the most part daily life is habitual. The most obvious example of what happens to us and our informants comes from the field of family history. Thompson's *The Voice of the Past* closes with a set of "model questions" for the conduct of interviews in family history. Among these questions are inquiries about the family wash, dinner table routine, family visits, etc.[24] We ask such questions because their answers tell us much about the internal organization of family life. Most people, however, have never considered this behavior questionable; it has been unconscious, habitual, without meaning in a historical sense until *we* ask about it and thereby give it a historical meaning.

We do the same thing in other fields of inquiry when we ask about paths not taken and try to explore why not. "I never thought of it that way before," "That's an interesting question, I wonder now why it wasn't considered," our informants reply. Aside from questions about what we are doing to historical memory in such cases, we are introducing our concerns as historians into the lives of others and asking them to see these questions as their questions, be they the questions we now ask or the questions we think the past asked of itself. Thus we make behavior problematic.

We thereby bring into consciousness what had been, until the interview, part of the socially or politically unconscious. A clear example of this phenomenon is found in interviews in biracial communities where, for many whites, segregation has been so ingrained a part of life that it has never been questioned or articulated. After the interview, such relationships become open to question. In a different vein, a work such as *Civil Rights and Civilities* brings to the community of Greensboro, North Carolina the questions and concerns of the community of historians, thereby subtly altering that southern community's vision of its past.[25] Such considerations raise in rather bald form the whole question of authority in the interview and authority in the interpretation of the past.

Glassie has written brilliantly about the oral historical traditions of a small corner of the North of Ireland. Noting this effect, he is at pains, he says, *not* to intrude his knowledge

or his views of the past of Ballymenone into that tradition.[26]
But he is an outsider to that community,. while oral historians
generally are not strangers in the same sense. We interview in
our own society and culture, and as citizens we have a deep
stake in our history. We are engaged. We are participants.
Indeed, this co-participation, this bringing to consciousness,
has inspired *The History Workshop* and various community
oral history projects which seek to use the interview as a
consciousness raising device. One only has to compare *Brass
Valley* and its conscious attempt to apply the interpretations
of the new social history to the oral histories to Glassie's work
to see the difference. Another example is offered in *Family
Time and Industrial Time* by Tamara Hareven and Randolph
Langenbach, where the authors note the difference in attitude
of the people of Manchester, New Hampshire after they saw
a presentation of their past and came to realize that it had
importance.[27]

That people's views of the use of history are affected by
the interviewing process seems undeniable. The long and short
term political effects of this altered view, however, are open to
debate, and that this is related to an inherent characteristic of
the interview has not been so obvious. It is in this way that new
interpretations of the past are developed by the oral historian,
and a different historical stance is encouraged. It is also one
way in which we aid people to become their own historians.

Such considerations bring us inevitably to the question of
rapport in the interview and the relationship between interviewer and interviewee. There can be no worthwhile interview
without rapport, but the social situation thus produced contains
within itself severe limits upon the information conveyed and
its manner of presentation.[28]

The interview is a social occasion. We have usually been
invited into someone's home, shared coffee and cake with them
(broken bread, so to speak), been shown family photographs,
and been treated as guests. We are being given a gift and
must reciprocate. For the time of the interview we are

involved in someone else's life. In addition the interview is usually an enjoyable experience. Most people enjoy talking about themselves to a sympathetic listener. In the glow of good feeling and honest caring the interviewer feels awkward asking the difficult questions, and often frames these questions in obscure euphemisms, confusedly attempts to explain why such a question is being asked, and tries to avoid offending. Respondents in turn try to present themselves as they think the interviewer would like them to be. They pick up on the subtle clues fairly rapidly. They want to help, to be forthcoming, to give information, even if they weren't involved or weren't even there.

The intricacies of such relations have been spelled out in detail by Robert Georges and Michael Jones in *People Studying People*.[29] They need not be repeated here except to note their conclusion that, contrary to "the view, widely held and generally reinforced by conventional fieldwork guides and manuals . . . individuals [cannot] conduct field work involving people studying people without being human."[30] Who would want to interview as an automaton, or as an adversary? Who can? To be brutally reserved or obnoxiously confrontational in such a situation is an insult to our hosts. To advance careers, and sometimes make money, without returning even a minimal human sympathy or commitment is to ignore one's responsibility to the people one is studying. It also creates testimony of questionable value when informants react as they would to welfare bureaucrats. As the current debates over the work of Margaret Mead reveal, fieldwork is an intensely human affair. It is a social situation with its own patterns and rules and this obviously affects the quantity and quality of the testimony.

But oral history fieldwork also contains a profoundly alienating potential as well, alienating in the deepest historical sense of that word. Because we usually interview one person at a time and ask people about what they themselves did, there is a tendency to move our informants to stage center, seeing the world through their eyes and attributing to them or allowing them to attribute to themselves a choice, prescience, or motive which may not be historically valid. Oral history, like all biography or autobiography, encourages the view that individuals shape their own destinies, that they are in some way historical actors, and this by choice. This is an especial problem in the United States where there is such a long tradition of seeing institutions as but the shadows of individuals.

We live in a world of limits: legal, ethical, ideological, economic, social, historical. We internalize these limits and make our choices within the ranges offered to us. Often, as noted earlier, we are unaware or unconscious of those limits and often there are strong political reasons for such ignorance. A good interview reveals the political unconscious, but that revelation cannot be accepted at face value. Concepts of the role of individuals in history are class based both at a deep structural level and at the level of social relations. They are not self evident as historical axioms, and since they carry within themselves their own language of motive they must be carefully judged.

I once had a fine student, but bad interviewer, who insisted upon asking first generation Italian longshoremen in Brooklyn why they hadn't "tried to better themselves." Part of the problem with this question was wording. What this student was interested in, he explained, was why these men hadn't looked for work other than longshoring since, at that time, it was difficult and dangerous seasonal work. But the class biases in the phrasing, the concept of choice, the idea of "betterment," all assumed a middle class vision of the world and history. The questioner failed to understand both the strengths and limits of the world of South Brooklyn. To ask such a question of men who had struggled for forty years in hard and demeaning labor to build a life for themselves, homes and protection for their families, and a powerful union was to ignore what they had succeeded in creating, and the limits imposed upon that creation by the structure of American capitalism. Such questions also assume, in the guise of the "new social history," that the victims were responsible for the limitations imposed upon them.

In this case the damage was slight because the question was simply not understood and was usually answered with references to family and home. It was redefined in terms of the culture of the docks, revealing the rules of that culture as well as the inventiveness of the human imagination. In other cases, however, amid populations less sure of themselves and their world, such a line of questioning is usually answered with vivid descriptions of full participation in the American dream and a strong accent upon success stories; the answers are defined by the interviewer's view of success. The result is a picture of people divorced from community and society, people who turn history into personal biography, people alienated from history.[31] If the oral history interview can make life anthropologically strange, it can also alienate it from context. Consciousness is formed and expressed in many ways.

If we face such problems in the creation, use and understanding of our materials, how do we resolve them? Critics of oral history, and by implication all fieldwork, will probably claim that they cannot be resolved and this simply shows the weakness and dubious nature of the whole enterprise. Yet, common sense, a review of the increasingly rich literature of oral history, and the way it is changing our view of the past cannot be denied. Neither can we deny the excitement of oral history fieldwork and its liberating effect on the way we practice our craft. For those of us who have committed ourselves to the creation and use of oral histories, it becomes necessary to face these problems and to resolve them both practically and theoretically.

While each interview is an intensely subjective experience depending upon the vagaries of the personalities of the interviewer and interviewee, in form an oral history is a conversational narrative. Pursuing the implications of that definition in detail will mediate theoretical and practical concerns and resolve the problems posed here. What do we mean by "conversation" and "narrative?" How are they structured? How do they reveal themselves in an oral history interview? How do we, once we understand what we mean by conversational narrative, organize our fieldwork to produce the richest document possible?

The answer to these questions relies very heavily upon the work of E. Culpepper Clark, Eva McMahan and Michael Hyde. In their collective and individual work which attempts to understand an oral history interview as a hermeneutic act,[32] they have provided a base from which we can construct some general principles of oral history conversations and through which we can integrate these principles into our earlier discussion. (These authors are not responsible for my particular reading of their work, my simplifications of their complex formulations, and my peculiar application of their thought.)

Assuming that language is an arena of struggle over interpretation, and beginning with the inherent conflict in the interview situation produced by the separate and different "understandings, interpretations and meanings" of a historical event formed by the interviewer and interviewee, and through an analysis of the transformations involved in conversation, Clark et al. have outlined three possible types of oral history conversations.

First are those conversations which cease to be conversations. When conflict becomes too great, conversation ceases. For reasons of personality, interpretation, or situation, the disagreement becomes so obvious that both parties simply stop talking to one another. There is no conversation.

A second form of conflict resolution in conversation is through "acquiescence." One or the other party simply gives in, hides his or her real views, goes along. A somewhat similar situation is one of full agreement. What happens in such conversations, whether they be acquiescence or total agreement, is that one party does all the talking and more important, the signifying, as in the unequal conversations of faculty members and students or parents and repressed children.   In other cases where there is total agreement, conversations are truncated; because so much is shared, it is unncessary to go into detail.   Such conversations can be conducted through nods, grunts, the use of key words and phrases. It is like telling a joke which everyone knows. One skips the details and gets to the punch line.

The third form of conversation, and this is the major contribution of Clark, McMahan and Hyde, is a situation not of conflict or agreement, but where "contrariety" prevails. These are the conversations which produce the most words, the most explanation, and the richest language. If we think back on those conversations which have been most satisfying, they have been conversations in which, while there was argumentation and conflict, there was also an agreement that the discussion itself was worth pursuing. There was an implicit assumption of an agreement to disagree. In such conversations the inherent conflict of different perspectives was not muted, yet both parties agreed to continue the dialogue, to keep exploring differences. In such conversations each party continues to test the other, to offer new facts to be explained, new interpretations to be dealt with, and new arguments to be answered. The narratives and explanations become more explicit and more detailed, the interpretations more complex, the contradictions clearer.

In structure, if not in exact form, this is the type of conversation we seek in an oral history interview. We want conversations which discuss more facts, offer more interpretations, and reveal contradictions. When we say, pursue in detail, we ask for more information. We do not take testimony at face value. We challenge. We ask, "How would you answer the claim of X (such as *The New York Times*, critics, etc.) that . . . ?" We introduce new evidence, "At the time the strike was called, the women were organizing. Was there a connection?" We seek alternatives: "Did you consider that . . . ?" We explore contradictions: "Earlier you said something that seems to contradict this. How do they go together?" "You said the treasury was ably maintained: why was there a grand jury indictment?"

We do this, however, without open conflict. We do not confront in an adversarial manner, not just because we are polite (and it is sometimes dismaying that it is so difficult to get across to students how important such politeness is), but also because the person we are talking to understands that we are embarked upon a joint creation and that it is right and natural that we should see the world differently, not sharing the same fund of knowledge. We are often of a different age; we have read different descriptions of the events under discussion; we were not there, they were. We are at the same time both more and less informed than one another. It is clear that Theodore Rosengarten knew more about the social history of the American South during the Great Depression than did Nate Shaw. It is equally clear that Nate Shaw knew more about what it was like to be a black sharecropper during that time in that place than Rosengarten could ever know.[33] In such situations it is expected that we will hold different views of history, but it is also expected that the enterprise is important to both of us, that we will continue to talk despite our differences, and that we will treat each other with respect.

Such a stance allows us to be both within and without, being sympathetic yet critical; to manipulate, in the best sense of that word, the rapport generated in the interview, and the history being told, in order to maximize the retelling of the story. In addition it allows us to, and explains to others why we should, make life anthropologically strange. We *are* strangers; often loving strangers, but strangers nonetheless. We have not lived through the events under discussion, but we do live with their history and their consequences. We are, both of us, involved in that history as a collective process but in different ways. By viewing the interview as a situation of contrariety and building upon the asset of rapport we can thus turn what appears to be a handicap into an advantage. There is nothing unique to this. It is what good fieldworkers have been doing for years.[34] Such practice does, however, allow us to move beyond sentimentalization without becoming rigid in our so-called "objectivity." It allows us to provide a sympathetic ear while maintaining critical distance, thus enriching the history.

The concept of narrative in an oral history is far more complicated, as we tried to point out in the earlier version of this volume.[35] The interplay of myth, ideology and history in the formulation of a vision of the past is complex, yet the way it is formulated in an interview through the joint efforts of both parties, how it is developed as narrative, is possible to describe. If, as Jameson notes, all historical interpretation is textual analysis because what we know of the past comes to us as a form of structured gloss,[36] then it is important to discover how the texts we create are created in order to help us produce the most vital texts we can. Again, the work of Clark, McMahan and Hyde points the way, once we strip it of its inherent Hegelianism.

When we interview people, they tell us about their experiences in such a way as to convey to us the meaning of those experiences. But the oral history interview is not necessarily the first time that experience was given meaning, was interpreted. That occurred, probably, during or shortly after the event itself was experienced. As it attained meaning over time it was told again but slightly differently depending upon the audience, the use of language deemed apt at the time and the shifting meaning of the interpretation.[37]

Contained in each telling, and interpretation, of the historical event is the linking of one event to another to form the tale and interpretation. Each time the story is told there are factual, logical and linguistic limits to what is told and how it is told. Imagine the event under discussion as a strike of 1920. Each telling relates the strike to other facts and events, such as the prevailing wage, shop floor regulations, the strength of the union, the union leadership, etc., in order to explain the strike. As the story is retold over time it changes. Perhaps in the first telling to a striker's wife, alcohol on the picket line was not mentioned, perhaps when told to the children, the role of the police was emphasized. When told in the 1930s, the role of a fiery Communist party strike leader was highlighted; when told in the 1950s, this leader disappears. Each time the tale is told there are also linguistic limits: in the structure of the language, in the ability of the person telling the tale and the ability of the audience to comprehend. Words too have a history, and at each telling certain words and phrases were used which were then current. There are also logical limits in each telling. Only certain events can be linked to the strike without the whole tale seeming or becoming unreal. But that logic changes over time. Because we are who we are at this moment of time, we feel it necessary and important to ask about the role of women in the strike and our informant feels it necessary and proper to answer, even though that may not have been an element in any previous telling of the tale. While we are concerned to discover the questions the past asked of itself, we are also concerned that the past answer the questions we ask of ourselves.

Rather than viewing this as a quandary, we should see it as an opportunity to resolve many of our fieldwork dilemmas. Because we have done our research prior to the interview, by reading the original and secondary materials available. we are aware of much of what happened as well as much of what has been said about what happened. We know how historians and others have given the events under discussion various meanings through various interpretations. We can therefore judge, as we listen, the fullness of the current interpretation, and also whether or not we are being given the nostalgic version of the 1930s, 1940s or 1950s, or a fuller interpretation than that of previous historians. More important, since, as historians, we have been trained to analyze and test historical interpretations, we can do so in the field and thus devise new questions in the light of new information. We can introduce new evidence: "What was the role of the Socialists?" We can offer conflicting interpretations for consideration: "Was there any evidence of the claim that . . . ?" We can explore contradictions and search for new evidence and examples to support the interpretation we are being given. Very often the best fieldwork question is precisely that: "Can you give me an example?" What we do is push to the fullest limit the logic of the story, the memory of the informant and the explanatory power of the interpretation. If each previous telling was only partial and this one is also, at least this partial telling under our guidance and prodding will be fuller and more complete than any previous telling. Because it tests all previous tellings and interpretations it encompasses and transcends them.

The latest telling, if it is a fuller narrative because it pushes memory and logic as far as possible, can thus bear the type of complex analysis sketched earlier in this volume or the type of analysis proposed by Portelli.[38] More complete, it allows us to relate our narrators more directly to the social and historical forces which govern their lives, in the way Daniel Bertaux and Isabelle Bertaux-Wiame have so brilliantly outlined.[39] It is also the fieldwork technique which most consistently tests the "self evident" truth of the narrative.

In many cases the rules of oral history interviewing are a matter of simple common sense. Prepare for the interview through intensive research. Know the subject under discussion. Pursue in detail. Keep a critical mind. Don't interrupt the flow of the narrative. Be prepared to follow up. Get examples. There are, however, deeper reasons behind these simple dicta that, when elaborated, make their commonsensical nature understandable. They are the rules necessary to construct the type of interview needed for a full historical analysis.

The view of the interview posited here offers a method whereby we can resolve the problems inherent in the oral history interview. It offers us a way to maximize the shifting nature of interpretation over time, to judge the complexity, tenacity, longevity, and use of deeply held ideologies, and to construct an interpretation of this interpretation—to develop the methodological principles of the interview. Such practice also allows us to place people in the fullest historical context possible and thus counters the alienating tendency of the interview situation. In addition, it encourages the fullest development of the expression of historical consciousness because it pushes both interviewee and interviewer to the limits of historical explanation. Earlier we argued that the goal of an analysis of the oral history interview was to understand people in history by understanding how history is formed in the imagination, and how it is used in the development of ideologies, and then to examine how these ideologies frame the material presented. In order to create the documents which will allow this type of examination, we must devise methods which will bring into articulation the deep structure of historical formulation inherent in historical dialogue. The method described here helps us to develop the hidden conversation of our narrators with their community.

In *Interpretation Theory*, Paul Ricoeur describes the goal of textual analysis. "What has to be appropriated," he argues, "is the meaning of the text itself, conceived in a dynamic way as the direction of thought opened up by the text. In other words, what has to be appropriated is nothing other than the power of disclosing a world that constitutes the reference of the text . . . the disclosure of a possible way of looking at things, which is the genuine referential power of the text."[40] If, as I have argued, an oral history is a text and it contains a narrative, and if the historian is deeply involved in the creation of that text, then we have the opportunity to create as complex a narrative text as possible in order to grasp the fundamental problematic of the imagination of the people we interview and thus make our document as rich as possible. But, further, it is not just that we enter the subjectivity of those we speak to. As John Berger has pointed out, "To talk of entering the other's subjectivity is misleading. The subjectivity of another does not simply constitute a different attitude to the same exterior facts. The constellation of facts, of which he is the center, is different."[41] What we seek is the way people make history;

their facts and their interpretations which we then play off of our facts and interpretations.

Such a goal and such a method allows us to develop complex historical documents. They also allow us to speculate upon some of the differences between oral history interviewing and other fieldwork practices using "qualitative methodologies." Earlier we noted briefly the differences between oral history and the collection of oral traditions. Much of that difference derives from the origin of the tale. Oral traditions are formed without the intervention of the historian. They exist without our activity. They have a cultural function quite similar to, yet very different from oral history, and much of that difference derives from the different relation of the historian and the person being recorded—the teller of the tale.

Again, using the example of the strike of 1920, if we were collecting the oral tradition of the strike, we would not necessarily concern ourselves with finding a participant in the strike. Rather we would look for those who stand at the end of the telling of the story. If, for instance, the tale of the strike of 1920 was told to children in 1930, who in turn told it to friends in 1940, who in turn told it to others in 1960, in 1983 we would seek out those who heard the tale in 1960 and ask for a retelling of the story. The concern here is to get as far back into the past as possible by collecting as true a rendering of the tale as possible, to try to examine the changes in the tale over time, and to understand change in the culture through an examination of the changes in the tale. While it is quite clear, as Vansina has shown, that we can use the tradition to grasp the event itself, it is a process quite different from an oral history interview.[42] In this situation the historian is far less active in the creation of the history. The search for new data is not necessarily the desired goal. As oral historians, we stand at the beginning of the creation of the tale, not its end. We try to speak to eye witnesses, not those who have had the tradition passed on to them.

The relationship of folklore and history is more complex. In some cases, such as the work of Richard Dorson, history is used to verify folk tales or legends, to test them. In other cases, such as the brilliant work of Edward Ives, history forms the context for the discussion of folk life and forms. In other cases, such as Glassie's work, history ofttimes becomes another form of myth or folktale. In yet other cases, folklore becomes just another aspect of intellectual history.[43] For our purposes here, the difference between oral history and folklore is best seen in *Passing the Time in Ballymenone* and I return to Glassie's work because it is such a sophisticated discussion of the relation of history to folklore and story telling. In his chapter on "The Topography of Time Past," Glassie notes: "History is a prime mode of cultural construction. That is how . . . history . . . is best addressed: as a way people organize reality to investigate truth to survive in their own terms." He lays out a series of topics in the chronicle of Ballymenone and a crosschecking of which topics each of his best storytellers included in their histories, and which they did not, and he discusses his own relationship with that history. "To fill in and write my own chronicle, I imported facts from histories preserved in other places. *That was wrong* [italics mine]. It is the analyst's duty to construct hidden relationships within a community's knowledge, but what a community does not know cannot exist within its culture, is not part of its own history." "Plugging a gap in culture with ideas not part of that culture falsifies its shape, because culture has no gap."[44] But to do history is to do exactly that. We must know the basis of selection. We must know why one event was left out and why another was included. We must bring that gap to consciousness. Do we know that certain topics were omitted because our interviewee did not read certain letters or books, or listen to certain conversations and certain people? We must know why Communists are not discussed while telling the tale of the strike. Was it because their efforts were only concentrated on the leadership? Was it because there is a concious political point in telling of the tale? Was it because they had no role? We must explore the gap in order to broaden the horizon of discourse and interpretation, as Hans Gadamer would put it.[45] In order to understand silences we must talk.

While to the folklorist culture may have no gap, to the historian individual historical constructions do and history as an artifact of culture does. The domain available for reference to storytellers is far greater than that used, as Albert E. Stone has shown in great detail in his discussion of the construction of autobiographies.[46] To understand the text we must be able to fathom the rules of selection; how myths and ideologies are created through history, and how they are transformed by people into "a usable past." It is not that we plug the gap with ideas not part of that culture; rather, we examine why certain individuals and classes of people leave gaps, or don't. To do this, oral histories strike a much more activist stance than simply recording stories. Furthermore, culture itself is historical; the rules, recipes, etc. change over time. For the historian this is a crucial concern, as is the pace of that change.

How involved one becomes in the lives of those one studies, how actively one intervenes in the creation of the history and what consequences one's research may have on the lives of those studied, are always difficult questions to answer. While Glassie may not have intruded his history upon his informants, certainly the book, when read in Ballymenone, will do just that. There is not an insurmountable gap between folk life studies and oral history, but the two do have different concerns when discussing consciousness, and somewhat different approaches to similar phenomena. Both are concerned with the way in which history becomes a cultural artifact and how culture lives in history. The historian is, however, not an outsider to the process and is always concerned with the political dimension of consciousness and the way it functions in actual social orders.

In other cases the distinctions are not so clear. Daniel Bertaux's work in the life history method and James P. Spradley's in ethnography show the close connection between oral history and their respective disciplines.[47] Yet at times, in some cases, work in these social science disciplines can become profoundly ahistorical. An example is found in Spradley's *The Ethnographic Interview*.[48] He discusses cultural rules through a description of an event in Hartford, Connecticut, when a group of Puerto Rican residents attacked a police officer who was giving mouth to mouth resuscitation to a woman from the neighborhood. Spradley uses this as an example of the conflict of cultural rules. Granted, saving lives is one of the cultural rules of police officers, but what kind of cultural rule prompted Puerto Rican city dwellers to attack someone giving mouth to mouth resuscitation? Would they have done so if it had not been a policeman, or in Puerto Rico? Does not the history of the relations of the police to the minority community have something to do with this behavior? Is not history, not cultural rules, the deciding factor here? While we are interested in culture and the way in which history and historical speculation formulates culture, our prime objective is always the understanding of the past and its lasting effects upon us as we live our lives. It is interesting that in Spradley's book, of the hundreds of example questions offered for students almost none are concerned with changes over time.

But the ethnographic stance is important for the historical fieldworker. In the first place it reminds us again that we must be aware of the fact that those being interviewed know and understand much more about their lives than do the interviewers who are there to learn, that what we search for are the rules governing the lives of those we speak to. Secondly, the goal of an ethnography is to move beyond individual tales to examine the culture itself. The study of hermeneutics alone often leads to the impossible task of examining each and every interview as a singular item. At all times our reference must be people in space, culture and time.

In "Movement Without Aim," we argued that the structure of history and its uses, as revealed in the interview, provide the key to understanding the interplay of myth, ideology and history, and therefore the context in which historical data is imbedded. In "Listen to Their Voices," we provided an example of such an analysis. To date, there have been two criticisms directed at that argument: one concerning the historical vision it encompasses, the other its application. Because they raise substantial questions about the view of history presented here, it is necessary to discuss them at some length before moving on to a consideration of our relations as oral historians to the historical enterprise, the communities in which we work and the people to whom we listen.

In 1980, in *Social Analysis*, Kenneth Brown and Michael Roberts raised two fundamental concerns about the relationship posed here between myth, ideology and history. Noting that "the distinction between myth and history is a vexing problem . . . ," they argue that I "set hard and fast parameters" and that oral tradition in both literate and nonliterate cultures may be mythical, historical, both or neither."[49] A hard and fast distinction was not the intention of the original essay. Its aim was to argue explicitly that it was the peculiar way in which history, myth and ideology were interwoven which provided the key to oral testimony, and that ideology, not mentioned by Brown and Roberts, provides the driving force to historical memory and subtly organizes its presentation. This can be found, as Jameson notes, at the deep level of political unconsciousness. Without the proper appreciation of the ways in which history becomes myth or ideology and ideology becomes history, we cannot comprehend that unconscious.

The second issue raised is idealism. Brown argues that the view of history proposed here "assumes that history is about progress."[50] This is not the case. The view of history proposed here is that history is the explantation of change over time, and that is what we ask people to do when we interview them. That explanation can take many forms, one of them being a concept of progess, and even there one finds very real distinctions as to the nature of progress. As I said (Chapter VII), it is possible to find quite complex formulations of historical explanation, in this case one cyclical, the other folkloric. While some aspects of some of these formulations may imply progress, nowhere is there the assumption that that is what history is. Such an interpretation is simply a misreading.

More deeply, Trevor Lummis questions "the value of establishing the informant's view of the past in terms of historiographical categories."[51] He argues that "individuals are bound to experience history as biography . . . . It is difficult to see how people are going to arrive at any other structure without a specific knowledge of alternative interpretations to the dominant ethos."[52] Thus an analysis of the structure of the interview is valuable for understanding present values but cannot be "assumed to illuminate their earlier values or attitudes."[53]

Lummis goes to the heart of the question. Behind his critique are three basic assumptions about how people construct historical narratives: 1. History is experienced, and therefore expressed as biography; 2. At any one time the historical repetoire is narrowly limited, dependent upon the availability of alternative interpretations; and 3. Values and attitudes, and their expression are fluid and changeable so that what is articulated now has only a doubtful relationship to what one's past views were.

Concerning the first two of these points, the interview strategy outlined here offers a corrective. If history is biography (and I do not think this is universally the case) the function of the interviewer is to move beyond biography, to relate praxis and consciousness in ways other than those of the dominant (individualistic) historical attitude, or to push that vision to its limits to discover the way in which it operates as politics, in the way Frisch's analysis of Terkel's interviews does.[54] In the second case, as noted here, one way in which this is done is by offering for consideration alternative interpretations and testing them against those currently held. This does not mean that one attempts to change the mind of the interviewee or rewrite the history. Rather we create documents which allow us to discover the complexity of the historical formulations and the precise manner in which dominant ideologies, whether their origins be in the classroom, the media, or whatever apparatus, are integrated into the consciousness of members of the culture.

Lummis's final point raises in bald form the issue of the role of ideology in consciousness. It is an issue which we must face because, as we noted earlier, we interview in the now about the then and the two are inextricably bound up with one another. It is the assumption here, and in the works upon which this work is based,[55] that while particular historical formulations may change over time, ideologies, since they express class relations, do not change significantly in structure over time unless there is a change in those relations or change in consciousness. Ideologies are formed early in life and emerge out of the full experience of a life in culture and they are deeply held. Therefore the historical articulation of today which reveals the ideological structure of consciousness does indeed tell us about the way in which event and ideas were related in the past.

In addition, Lummis's claims fly in the face of the whole thrust of the new social history. They assume that ordinary citizens have no independent power of cultural construction, can only respond to the stimulus of the hegemonic ideology, and are doomed to view history as biography (unlike the historian presumably). The elitism of such a view need not be commented upon, but the narrowness of the end result—that we can only validate oral history by reference to social data (aggregate statistical tabulations)—is a retreat to positivism, despite Lummis's disclaimers.

It is to break this boundary that it was first proposed that we look at an oral history as a historiographic act and that we examine the structure and use of history as articulated in the interview. Most importantly, this view gives proper respect to those we interview. It assumes that they are capable of complex cultural formulations, that they can interpret their own pasts, that they can look at themselves and us critically. It also assumes that they can and do use history, and that they can use it to actively involve themselves in the cultural dialogue in a fully participatory manner. People become not simply objects of study but part of the community of discourse. Thus we live up to the democratic promise of oral history and, as citizens, engage our past in a collective enterprise. It is in this way that the promise of oral history is realized.[56]

Footnotes

1. Renato Rosaldo, "Doing Oral History," *Using Oral Sources: Vansina and Beyond*, in *Social Analysis*, No. 4 (September 1980), p. 89.

2. See for example: Paul Thompson, *The Voice of the Past: Oral History* (Oxford and New York, 1980), Chs. I and II; Alessandro Portelli, "The Peculiarities of Oral History," *History Workshop*, Number 12 (Autumn 1981), pp. 96-107; Tamara Hareven, *Family Time and Industrial Time* (New York, 1982), Appendix A; Sven Lindquist, "Dig Where You Stand," *Our Common History: The Transformation of Europe*, ed. by Paul Thompson (Atlantic Highlands, 1982), pp. 322-330; Linda Shopes, "The Baltimore Neighborhood Heritage Project: Oral History and Community Involvement," *Radical History Review*, 25 (October 1981), pp. 27-43.

3. See in particular: Luisa Passerini, "Italian Working Class Culture Between the Wars: Consensus to Fascism and Work Ideology," *International Journal of Oral History*, Vol. 1, No. 1 (February 1980), pp. 4-27; and in the same issue: E. Culpepper Clark, Michael J. Hyde and Eva McMahan "Communicating In the Oral History Interview: Investigating Problems of Interpretating Oral Data," pp. 28-40. See also: Alessandro Portelli, "'The Time of My Life': Functions of Time in Oral History," *International Journal of Oral History*, Vol. 2, No. 3 (November 1981), pp. 162-180; Daniel Bertaux, "Stories as Clues to Sociological Understanding: The Paris Bakers," in Thompson, *Our Common History*, op. cit., pp. 93-110; Sidney W. Mintz, "The Anthropological Interview and the Life History," *Oral History Review* (1979), pp. 18-26; Charles Joyner, "Oral History as a Commmunicative Event: A Folkloristic Perspective," *Oral History Review* (1979), pp. 47-52; and Gary Y. Okihiro, "Oral History and the Writing of Ethnic History: A Reconnaissance into Method and Theory," *Oral History Review* (1981), pp. 27-46.

4. Henry Glassie, *Passing the Time in Ballymenone: Culture and History of an Ulster Community* (Philadelphia, 1982). The notes in this volume, pp. 721-800, are a rich and complex introduction to folklore fieldwork. For a view of the current literature in ethnography, see John L. Caughey, "The Ethnography of Everyday Life: Theories and Methods of American Culture Studies," *American Quarterly*, Vol. 34 (1982), pp. 222-243. See also James P. Spradley, *The Ethnographic Interview* (New York, 1979).

5. V. William Bathorp, "Argumentation and the Critical Stance: A Methodological Perspective," *Advances in Argumentation Theory and Practice*, ed. by J. Robert Cox and Charles H. Willard (Carbondale, 1982), p. 240.

6. Portelli, "Peculiarities of Oral History," *op. cit.*; Passerini, *op. cit.* See also the version of Passerini's essay in Thompson, *Our Common History, op. cit.*, pp. 54-78.

7. Passerini, *ibid.*

8. David Lance, *An Archive Approach to Oral History* (London, 1978), is the clearest statement of this position. See also David Lance, "Oral History Archives: Perceptions and Practices," *Oral History*, No. 18 (Autumn 1980), pp. 59-63; Ch. IV of this volume; and Portelli, "Peculiarities of Oral History," *op. cit.* There is also some reason to believe that listening, rather than viewing, is a far more potent mode for remembering. See Elizabeth Loftus, *Memory: Surprising New Insights Into How We Remember and Why We Forget* (Reading, 1982), pp. 16-17.

9. Jan Vansina, *Oral Tradition: A Study in Historical Methodology*, trans. H. M. Wright (London, 1965). Jan Vansina, "Mem-

ory and Oral Tradition," *The African Past Speaks: Essays on Oral Tradition and History*, ed. by Joseph C. Miller (Folkestone, Kent, 1980), pp. 117-132, and by the same author, "Once Upon a Time: Oral Traditions as History in Africa," *Daedalus*, Vol. 100 (Fall 1978), pp. 422-468.

10. Frederic Jameson, *The Political Unconscious: Narrative as a Socially Symbolic Art* (Ithaca, 1981), Ch. I. For a discussion and critique of the work of Jameson, see Terry Eagleton, "The Idealism of American Criticism," *New Left Review*, No. 127 (May-June 1981), pp. 53-65.

11. See above, Ch. VI: "Can Anyone Over Thirty Be Trusted?"

12. Glassie, *op. cit.*, pp. 649, 651.

13. Thompson, *The Voice of the Past*, pp. 100-119.

14. Vansina; *Oral Traditions*, Glassie, *op. cit.* See also Barbara Allen and William Lynwood Montell, *From Memory to History: Using Oral Sources in Local Historical Research* (Nashville, 1981).

15. It is for this reason that we do not encourage people to talk off tape. The twice told tale, in an oral history interview, is never the same. It is always shorter and less spontaneous when repeated.

16. See esp. Ernst Schachtel, "On Memory and Childhood Amnesia," in *Metamorphosis* (New York, 1959). Two interesting and complex discussions of memory in the oral history fieldwork situation are Tamara Hareven, "The Search for Generational Memory: Tribal Rites in Industrial Society," *Daedalus*, Vol. 107

(Fall 1978), pp. 137-149; and Samuel Schrager, "What is Social in Oral History?", *International Journal of Oral History*, Vol. 4, No. 2 (June 1983), pp. 76-98. Much of this discussion follows, very closely, points raised by Jan Vansina: "Memory and Oral Tradition," in *The African Past Speaks*, pp. 262-79.

17. Loftus, *op. cit.*

18. Michael Frisch, "The Memory of History," *Radical History Review*, No. 25 (October 1981), pp. 9-23.

19. Jameson, *op. cit.*, Ch. II. This concept of ideology draws heavily upon Louis Althusser, *Lenin and Philosophy*, tr. by Ben Brewster (New York, 1971).

20. This use of nostalgia varies somewhat from the more optimistic view of Fred Davis, "Nostalgia, Identity and the Current Nostalgia Wave," *Journal of Popular Culture*, Vol. XI (Fall 1977), pp. 414-424, yet is less pessimistic than M. Mile Nawas and Jerome J. Platt, "A Future Oriented Theory of Nostalgia," *Journal of Individual Psychology*, Vol. 21 (May 1965), pp. 247-263.

21. Gelya Frank, "Finding the Common Denominator: A Phenomenological Critique of Life History Method," *Ethnos*, Vol. 7 (Spring 1979), pp. 68-94.

22. See above, Ch. I.

23. Harold Garfinkle, *Studies in Ethnomethodology* (Engelwood Cliffs, 1967), pp. 3-4.

24. Thompson, *The Voice of the Past*, pp. 243-352.

25. William Chafe, *Civil Rights and Civilities* (New York, 1982).

26. Glassie, *op. cit.*, pp. 653-654.

27. See esp. The Brass Workers History Project, *Brass Valley: The Story of People's Lives and Struggles in an American Industrial Region*, compiled by Jeremy Brecher, Jerry Lombardi and Jan Stackhouse (Philadelphia, 1982), Part V, pp. 269-277. See also Tamara Hareven, *Family Time and Industrial Time* (Cambridge, 1982), Appendix A, pp. 371-382.

28. Lewis Anthony Dexter, *Elite and Specialized Interviewing* (Evanston, 1970) is useful. See also the bibliography in Caughey, *op. cit.*, and Edward D. Ives, *The Tape Recorded Interview* (Knoxville, 1980).

29. Robert A. Georges and Michael O. Jones, *People Studying People: The Human Element in Fieldwork* (Berkeley, 1980).

30. *Ibid.*, p. 153,

31. Studs Terkel, *Hard Times: An Oral History of the Great Depression* (New York, 1967). See also Michael Frisch, "Oral History and *Hard Times*: A Review Essay," *Oral History Review* (1979), pp. 70-79. Oddly enough, Robert Nisbet, "The 1930s: America's Major Nostagia," *The Key Reporter*, Vol. 38 (Autumn 1972), pp. 2-36, believes the 30s to have been a better decade.

32. Culpepper, McMahan and Hyde, *op. cit.* See also Michael J. Hyde, "Philosophical Hermeneutics and the Communicative Experience: the Paradigm of Oral History," *Man and World*

(1980), pp. 81-98; E. Culpepper Clark, "Argument and Historical Analysis," Cox and Willard, *op. cit.*, pp. 298-317; Eva McMahan, "Communicative Dynamics of Hermeneutical Conversation in Oral History Interviews," *Communicative Quarterly*, Vol. 31, No. 1 (Winter 1983), pp. 3-11.

33. Theodore Rosengarten, *All God's Dangers: The Life of Nate Shaw* (New York, 1974).

34. Georges and Jones, *op. cit.*

35. See Ch. IV.

36. Jameson, *op. cit.*, pp. 20-23.

37. Clark *et al.*, pp. 32, 33-38.

38. See Ch. IV; also, Portelli, "The Time of My Life," *op. cit.*

39. Daniel Bertaux and Isabelle Bertaux-Wiame, "Life Stories in the Baker's Trade," *Biography and Society* (Beverly Hills, 1981), pp. 169-190.

40. Paul Ricoeur, *Interpretation Theory: Discourse and the Surplus of Meaning* (New York, 1976), p. 92.

41. John Berger and Jean Mohr, *A Seventh Man* (London and New York, 1981), p. 94.

42. Vansina, *Oral Traditions*.

43. Richard Dorson, *America in Legend: Folklore from the Colonial Period to the Present* (New York, 1973), and by the same author *American Folklore and the Historian* (Chicago, 1971). Edward Ives, *Joe Scott: The Woodsman Songmaker* (Urbana, 1978). Glassie, *op. cit.* Guiseppe Cocciara, *The History of Folklore in Europe*, translated by John McDaniel (Philadelphia, 1981). Michael Herzfeld, *Ours Once More: Folklore, Ideology and the Making of Modern Greece* (Austin, 1982).

44. Glassie, Ch. XXIV.

45. Hans-Georg Gadamer, *Truth and Method*, ed. by Garrett Barden and John Cumming (New York, 1975), p. 269.

46. Albert E. Stone, *Autobiographical Occasions and Original Acts: Versions of American Identity from Henry Adams to Nate Shaw* (Philadelphia, 1982).

47. Daniel Bertaux, *op. cit.* Ken Plummer, *Documents of Life: An Introduction to the Problems and Literature of a Humanistic Method* (London, 1983).

48. Spradley, p. 5.

49. *Social Analysis*, "Introduction," p. 6.

50. *Op. cit.*, "Postface," p. 119.

51. Trevor Lummis, "Structure and Validity in Oral Evidence," *International Journal of Oral History*, Vol. 2 (June 1981), p. 112.

52. *Ibid.*

53. *Ibid.*, p. 113.

54. Frisch, *Hard Times*, *op. cit.*

55. Althusser, *op. cit.* Jameson, *op. cit.*, Ch. IV, n. 5, 7, 10.

56. As this work was going to press three new and slightly different criticisms were leveled at oral history. In her comments
at the Fourth International Conference on Oral History held
in Aix-en-Provence, France, Dominique Aron-Schnapper argued that oral historians should not concern themselves with
elaborate constructions to understand subjectivity but should
rather concentrate upon the archival task of filling in the gaps
in the written record. Since this narrow view of the task of
the oral historian has been dealt with again and again in the
American literature we need not discuss it here. The second
critique was mounted by Patrick O'Farrell in the latest issue of
the *Oral History Association of Australia Journal*, Number 5
(1982-83), pp. 3-9. O'Farrell in a critique of the work of Paul
Thompson argues that the use of oral history for social history
has been a feckless effort to fill the pages of history with the
history of "ordinary" people whose history, basically, is uninter-
esting. This attack was followed in the journal with a number
of responses and the reader is urged to consult that issue.
    The third critique was a bit more substantial. Writing in
Social Science History, Vol. 7, No. 4 (Fall, 1983), pp. 457-
474, Louise Tilly, reviewing the work of Portelli, The History
Workshop and several French oral historians, raises serious
questions about the goals and methods of those who attempt to
explore the "subjective" in history. She argues, essentially, that
the concern of history is with the verifiable or what happened,
and that the historian's stance must always be that of critical

judge. This article and a variety of responses will be presented as a special issue of the *International Journal of Oral History*, where readers will be able to find the full debate. While all three critiques raise interesting questions, none of them has caused me to change my thinking about what it is we, as oral historians, do or should do.